PENGUIN BOOKS

MORE FUTU... F

malcolm abrams is a magazine consultant and writer. A native of Toronto, he lives in New York City.

harriet bernstein, a native New Yorker, is a researcher and writer with a special interest in social trends.

OVER
250 INVENTIONS
THAT WILL CHANGE YOUR LIFE
BY 2001

ILLUSTRATIONS BY BOB JOHNSON

MORE future stuff

MALCOLM ABRAMS

HARRIET BERNSTEIN

PENGUIN BOOKS

PENGUIN BOOKS
Published by the Penguin Group
Viking Penguin, a division of Penguin Books USA Inc.,
375 Hudson Street, New York, New York 10014, U.S.A.
Penguin Books Ltd, 27 Wrights Lane,
London W8 5TZ, England
Penguin Books Australia Ltd, Ringwood,
Victoria, Australia
Penguin Books Canada Ltd, 10 Alcorn Avenue, Suite 300,
Toronto, Ontario, Canada M4V 3B2
Penguin Books (N.Z.) Ltd, 182–190 Wairau Road,
Auckland 10, New Zealand

Penguin Books Ltd, Registered Offices:
Harmondsworth, Middlesex, England

First published in Penguin Books 1991

10 9 8 7 6 5 4 3 2 1

LIBRARY OF CONGRESS CATALOGING IN PUBLICATION DATA
Abrams, Malcolm.
More future stuff: over 250 inventions that will change your life by 2001/Malcolm Abrams, Harriet Bernstein.
p. cm.
Includes index.
ISBN 0 14 01.4523 0
1. New products—United States. I. Bernstein, Harriet.
II. Title.
HF5415.153.A274 1991
338'.02'0973—dc20 90-26856

Printed in the United States of America

Set in Bodoni Book
Designed by Beth Tondreau Design
Illustrations by Bob Johnson

for

Mildred

In Memory of Allan Abrams

• • • • •

In Fond Memory

of Seymour Bernstein

INTRODUCTION

It's hard to park a car, so Volkswagen engineers design a car that parks itself. For computer operators who need to use their hands away from the keyboard, scientists at LC Technologies create a computer that is "eye" operated. Six-year-old Brett Racine is a messy burrito eater, so his sister Sarah, eight, invents "food tape" to hold crumbly snacks together.

Welcome to *More Future Stuff.* Like an old-time carnival show,

there's something amazing, spectacular, fantastic, and unbelievable everywhere you look.

But the best part of *More Future Stuff* is that all of the 260-plus inventions are real. They're all designed to make your life better. And almost every product will be here before the year 2001.

In case you missed our opening act, *Future Stuff* (Penguin Books, 1989), it contains a lot of wonderful things like High Definition TV, virtual reality, and flying cars.

What we learned from writing that book is that somewhere, every day, someone has a bright idea that solves a problem, big or small, or adds something to enhance the human experience. It happens in a Cornell University laboratory, a German automotive plant, a Japanese electronics company, or a basement workshop in Ellijay, Georgia.

More Future Stuff is a look at the latest and the very best of those products, as well as the people possessing that special mix of creativity and resolve, who think them up.

From flying boats to fish dogs, from robot bartenders to computerized shrinks, from ornithopters to holographic foods, from peanut-oil breast implants to permanent buttons, from floating furniture to fat prevention drinks, there's something for everyone just around the corner.

So come with us on a trip into the near future—a kind of window-shopping expedition to the year 2001.

We hope you enjoy the journey.

Malcolm Abrams

Harriet Bernstein

THE HEADINGS EXPLAINED

Below the title of each product, there are three headings: *Odds*, *ETA*, *Price*. A few words of explanation are needed for each.

ODDS: This is a probability, measured as a percentage, that the product will actually be on sale by the year 2001. When the odds are listed as 100%, that means the product exists now and that there's a manufacturer and distributor.

In most cases, the odds of a product reaching the market have been projected by the inventor or manufacturer. In some cases, though, the authors have made this projection based on the available information.

ETA: This is the Estimated Time of Availability—the year that the product is expected to arrive in stores or become otherwise available nationwide. In some cases, when the ETA is listed as 1992, the product is already being sold in a limited fashion, either directly from the manufacturer, through a mail-order house, or in a test market.

In most cases the ETA has been supplied by the inventor or the manufacturer. However, on a few occasions, the authors have made the projections.

PRICE: This is what the inventor or manufacturer believes the product will sell for in today's dollars when it arrives on the market. When the price is listed as NA, that means it is not available because it has not yet been determined by the inventor or manufacturer.

ACKNOWLEDGMENTS

It takes a lot of people to put together a voyage into the future. The fact that this second expedition to the world of the twenty-first century stayed buoyant is due to the cooperation and enthusiasm of a large crew. We owe many thanks to our loyal team of researchers who stayed up late, got up early, and often gave up weekends to help us focus on this glimpse into the future. Thanks go out to Trish Arbib, Trudy Balch, Suzanne Carmick, Robin Eisgrau, Mary Fratto, Lauren Freudmann, Jim Gerard, Cecily Harrison, Ira Hellman, Alan Horing, Gill Kent, Linda Keslar, Ellen Liebowitz, Elizabeth MacDonald,

Norm Meyersohn, Bruce Meyerson, Jennifer Newman, Margery Newman, Judy Sawyer, Christina Schlank, Rob Schwartz, Linda Simone, Miranda Spencer, Sunsh Stein, Susan Storms, Margaret Talcott, and Lisa Towle for their fine efforts on our behalf. We are especially indebted to Laura Schenone for her tenacity in sniffing out stories, and to Trilby Schreiber for her excellent skills and her unique sense of humor. Thanks also go to Madeleine Morel, Mindy Werner, and Janine Steel for believing we could find 250 products for the future that weren't already in our first book; to Phyllis Romanski and Susan Rothenberg, our computer whizzes; and to Jill Sotnick, Peter Cerbone, Cheryl Perry, and Christine Brodbeck for their unerring patience in tending to administrative details.

We were also fortunate to have been assisted by a huge network of people who were eager to help us locate inventors, scientists, CEOs, marketing directors, researchers, public relations officers, engineers, professors, doctors, and dentists who have "stuff" that will soon enhance our lives. Help came from all parts of the globe, and although some names may be lost somewhere on small slips of paper, most of them are ever present in our minds. There was Pam Michaelson and her husband Tom of the *International New Product Newsletter*, Dan Seamens of *East West* magazine, Edmund L. Andrews of *The New York Times*'s patents column, John Preston and David Lampe of MIT, Molly Bancroft at the MIT Media Lab, Patricia Roe of *IC*² from the University of Texas at Austin, Linda Kowano at Northwestern University, Neils Rheimers at the University of California at Berkeley, Martin Bernard of Argonne National Laboratory, Kathy Howe of MRI Ventures, Marilyn Brown of Oak Ridge National Laboratory, Dr. Pepi Ross of the Lawrence Berkeley Labs, the people at SERI International, Tom Lauderback of the Consumer Electronics Show, Bill Pritchard of Panasonic, Oscar Mastin of the U.S. Patent Office, the New York Patent Library, Linda R. McElreath from the U.S. Department of Agriculture, the Franklin Institute Science Museum, Bob Harrison of the Tech Transfer Society, Marion Stamos of the Association of Home Appliance Manufacturers, Phil Wells and Tom Manning of Tech Ex, Leslie Clay and Todd Whitaker from Seventh Generation, the publicity department of Hammacher Schlemmer, Roger Hanson of the Small Business Innovation Research and Development Program, the staff at Invent America, Kathryn Shafer and Rich Barnett of the

National Invention Center, Clayton Williamson of the Inventors Workshop, Penny Becker of the Minnesota Inventors Congress, Shelly Beauchamp of the Women Inventors Project in Canada, Inventors Association of New England, Inventors Workshop International Education Foundation, Donald Moyer of the Inventors Council, Dick Wantz of Kessler Sales, Lou Eckebrecht of Lomar Associates, Joanna Patterson of the Invention Company, M & M Associates, the Australian Trade Commission, the Japan Trade Board, Wang Tie Ying from the Shanghai Union Trading Company in China, Frank Hilf, David Freedman, Lynn Klotz, Ashley Stevens, and Myron Krueger (arguably the true father of virtual reality). Special thanks to Dr. William Rosenberg for sharing so willingly his wealth of contacts in the world of technology transfer, and to Michael Mascioni of Intertainment '90 for his kindly, last-minute help in leading us to important technologies. An especially warm thanks goes to Michael Thomas of *Business Tokyo* for acting as such a friendly intermediary between us and Japan.

Add to all the above our deep appreciation for the people who explained to us, patiently, what their contribution to the next decade will be. To see the future through their eyes, though sometimes hard to grasp, was always enlightening.

Many thanks to all our friends and members of our families who withstood some neglect yet never faltered in their ever-crucial show of support. Without their constructive criticisms, their hours of listening, and their ability to laugh at us and with us, life would be grim. Nancy, Barbara, and Larry Abrams, Seena Parker, Joe Giarraputo, cowboy Vincent Inconiglios, Katherine Bolman, Peter Cerbone, Elizabeth Masi, Susan Cass—you know how much you mean to us.

CONTENTS

INTRODUCTION vii

THE HEADINGS EXPLAINED ix

ACKNOWLEDGMENTS xi

1. STUFF YOU WOULDN'T BELIEVE! 1
2. WHO THINKS OF THIS STUFF, ANYWAY? 23
3. ENVIRONMENTAL STUFF 35
4. LOOKING GOOD, FEELING GOOD 55
5. HOUSE STUFF 73
6. ENTERTAINMENT STUFF 97
7. PHONE STUFF 113
8. FOR THOSE WHO HAVE EVERYTHING 121
9. TRAVEL STUFF 133
10. SUN, SAND, & SURF 143
11. HIGH-TECH MATCHMAKING & OTHER ESSENTIAL SERVICES 157

12. LEARNING 169

13. HOBBIES 175

14. SPORTS STUFF 183

15. BIKE STUFF 199

16. HEALTH & SAFETY 207

17. SLEEP-EASY STUFF 235

18. FOR PARENTS 243

19. FOOD STUFF 255

20. SNACKS 271

21. RODENTS & BUGS 281

22. HOME OFFICE STUFF 289

23. CAR STUFF 299

24. WHY DIDN'T I THINK OF THIS? 313

25. END STUFF 327

ALPHABETICAL LIST OF PRODUCTS 333

C H A P T E R 1

stuff you wouldn't believe!

FLARECRAFT

The great new transportation toy of the nineties is about to take off. The Flarecraft is a fish/bird hybrid, 32.5 feet long with a 24.6-foot wing span, that's right out of a futuristic comic book. It's fast. It's smooth. It flies above the water. It's *not* a boat, plane, or Hovercraft. It *is* very cool.

• • • • •

ODDS: 95%

ETA: 1992

PRICE: $45,000–$60,000

• • • • •

A pilot's license is not required, as the Federal Aviation Administration does not classify it as a plane. But fly it does. With only a 70-horsepower engine and 3 gallons of gas an hour, the Flarecraft gets airborne with a cruising speed of 75 miles per hour.

How is this possible? The main reason is the shape of the wings. They're designed to capture and compress air against the water, exploiting a scientific phenomenon known as *ground effect*, a trick birds have been using for some time.

According to Bill Russell, the entrepreneur who plans to bring Flarecraft to the world, "Ground effect, in simple terms, is an increase in pressure under the wing. What you're doing is slowing the air down."

To understand what ground effect is, Russell suggests, observe a water bird as it comes down for a landing. It tilts or flares its wings downward as it nears the water. This slows the air and increases the air pressure between the bird's wings and the water. The pressure keeps the bird airborne, even though technically it's no longer flying.

At slow speeds, Flarecraft operates like a boat. But at 45 mph, ground effect takes hold and the craft starts to lift. The faster you go, the higher you lift. Maximum height is 8 feet, although the current prototype is designed for a height of 3 to 6 feet.

What's the difference between a Flarecraft and a Hovercraft? They operate under similar principles, but a Hovercraft is much slower and hits the waves hard. And a Hovercraft requires four times the engine power of a Flarecraft to create thrust.

"The Flarecraft goes over waves smoothly," says Russell. "It's even better in waves because the ground effect is greater. You can put a glass of water on the dashboard, and it won't spill. If you dig a wingtip in the water when turning, you don't spring or catapult."

A Flarecraft, however, will sell for several times the price of a recreational Hovercraft (see page 123).

In addition to ground effect, the Flarecraft gets lift from low-pressure forces above its wings. This is known as the *Bernouli effect*, the principle of suction that causes the flight of all planes. Russell compares the Bernouli effect to a string lifting the plane from above, while ground effect acts as a stick pushing up from below. When these forces are balanced, the Flarecraft kicks into "automatic height stability." At this point, you can take your hands off the controls and just cruise.

Russell got the idea for Flarecraft when he was living in Westport, Connecticut, and commuting ninety minutes each way to New York City. He decided to build a craft that would take him to work quickly. Although not an engineer, Russell knew about ground effect and managed to construct a model. Later, however, he learned that a deceased German scientist, Dr. Alexander Lippish, had patented the invention years earlier.

Russell bought the patents for the Flarecraft from Dr. Lippish's widow. In Germany, Russell also found Hanno Fischer, who had worked with Dr. Lippish for ten years developing the craft. They joined forces, manufacturing the Flarecraft in Germany and marketing it from the U.S.

The craft they are turning out has a 7-foot long, 4-foot wide cockpit with two contoured seats enclosed in glass. It can be air-conditioned and heated, and can take 550 pounds of payload. Should you decide to park on water overnight, the seats fall back to provide cozy sleeping quarters.

Driving the Flarecraft is simple, mostly based on using a throttle and a steering wheel. You can fish, scuba dive, and water ski from it.

The Coast Guard has ruled that it is a boat, and therefore must comport to the rules and regulations of the sea.

Russell believes that Flarecraft will gain wide acceptance as a recreational and commuter vehicle with many future adaptations. He also thinks it will take over a large segment of the boat market. "Why drag a hull through the water when you can go over the top?"

SYNTHETIC VOCAL TRACT

Strings, flutes, drums—they've all been duplicated by electronic sound. Soon, so will the singer!

That's right, a beautiful-sounding, lead-singer-quality human voice will soon come to us via computer. And not long afterwards, specific human voices will be cloned by machine. Fabulous long-gone entertainers will be heard again, singing songs of today.

ODDS: 90%

ETA: 1993

PRICE: COMPARABLE TO CURRENT COMPUTER MUSIC PROGRAMS

Imagine Caruso's voice performing the score of *Les Miserables!*

Perry Cook, a singer and electrical engineer doctoral candidate at Stanford University, is the developer of the synthetic vocal tract. When the computer program begins, a cross-sectional drawing of the side of a human head appears on the screen. The size of the nasal cavity, the throat, the mouth, and both nostrils can be manipulated by the computer mouse to shape the sound that's emitted from the "voice."

"It's a composer's tool," says Cook, "as well as an educational tool. You can study how sound is made."

For the layman, it's more like magic. The computer voice can be made to sing with a stuffed nose, or three noses. With the attachment of a joystick, the voice can be driven up, down, and around the scale faster than you'd ever want to hear it.

Eventually, says Cook, it could be so finely tuned that it would indeed be possible to duplicate the voice of any singer who ever lived. We could hear singers from Jolson to Joplin and from Lanza to Lennon all performing songs not even written when they were alive. (Cook notes, though, that legal complications are likely.)

The vocal tract system will someday be incorporated into electronic synthesizers. Next to the buttons for clavichord and strings will be a button marked "singer." Cook figures that's about seven years away. But the computer program will be available for consumer use by 1993.

IRIDIUM CELLULAR TELEPHONES

4

Explorers in Antarctica, pilots over the Himalayas, geologists on the floor of the Grand Canyon, you on vacation at the beach—anybody, anywhere on this planet will be reachable at their personal telephone number when the Iridium Global Personal Communications System is set up.

ODDS: 95%
ETA: 1997
PRICE: $3,500

This remarkable system is a satellite-based network being created by the Motorola Electronics Company. Between 1994 and 1996, Motorola will deploy a constellation of 77 satellites in 7 circular orbits around the earth, putting every point on the planet's surface within the system's range. (The name Iridium was chosen because it's a mineral with 77 electrons orbiting its nucleus.)

These "low earth orbit" satellites will be only 413 nautical miles away from the planet. The low altitude of Iridium will mean that we'll need only small antennas, not satellite dishes, to use the system. The signal will go directly from your phone to the satellite and/or to the person you are calling.

The most amazing feature of Iridium is that you don't need to have the faintest idea where your party is in order to reach them by phone. For example, you call your neighbors down the street, assuming they're at home. As it happens they're on vacation in China. In fact, at the exact moment you call them from your Iridium phone, they are walking on the Great Wall. Fortunately, they have their Iridium Cellular Telephone with them. Ring, ring.

It's almost scary, isn't it? No place to hide. No place your boss can't reach you. No excuse for not checking in.

In traditional cellular phones, the cellular message moves like a baton in a relay race: The information is passed from cell to cell using radio waves that rely on a transmitter. These systems have a fixed number of unmoving cells that service a number of mobile users within a fixed area.

Iridium is similar in that it also relies on cells. However, the Iridium satellites move, and fast—at a rate of 7,400 meters per second. So, relatively speaking, the users appear static, and the cells travel to "hand off" the messages to the next cell. These mobile, intelligent satellites are what give Iridium its greater range and capacity.

Despite its similarities to Iridium, your old cellular telephone won't work with this new system. You'll have to buy an Iridium Cellular Telephone that will sell for about $3,500. Models available will include a lightweight portable, a mobile, and a small fixed unit.

Iridium is best suited for low-traffic, underpopulated areas, where setting up of traditional cellular phone networks is economically infeasible. "The traditional cellular is still best for well-developed areas," explains Lawrence Moore, public affairs manager for Motorola

GEG. "Because of the way the Iridium cell structures are set up, the technology can't handle the number of callers and users in populated areas with developed communications infrastructures."

Still, Iridium will become available in every city and town in America. "Each country will probably have at least one company to provide Iridium service," says Moore. "Billing will depend on the market in each location." Rates will run about $1 to $3 per minute. "This is a high-end item, but you have to remember that it will service some areas that can't be serviced any other way."

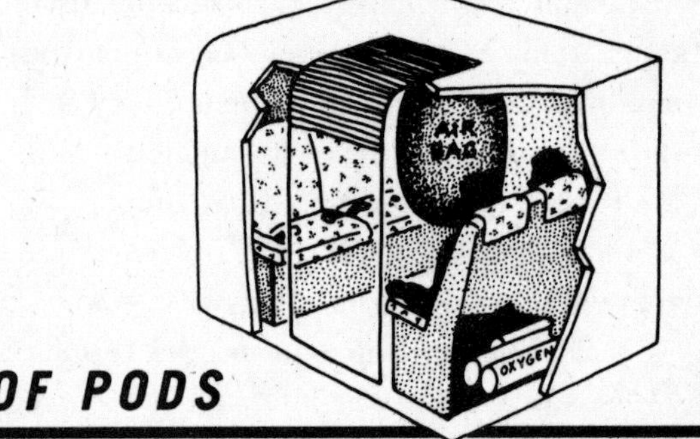

AIRPLANE CRASHPROOF PODS

ODDS: 95%

ETA: 1995

PRICE: MORE THAN A FIRST-CLASS SEAT

If you are a frequently nervous flyer, what follows is the best news you are ever likely to hear about leaving the ground.

A company in Long Beach, California, is manufacturing seating compartments that fit inside commercial airplanes. These safety enclosures automatically seal off in an emergency, keeping those passengers inside safe from shock, water immersion, flying debris, dramatic pressure changes, and temperatures up to 2,000 degrees Fahrenheit coming from open flames and thermal radiation.

George Fukuda is the CEO of Life Protecting Systems, the company that is developing the safety enclosures, which are called Aeronautical Life Preserving Security Systems (ALPS). According to Fukuda, years

of research and development has shown that "the ALPS systems reduce the force of impact to something survivable to many passengers."

The individual safety enclosures, which will cost about $17,500, fit into airplanes like private compartments in passenger trains. The safety enclosures come in different sizes, seating three, four, six, or eight passengers. The specially designed seats are much more comfortable, and their impact-absorbing capability goes beyond that of industry standards, says Fukuda.

In an emergency, the door on the enclosure automatically closes and the life-protecting systems are activated. These systems include a specially designed airbag to assist breathing, a cooling and oxygen system, and a communication system so that passengers will be able to communicate with search-and-rescue teams.

Life Protecting Systems is a private company that was founded by a group of Ph.D.s and engineers who have now worked on the ALPS design for over four years.

THE SELF-PARKING CAR

ODDS: 75%

ETA: 1999

PRICE: NA

Sometime in the next ten years (and not a moment too soon) Volkswagen may market a car that will park itself. The driver could simply press a button to confirm the maneuver, then relax while the computerized, sensor-equipped car slips perfectly into the tightest of spaces.

Ahhh. This is what the future is supposed to be about.

The technology for automatic parking has already been incorporated into a research vehicle called the Futura, a concept car with 2 + 2 seating, gull-wing doors, electronic four-wheel steering, and a 1.7 liter, 82-horsepower engine with direct fuel injection.

More than anything, it has been the advances in four-wheel steering technology that enabled VW researchers in Germany to develop the self-parking system. They aggressively pursued this innovation because the wedge shape on most new cars, while aerodynamically advantageous, was making it more difficult for drivers to see the extremities of the car—and thus to park. Also, in Europe, parking spaces seemed to be getting scarcer and smaller.

The Futura is equipped with laser, ultra-, and supersonic sensors, as well as a computer that stores, monitors, and calculates all data pertinent to a particular parking space. The parking system controls the front and rear steering, acceleration, braking, the handbrake, and the selector level position on automatic gearboxes.

As the car approaches the empty spot, the sensors determine if the space is long enough and whether a front or rear approach is preferable. If the space is adequate, a display panel then indicates its choice of five maneuvers (forward, back, parallel, straight, or tail wagging). The driver confirms the selection by pushing a button. The automatic parking pilot then goes into action.

During the actual parking, the space is constantly scanned by the sensors to register any obstacle fore or aft, as well as the curb. All the maneuvers have been designed to minimize interference with oncoming traffic. The automatic system leaves the car in the best possible position for a quick, one-move exit, which is also automatic.

At any time while going into the space or out of it, the driver can interrupt the automatic process and resume control of the car.

The sensors that regulate self-parking can also be used during normal driving to measure the distance to cars in front and behind as well as to other road obstacles. A separate electronic system evaluates the distance relative to speed and issues a visual warning on the dashboard if there is danger. Volkswagen engineers believe this system will help avert "pile-up" accidents.

FOOD TAPE

Eight-year-old Sarah Cole Racine and her six-year-old brother, Brett, were having Mexican food for dinner one night when Brett's burrito fell apart.

It wasn't the first time, either.

So Sarah invented food tape.

ODDS: 40%

ETA: 1993

PRICE: $3 PER 10-FOOT ROLL

Food tape? Think of it as edible adhesive tape. You can use it to hold together yummy but messy concoctions like Dagwoods, burritos, tacos, sloppy Joes, big burgers, and subs. (Hey, even grown-ups have a hard time eating neat.) Food tape will come in a roll packaged in a dispenser, so you can tear off the exact amount you need. It will have the consistency of fruit leather, but will come in flavors like cheese, cranberry, chocolate, and nacho. Sarah's winning attempts were made from dehydrated (each separately) ketchup, mustard, applesauce, and whatever she found around the house. Each dehydrated condiment efficiently stuck to itself, though ketchup and mustard didn't look too appetizing, according to Sarah's father, Bruce.

Food tape even has decorative potential. Think of the stuff as ribbon instead of tape and a world of possibilities opens up. Cranberry bows on your turkey club! Lemon-flavored curlicues on bundles of asparagus! Layer cake wrapped in raspberry ringlets!

And think of the snacking possibilities—all those times when you just want a little something . . .

Sarah's parents, Susan and Bruce Racine, of Carnation, Washington, are understandably proud of their daughter's creativity, while for Sarah, food tape has brought fame and acclaim. She won first prize in the second-grade category of the 1990 Invent America contest sponsored by the U.S. Patent Model Foundation. And you may even have seen her on "Good Morning America" or hamming it up with Johnny on "The Tonight Show."

By the way, Brett has got his burritos under control. They're tied in knots.

TV THAT PUTS YOU IN THE PICTURE

Vivid Effects TV puts *you* on the screen to interact in video worlds.

• • • • •

ODDS: 100%

ETA: 1992

PRICE: $11,500

• • • • •

- The next time you watch "Cheers," pull up a bar stool next to Norm and Cliffy. Bring your own beer.
- Care for a game of tennis . . . with your friend who lives in Los Angeles, 2,000 miles away? Call him up. "Tennis, anyone . . ." You'll both be there on your TV screens, on an animated tennis court, rackets in hand, whacking the ball back and forth.
- Buy the new hockey, basketball, or baseball video game. See all those little players moving around on the video. "Hey, wait a minute . . . one of them is me!"
- Step up to the bandstand. Take your place behind the drums. Pick up the sticks and hit those skins. Play any song you like. Yet the instrument exists only in videoland.
- Making an important business presentation? Lots of graphs and pie charts on video. Now add you . . . walking up to those graphs, pulling pieces out of those pie charts. Knock their corporate black socks off!

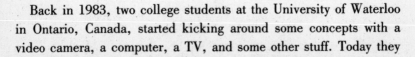

Back in 1983, two college students at the University of Waterloo in Ontario, Canada, started kicking around some concepts with a video camera, a computer, a TV, and some other stuff. Today they are the Vivid Effects Company of Toronto, creator of the Mandala System of animated video worlds and right up there on the cutting edge of virtual-reality technology.

Vincent John Vincent, a thirty-one-year-old psychologist, is president of Vivid Effects. Frank MacDougall, twenty-eight, is "the computer genius behind it all." Together, what they've created has been hailed as sensational from Washington to Tokyo.

And starting in 1992, for about the price of an inexpensive family sedan, you'll be able to buy the system for your living room. What you'll get, Vincent explains, "is a full system wired together that includes five different screens, a camera, TV, computer, and synthesizers." And, of course, the patented video digitizing processing equipment and software called the Mandala System.

When you get all this stuff home, you might want to start with something easy, like the hockey goalie game (on display at the National Hockey League Hall of Fame in Toronto, by the way). On the TV screen, you see the posts and hockey net. Now step in front of the video camera set up in your living room. Suddenly, there you are, digitized, looking every inch the hockey goaltender, standing in front of the goal mouth. Move your right arm in the living room, the little man on the screen moves his right arm. Now what?

Suddenly, swooping into the picture is a fierce-looking animated player. He brings his stick back and fires the puck 90 miles an hour. Oh no! Aw, but the fearless goaltender (you!) kicks out his right leg and miraculously stops the puck just before it enters the net. The crowd cheers. But wait, here comes another puck, and it's aimed right at your head . . .

Get the picture?

"What's really unique," says Vincent, "is the combination of everything—a standard video camera that's brought into a computer system, that has a graphical base to it so we can digitize people's images in live, real-time video so they can see themselves on a television screen and they're a part of the television world.

"It's sort of like being with a live Roger Rabbit," Vincent chuckles.

ROBOT BARTENDER

Did you hear the one about the 750-pound, one-armed bartender who had no head? If you did, turn the page. If you haven't, stick around, because readers, this is no joke.

ODDS: 95%

ETA: 1993

PRICE: $175,000

It seems there's this little robotics firm . . . It's situated above a muffin bakery in the Little Italy section of New York City. The name of the company is Honeybee Robotics Inc. Its president, a former piano tuner, is thirty-five years old. Altogether, Honeybee has ten employees. And, oh, yes, Honeybee makes stuff for NASA. Important, million-dollar stuff, like hands for robots that will assemble the space station *Freedom*.

Everything else about this company is pretty normal . . . except for one thing: RoboTender (no relation to RoboCop), the robotic bartender that the Honeybee people have put together in their spare time.

Don't laugh. You may someday enter your favorite bar or nightclub and find a robot has taken the place of Sam or Woody. Because RoboTender can do just about anything that HumanTender can do.

Operating inside a specially designed, circular work station, RoboTender stands 8½ feet tall with an arm reach of 4½ feet. He's programmed to mix more than 100 drinks, and he can learn any variation or new concoction that anyone cooks up.

When you want service, you enter your order on a keypad at the bar, or, if you prefer, just call it out. RoboTender has voice recognition. He will grab a plastic glass in his single stainless-steel hand, put it down, and pour in all the necessary ingredients, add ice, and shake or stir. He will then proudly deposit the finished drink at a "delivery station" where a waitress or customer can pick it up.

Ah, but can he tell bad jokes or boring stories like a regular bartender? The answer is yes! If he is equipped with the optional "video head," RoboTender can use laser disc technology to amuse his customers with anecdotes, music videos, even individualized stories about the drinks he mixes.

If that's not enough, RoboTender comes with his own light show. A special beam illuminates the drink he is preparing, while a series of spotlights shine on the part of the work station where he's engaged.

All this for $175,000.

The first RoboTenders should start popping up in high-tech taverns in about 1993. A home version might someday be available for lottery winners.

UBIQUITOUS COMPUTING

• • • • •

ODDS: 80%

ETA: 1998

PRICE: $2–$5 FOR SMALLEST
$50 FOR MIDSIZE
$5000 FOR LARGEST

• • • • •

In the not-too-distant future, computers will disappear. Disappear in the sense that they will become so small, specialized, disposable, and commonplace that they will fade into the background of our daily lives, just like pencils, notepads, can openers, and coat hangers.

When was the last time you paid any attention to the ubiquitous ballpoint pen? *That* was a technological marvel not so long ago. So what we're talking about here is ubiquitous computing.

Dr. Mark Weiser of the Xerox Palo Alto Research Center calls it "embodied virtuality." The idea is that these little computers will become so cheap and convenient, you'll get used to having a variety of sizes and styles on hand all the time—cluttering up your desk drawers, your kitchen counter, glove compartment, ladies' purses, and briefcases.

These will not be full-powered computers. Rather, they will be links in a network that reports to and from a centralized processing unit via infrared, radio, or other wireless transmission. For instance, in your office you might grab a notepad-size computer and scribble a memo on it (or dictate one). The memo will be stored as data elsewhere, to be later rewritten, circulated, or ignored, as the user sees fit.

Inch-size computers can be attached to things like books, cashmere sweaters, and the keys to the family hydrofoil. Should you lend these items out, you can track their whereabouts on the map you can call up on the computer-wall of your living room.

The possibilities for information and communication using ubiquitous computers seem almost endless. Are you an antiques buff? Looking to add to your collection of Early American pipe reamers? As the computing infrastructure grows, you'll be able to ask your glove-compartment model to keep an ear out for antique shops broadcasting on a special frequency. The computer will also alert you when you're nearing some Ye Olde Shoppe in the course of a Saturday afternoon drive.

The amazing part is that you'll take this for granted. Computers won't be these big, cumbersome, intrusive, alienating "things." They'll be part of the landscape, everywhere and nowhere.

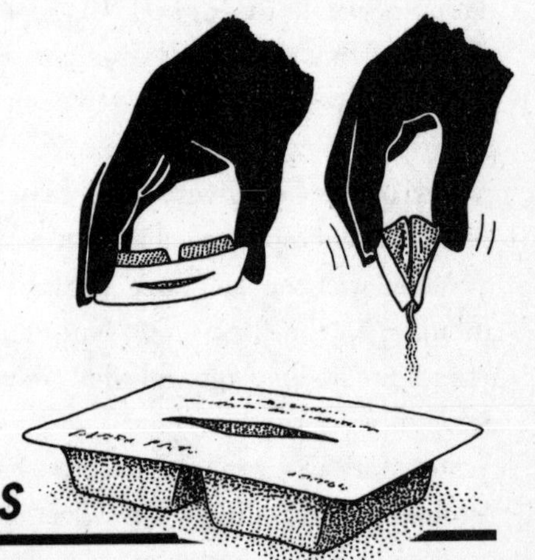

ONE-HAND DISPENSER PACKS

Do you hate those vile little condiment packages that say TEAR HERE but never really do? Do you despise those leechlike vessels that squirt the mustard on your hand instead of on your hot dog? Do you use foul language while squeezing

ODDS: 100%
ETA: 1992
PRICE: NA

out the contents of ten of those despicable packets to get enough ketchup to cover one medium-size order of fries?

Hey, if you don't like them, just say so, because one of the great inventions of the twentieth century is about to take over fast-food restaurants from coast to coast. The new product is dispenSRpaks. They're great because, unlike the "portion packages" now in hamburger joints, they don't force you to use two hands, a knife, a scissors, and your teeth to open them.

One hand only. Plus, the patented dispenSRpaks squirt straight (you can write your name in mayonnaise). And you get every last drop.

The dispenSRpak is the simplest, smartest, most useful product since the introduction of the Post It pads. And it is headed for equal, if not greater, success.

Sanford Redmond, a sixty-six-year-old New Yorker, is the man responsible for dispenSRpak. While a young soldier, Redmond worked on the A-bomb at Los Alamos. Recently the Mitsubishi Corporation bought exclusive Japanese rights to his condiment packages.

DispenSRpak is made of two soft miniature sacks resting on a stiff layer of plastic with a patented pyramidal stress concentrator (a raised bump of thin plastic that is easily broken) formed on it. Across the stress concentrator is a fault line. Hold the two edges of the package between thumb and forefinger and bend. The stress concentrator ruptures along the fault line creating a small nozzle from which the condiment is ejected.

Will he really get rich with an invention the size of a matchbox? $illions. "There isn't a major company in the United States that doesn't have a hand in progressive packaging," says the inventor. And he already has about 300 of those companies wanting to license the use of dispenSRpak, in addition to other companies that want to manufacture it. "This is bigger than the tin can," says Redmond.

DispenSRpaks can be made in sizes from 1 gram to 2 ounces and hold anything from condiments to medicine to cosmetics. The demand for his product right now would require 10,000 to 15,000 of Redmond's patented SuperStarter machines to make the packages. Currently he has only twenty machines. He has already sold ten to various companies for about $350,000 apiece.

Also worth noting, says Redmond, are the cost and the environmental aspects. "Eight 1-ounce dispenSRpaks cost 50 percent less than an 8-ounce bottle of salad dressing with a plastic cap. More importantly, dispenSRpaks use 50 percent less plastic and may be made of environmentally recyclable unmodified polyester."

$illions and $illions.

EYE-OPERATED COMPUTERS

ODDS: 95%

ETA: 1995

PRICE: $5,000 AND UP

The idea of operating a computer simply by *looking* at it seems so futuristic that you wouldn't expect to see this advance until well into the next century. The fact is, that on a very small scale, eye-operated computers are already being sold.

The system is called Eyegaze and it comes from LC Technologies in Fairfax, Virginia. The Eyegaze Computer sends out an infrared beam to the user's face. The beam allows eye movement to be tracked. Pictured on the screen is a keyboard which the user can operate by visually "pushing" the keys. The computer is able to determine which button the user is looking at.

Joe Lahoud, president of LC Technologies, sees the Eyegaze system as ideal for people who are "disabled, required to use their hands for something else while using the computer, or people who have to keep their hands clean."

Lahoud also thinks that Eyegaze could revolutionize the computer-game industry. "This will open up a new dimension in eye-hand coordination."

Another interesting application of Eyegaze is in the evaluation of advertising and commercials. By monitoring eye movement, researchers can determine which parts of an ad draw the viewer's attention.

Lahoud acknowledges that some people have raised a question

about the infrared beam emitted by the Eyegaze Computer. "We examined the possibility of health risks and found that there is no danger," he explained. "The light we are using is not in a dangerous area of the spectrum and the levels we use are far below what the government has established as dangerous."

TOBACCO FOOD

The tobacco plant, long scorned for its association with life-threatening cigarettes, may redeem itself as a major food producer before the end of the century.

ODDS: 75%

ETA: 1998

PRICE: NA

According to a leading scientist at the University of Kentucky, protein extracted from tobacco leaves is healthier for humans than the protein found in egg whites, milk, cheese, and even soybeans.

Dr. Shuh J. Sheen is a plant geneticist and pathologist who has spent the past twenty-five years studying tobacco. He has reported that tobacco-leaf protein (which, incidentally, contains no nicotine) is composed of 99.5 percent amino acids, the basic structural unit of protein. Soy protein, on the other hand, contains 80 to 90 percent amino acids, while milk has a mere 70 to 80 percent. The rest of these foods are made up of carbohydrates and lipids (fats).

What makes tobacco even more valuable, according to Dr. Sheen, is the fact that not all amino acids are alike. There are "nonessential" amino acids, which the body can produce on its own, and "essential" amino acids, which must be consumed from external sources.

As it turns out, the essential amino acid content of tobacco-leaf protein is higher than that found in any other food source and exceeds the amount recommended by the National Academy of Sciences. "Therefore," says Dr. Sheen, "you don't need to eat a lot of tobacco protein to satisfy your dietary needs."

Food manufacturers should have an easy time with tobacco protein since it can be subjected to boiling temperature and remain an odorless, tasteless, clear liquid. It also can be whipped, gelled, and baked like an egg white. To the average consumer, this means that many nutritionally useless foods, like sodas and whipped toppings, can be made protein rich.

According to Dr. Sheen, FDA approval of tobacco protein is still a few years away. And while the scientific community has accepted the discovery of tobacco protein as a viable food source, it may take longer for the American public to accept the idea that tobacco can be good for you.

TWO CARS IN ONE

ODDS: 25%

ETA: 2001

PRICE: NA

Chrysler Corporation's Voyager III concept vehicle is the car of the future for the two-car family that really doesn't want to be. If you fall into that category—a family where the priority is not quantity but rather different types of vehicles—the Voyager III may offer a less expensive, more efficient alternative to owning two cars.

The Voyager III separates into two pieces. The front half is a self-contained three-seater, commuter automobile that's 104 inches long, powered by a four-cylinder, low-emission propane engine. The rear module is an extension that will hold another five people or a lot of cargo.

The back half of the Voyager III sits in the garage until you need a van-size vehicle. When you do, you back the commuter car into the separate rear module, a process called docking. The commuter car's rear tires retract up into the wheel wells while the rear wall flops back to become the floor. The whole procedure only takes about one minute.

When the two pieces are snugly together, you have a minivan, complete with a second four-cylinder gasoline engine in the rear module.

The Voyager III is the brainchild of Chrysler president Robert A. Lutz. Stuck in traffic one day, he noticed how much gridlock was caused by cars pulling trailers. So, back at the office, he put his designers to work creating a vehicle that would combine efficient commuter transportation with expandable family use.

The concept vehicle looks downright spiffy. But there's a traffic jam of problems before this machine is ready for the roads. A few obstacles—like emissions controls, fuel and safety considerations, and insurance concerns—need to be addressed. More pressing, according to Neil Walling, Chrysler's director of advanced and international design, is structural solidity. "The combined unit has to be as solid as each unit is separately," he says.

The docking procedure is also very cumbersome. The driver backs the commuter car to within a few inches of the van section. Then the van section must be rolled forward by hand until the two are nearly engaged. Finally, an electric motor pulls the two sections together.

"If we decided tomorrow that we had to do this," explained Walling, "we would have to make it simple enough to dock so someone other than an expert could do it."

The Voyager III is full of exciting possibilities. The commuter car could be driven by alternative fuels or electricity. And the back half could be anything from a camper, to a pickup, to a twenty-person bus.

Oh, yes, there's one final little problem that needs to be resolved: Where do you put the rear license plate?

COMPUTERIZED SHRINK

ODDS: 100%

ETA: 1992

PRICE: $199

Are you blue?

Are you tired all the time? Anxious, cantankerous, and irritable? Does fun make you ill? In other words, are you depressed?

Maybe you could use a shrink? But you may be broke or unwilling to spend $100 an hour for years and years. Or you could be shy. Or ashamed. Or too busy.

So maybe what you need is a *computerized shrink*. Freud on a floppy disc.

He/she/it never gets bored or tired. He's always available when you need him, and he never ever gives a little cough in the middle of your dream about the boa constrictor, looks at his watch, and says, "I'm sorry, but our time is up."

In fact, for a one-time-only investment of $199 (assuming you have an IBM or IBM-compatible PC with hard disc and 640 RAM), he's all yours. Forever.

All kibitzing aside, "Overcoming Depression," a software package from Malibu Artifactual Intelligence Works, is a serious product designed to offer genuine relief from depression to the millions of people who could benefit from cognitive therapy. Its developer, Dr. Kenneth Mark Colby, a psychiatrist and computer scientist with over twenty years' experience as a psychotherapist, explains that 25 percent of Americans endure depression—the common cold of mental illness—at some point in their lives, yet the vast majority never seek treatment.

Cognitive therapy is not as simple as taking vitamin C for a cold. But it is a straightforward and systematic approach whose premise is that depression is often precipitated and reinforced by certain types of negative thought patterns, which, once identified and examined, can be altered to provide the depressed person with a more realistic—and positive—outlook.

You could call it . . . reprogramming.

Which is exactly why it can be done so effectively using a computer. The software program carries on a real dialogue with you. It asks questions. You give answers. You can misspell words or garble your syntax; it understands and responds.

If you get distracted, it guides you back to the issue at hand. If you get upset, it stays calm and reassuring. You can insult it, but you can't hurt its feelings. You could say that "Overcoming Depression" is more than software. It's almost a meaningful relationship.

Through dialogue and tutorials, the user is guided toward insight and reevaluation of his or her problems.

The program is available now directly from Malibu Artifactual Intelligence, 25307 Malibu Road, Malibu, CA 90265; 213-456-7787.

CHAPTER 2

who thinks of this stuff, anyway?

HOLOGRAPHIC FOOD

Who thinks of this stuff? Little holograms on lollipops, breakfast cereal, chocolate bars, and pills!

No doubt a cartoon character moving around inside a giant sucker is a heck of a lure for any four-year-old (or forty-year-old, for that matter). And granted, watch-

• • • • •

ODDS: 85%

ETA: 1992

PRICE: SAME AS REGULAR FOODS

• • • • •

ing little canoes race through your cornflakes is more entertaining than reading the back of the cereal box. But is this important?

Well, the folks at the Dimensional Foods Corporation in Boston think so. They're busy developing those wonderful, double-image, three-dimensional pictures (yes, like the ones on your Master Card) for edibles.

And, no, there will not be harmful additives added. According to Neal Winneg, Dimensional's executive vice president, the hologram is a particularly benign way of adding visual interest to food.

"Instead of using dyes or chemicals," he explained, "we are using a physical basis for food decoration." That means the colors, like the colors in a rainbow, are produced simply by the defraction of light. Like rainbows, holograms are illusions.

Light that bounces off microscopic ridges molded onto the food behaves the same way as light passing through a prism—it bends and breaks up into patterns of different colors.

The specific process being used by Dimensional Foods was developed by the company's president, Eric Begleiter. It's similar to the method of putting holograms on credit cards, except that the images go on edible materials rather than plastic film.

So, the next time you look into your cereal bowl and see someone else looking back up—and winking—relax, it's only a hologram.

EXERLOPERS

In 1990, the people of Pittsburgh got a sneak preview of what will likely be the next physical fitness craze to hit the U.S. And, in the true spirit of '90s internationalism, its inventor is a Canadian who emigrated from Russia.

ODDS: 90%

ETA: 1993

PRICE: $199 PER PAIR

It happened at the Invention/New Product Exposition (INPEX) in Pittsburgh. Some zany guy was bouncing around (and around) the convention hall wearing these strange, skatelike boots. But instead of wheels or blades, these boots had elliptical soles made of two surfaces bowed in opposite directions. Made of flexible plastic, they are held together by a central bar that acts like a spring.

This weird runner was bouncing high and far as he casually jogged up and down the rows of the inventors' convention. It looked easy, it looked like fun, and he covered a lot of ground with each bound.

Gregory Lekhtman of Montreal is the inventor. Exerlopers is the name he's given to his revolutionary running boots.

Lekhtman has a lot to say about fitness and health. The inventor of a heart monitor and other health accessories, he feels strongly that regular running is too jarring on the joints and skeletal system. "We're running to destroy ourselves!" he says. "Bang your hand on the table . . . that's not exercise, that's destroying!"

Exerlopers, on the other hand, are not "destroying." "If you are standing in a pair of these, the elliptical sole won't collapse, it will stay curved," he explains. "When you start running, the sole flattens and bounces, flattens and bounces, giving your feet a cushioned landing and send-off."

Exerlopers also give you quite a workout, according to Lekhtman, who came to Montreal from the Soviet Union in 1974. "They give four times more cardiovascular workout than running," he says, "because 75% of the 'shock factor' normally absorbed by your bones when running is absorbed by the springs and reapplied to your muscles."

However, what should make Exerlopers a hit is that they look "cool," and you just know that the workout is good for you.

So move over, mountain bikes, stair climbers, and roller blades.

DRIVER'S TV

It's hard to believe that when car radios were introduced sixty years ago, lawmakers considered them dangerously distracting and banned them in many parts of the country. Well, if you're just getting used to car phones, you'd better sit down, because the car TV is just around the corner.

ODDS: 90%

ETA: 1995

PRICE: $2,000

Driving and watching television at the same time is not outlandish nor dangerous, according to Jay Schiffman, an electrical engineer and consultant in Ferndale, Michigan, who conceived the idea fifteen years ago. Schiffman was then designing Heads Up Display (HUD) systems for military aircraft. Those are the systems (now in some cars) that project navigational and other information into space ahead of the vehicle so that the operator never has to look down at the control panel.

The car TV operates on the same principle. A miniprojector attached to the car's ceiling projects the image through a combining mirror to a point just above where the horizon meets the road. The combining mirror is a specially ground lens that reflects a "virtual image." This image appears to float above the road, about 15 feet in front of the car.

It would seem that watching "L.A. Law" and traffic simultaneously at 55 miles an hour might be a problem. Not so, says Schiffman. "We've tested 300 drivers over 300,000 miles without so much as a scratched fender.

"A person operates in terms of survival," Schiffman continued. "Five hundred thousand years ago, if a human ancestor was picking berries and noticed a shadow or change in light indicating a tiger approaching, he'd stop what he was doing and see about it. We're imprinted with the instinct to protect ourselves. If I was watching TV and the car in front of me slammed on its brakes, I'd know which was more important.

"The general consensus holds that it's not safe, but that's based on uninformed opinions. Years of research have proven it safe. In fact, it's much less distracting than a car phone."

Schiffman believes TVs for drivers will surface first in Europe and the Far East, probably in the next couple of years. "There are no perceived liability problems in some other countries, like in our too-litigious society," he says. He expects the TVs to catch on here in about five years, after lawmakers see them work safely overseas.

"The technology is here, the market is here. Now it's just a matter of convincing people."

Market analysts predict that there's a mind-boggling $20 to $30 billion annual sales potential in this country. Initially, Schiffman says, car TVs will sell for about $2,000. Then, like prices of VCRs and digital watches before them, prices of car TVs will come tumbling down to about $500 as the product catches on.

RAZOR WITH COUNTER

ODDS: 85%

ETA: 1993

PRICE: SAME AS OTHER DISPOSABLE RAZORS

The idea of a disposable razor with a shave counter is so simple and so promotable, it's bound to catch on with one of the giant razor companies.

But the man they'll have to see first is Elliot Rais, a versatile New York inventor (see Hamster Fitness Center, page 284 and Remote Control Call Forwarding Phone, page 118).

For the consumer, this razor should cut down on nicks and scrapes. After all, how often have you cut yourself with a blade you thought was okay, then remembered (after the fact) that it was actually about a dozen shaves old?

Rais's razor utilizes small tabs that run along the length of the handle. Each time you shave, simply fold in a tab or break one off.

Next time, just count the empty spots to know how many shaves your blade has been through.

"The time is right for this razor," says Rais. "Before disposables, you wouldn't want to bend or throw away any part of your razor. But since you're going to throw it out anyway, why not?"

Why not, indeed. With the razor wars played out nightly in TV commercials, a razor with a counter could have a heck of an edge.

3-D GLASSES THAT WORK ANYWHERE

ODDS: 85%

ETA: 1993

PRICE: $100

We know, we know, the very mention of 3-D makes you want to turn the page. Three-dimensional means silly glasses and B-grade monster movies; a 1950s fad that rears its ugly head every decade or two.

Bear with us. This is a different 3-D. This is 3-D that will work anywhere; 3-D that might even save lives.

With these 3-D glasses you don't need special movies that look blurry without the glasses or comic books with all those extra lines. With these 3-D glasses, any picture, movie, TV show, computer graphic, or photograph that's in color will leap right out at you. The reds will recede, the blues will come forward, and the greens maintain middle ground, making everything 2-D look 3-D.

Invented by scientists at Technology Development Corporation, a German company, the glasses have precision prisms, one for each eye, that alter the color spectrum so that it appears different in each lens. As a result, the brain sees two images. For example, it will see red in the foreground in one image and red in the background in the other. The brain reads the combined images, which register as one three-dimensional image.

According to Alan Korn, an American representative of Technology

Development Corporation, the glasses have a wide range of uses. "Doctors can use them to read CAT scans, and people can use them to enjoy their old photos in 3-D."

But perhaps the most beneficial use will come in air-traffic control towers. Wearing the 3-D glasses, controllers will actually be able to see the altitudes of stacked planes, thus helping to prevent collisions. "The FAA has two pairs of our glasses that they are already looking at right now," says Korn.

EDIBLE PENCILS

ODDS: 70%

ETA: 1995

PRICE: $10 PER DOZEN

Frustrated writers who believe that chewing on pencils improves concentration are in for unperturbed times when the totally edible pencil becomes available.

Developed in mostly nutty flavors, like almond and hazelnut, the edible pencil is made of graphite, a carbon generally useful to the human body, and mixed with a claylike organic substance. After being baked at a high temperature, the pencil is given a coating of dough. The pencil is then baked again at a lower temperature.

The creation of New York designers Constantin Boym and Laurene Leon, the edible pencil, they say, is not as crazy as it sounds. "It may surprise a lot of people to know that carbon is consumed quite a bit—every time we eat a burned hamburger or overdone toast," says Boym.

The edible pencil has already won an award from the Industrial Designers Society of America for new concepts in writing instruments, and an honorable mention in the Annual Design Review of *ID* magazine.

In this decade of environmental awareness, edible pencils may be the ultimate recyclable product.

VOICE BOX

ODDS: 40%

ETA: 1993

PRICE: $50

Worried that the kids won't wipe their feet while you're out of town? Wondering if the housekeeper will remember not to water your drenched African violet? Or maybe you want to leave word for intruders—tell them Granny's precious brooch is all zircon, not the real thing, so leave it alone!

Dr. Alan Mills of London, England, has a solution. An expert in solid-state voice reproduction, he has invented a box that will play a prerecorded message whenever someone comes near it.

A broad infrared beam picks up the body heat of anyone approaching the box and starts the playback. The box is small enough (6 inches by 3 inches by ¾ inch) to fit neatly atop any electronic equipment or even in a drawer or jewelry box. The quality of the sound depends on the case. Right now, Dr. Mills is using a plastic case, which results in moderate sound quality.

According to Brian Padgett, president of The Technology Exchange Ltd. of the United Kingdom, the company that is helping to market the Voice Box, messages last only about ten seconds, so batteries will last for years.

Uses for the Voice Box are almost infinite, he claims. "You can even use it to keep the cat off the commode!" How very British.

HOT/COLD FOOD CONTAINER

A single container for hot food and a cold drink that will heat up some stuff and cool other stuff at the same time just by opening a valve between the two chambers? Nah. Can't be.

It's true. And it's all based on a simple high school–level law of physics that says things boil easier in a vacuum. But you don't need high-school physics to be able to use this container.

ODDS: 90%

ETA: 1993

PRICE: ADD 25 TO 50 CENTS TO PRICE OF LUNCH BOX

According to Dr. Israel Siegel, the biologist/inventor behind this product, it works because of a vacuum. "The container removes heat from the food being cooled and transfers it to the food you want to be hot. The total heat is the same to your body. We just redistribute it."

When snapped open, the valve between the chambers will give the heat from one container a one-way ticket to travel to the other container. A desiccant surrounding the heating chamber will pull whatever heat it can from the water around the cooling chamber. The water around the cooling chamber will be getting heat from the room-temperature food it contains, thereby "cooling off" the food or beverage inside.

You'll see burgers and sodas packaged together at convenience stores and fast-food restaurants. You can keep the double-chamber package with you at work or in the car for hours. Two to three minutes before you're ready to eat, just open the valve and let the container regulate the temperatures.

Siegl thought of the idea while looking for a way to use this process to build solar engines. He has licensed the container to Zephyr Associates, a manufacturer in East Farmingdale, New York, that hopes to market the product in the next two to three years.

NAIL-POLISH-REMOVER WAND

The Nail-Polish-Remover Wand is an insignificant little gadget, sure, but to women everywhere who "do" their nails, it will be as big a deal as the invention of the ballpoint pen. Like the ballpoint, the wand makes life easier and less messy.

ODDS: 80%

ETA: 1994

PRICE: $5

Invented by Louise Smith, a professional manicurist in Phoenix, Arizona, the Nail-Polish-Remover Wand looks like a felt-tip pen. Ten disposable pads made of cosmetic sponge are stacked inside and connected to one another by a thin piece of tape. The pad to be used protrudes from the bottom of the tube. You simply dip it in nail-polish remover and apply to your nails.

Like many inventors, Ms. Smith saw a problem in her profession and set out to solve it. A manicurist for six years, she found working with cotton swabs messy and ruinous to her own nails. "I always had my nails done for me before I went into this profession," she explained, "but it was hard to keep my own manicure done while I was doing other people's."

In her first attempt at designing a wand, Ms. Smith used pieces of cotton inside a hollow tube. But the cotton kept sticking to the nail polish. She then came up with the idea of using cosmetic sponges. Connected by the thin piece of tape, the ten sponges form a cartridge that slides into the wand. A thumb slide on the side of the wand is pushed down when it's time to discard a soiled pad. A clean pad automatically takes its place. When all ten have been used, a new cartridge is inserted.

Ms. Smith and her co-inventor, Frank Kautman, have a patent but not a manufacturer yet, although a couple of major companies are testing the wand.

"My ladies love it," says Ms. Smith. "If it was available now, I could sell a wand to every one of them."

SPAGHETTI SIPPER

For pasta lovers who don't have time to sit at a table, wind spaghetti around a fork, drink a glass of wine, dab up the sauce with bread, and finish off with a nice capuccino or espresso, Nicholas A. Ruggieri has something for you: pasta to go.

ODDS: 75%
ETA: 1994
PRICE: $2

It had to happen. Italian food is the most popular ethnic cuisine in America. Now spaghetti is about to join hamburgers, hot dogs, and its cousin, pizza, as foods you can eat while walking down the street.

Ruggieri calls his invention the Spaghetti Sipper. It looks like a milk shake container but inside there is a single 4-foot-long strand of Ruggieri's homemade pasta. Wound around the inside of the cup, it enters into your mouth through a straw. When you suck on the spaghetti, it is drawn through a tomato-sauce compartment inside the container. Teeth at the base of the straw prevent the spaghetti strand from slipping away when you pause.

"I was sipping a soda in the car one day, and I thought, 'Why not spaghetti in a hurry?' " Ruggieri explained. An Italian immigrant, he had worked at an overnight mail delivery service, so he knew all about eating on the run. The Spaghetti Sipper, he explained, is the no-mess, no-hassle way to eat pasta.

Ruggieri, thirty-six, who now manages real estate in Rochester, New York, believes that his Spaghetti Sipper is perfect for this country because "America is filled with accelerated people, more and more on the go."

For mothers on the go, Ruggieri foresees a microwave version of the Spaghetti Sipper on supermarket shelves sometime around 1997.

CHAPTER 3

environmental stuff

SCRAP-HEAP HOMES

A house built of old tires, earth, and aluminum cans isn't exactly where you would expect to find a famous screen actor making his home. Unless, of course, that actor is an ecological advocate who wants to show the world that we can reuse what we throw away to make amazingly wonderful abodes!

• • • • •

ODDS: 90%

ETA: 1993

PRICE: $40,000

• • • • •

The actor is Dennis Weaver of "Gunsmoke" and "McCloud" fame. His home is an 8,500-square-foot, $500,000 structure built into a hill near Telluride, Colorado. It was constructed using 3,000 old tires and 200,000 aluminum cans. Everything in Weaver's home is run by the sun, including the hot tub and the pump, which operates the living-room waterfall.

The house was created by forty-four-year-old visionary architect

Michael Reynolds of Taos, New Mexico, who has built more than fifty of these energy-saving structures he calls Earth Ships.

A Walter Cronkite/Charles Kuralt environmental report nearly twenty years ago first inspired the young Reynolds to work at creating ecologically sound homes. After considerable experimentation, he found that a combination of old tires, cans, and earth formed ideal building blocks for his self-sufficient homes.

"The house is like a battery," Reynolds explains. "The dense mass of the materials [3 feet thick] stores and then holds energy from either the sun or conventional heat sources."

Weaver's home, for example, after a year of warming will hold a constant temperature of about 68 degrees Fahrenheit in winter and summer. The house is not even hooked up to a power line. Photovoltaic cells provide juice for lights.

Weaver has 300 square feet of planters for vegetables and fruit, which are irrigated by a system that filters gray runoff water from five baths and a laundry. "This is a house you don't have to take care of—it takes care of you," says the actor.

If you don't have $500,000 or so to spend on a self-sufficient home of your own, you can build it yourself using architect Reynolds's step-by-step guidebook, *Earth Ship*. The ambitious do-it-yourselfer, says Reynolds, can build his own home from tires, dirt, and cans and save up to 75 percent on the cost of conventional materials. A 2,500-square-foot home could run about $40,000 if you work on it yourself.

Reynolds expects whole Earth Ship communities to spring up around America in the next half-dozen years.

NATURAL GAS–POWERED CARS

If you're concerned about air pollution and/or American dependence on foreign oil, you might think seriously about converting your car to natural gas. This clean-burning fuel, available now in some regions, will be a viable option throughout North America very soon.

ODDS: 85%

ETA: 1993

PRICE: $3,000 FOR COMPRESSOR AND INSTALLATION; $2,000 TO CONVERT CAR ENGINE

There are, however, upsides and downsides to natural gas conversion. Besides the advantages stated above, the most interesting plus is that you'll be able to fill 'er up at home. And at a far better price than if you used petroleum. The major negatives are the high cost of converting the car and paying for a home compressor. Also, for the time being it takes hours to fill a car's tank.

The home compressor is the piece of breakthrough equipment. About the size of a 21-inch TV set, it's mounted on a concrete slab next to your driveway. The natural gas that's fed into your home through the basement is the same fuel that's going to power your car. The compressor takes the gas, which enters your home under very low pressure, and pumps the pressure up.

"For any situation—personal or commercial—where the vehicle is parked for several hours, the Fuelmaker home compressor is an ideal way to refuel and save," says Warren Shott, manager of administration for Fuelmaker Corporation in Vancouver, Canada. You'll need to park for a while since it takes an hour to pump a single gallon into your car.

Until compressors are mass-produced in large quantities, they'll sell for $3,000, and the removable converter in your car's engine will cost another $2,000. The big savings is that natural gas sells for a lot less than petroleum—about 80 cents a gallon in New York and 68 cents in Pittsburgh. Natural gas gets the same mileage as regular gas and burns cleaner.

The one-gallon-an-hour filling rate is a major drawback for any driver who goes great distances. But for commuters and homemakers who drive short distances, a natural gas–powered vehicle can make sense.

POTATO PLASTIC

ODDS: 80%

ETA: 2000

PRICE: NA

Every soldier ever stuck on KP, every homemaker, every cook—anyone who has ever had to peel a potato—knows about the downsides of potato scraps. Now, it appears, those same peels could solve one of man's most pressing environmental problems. Scientists have begun making a plastic from potatoes that is completely degradable either by bacterial action or by sunlight, or by a combination of the two.

This is a huge breakthrough because, unlike other so-called degradable plastics, this one breaks down completely, leaving only a harmless residue. When the plastic is used in agricultural applications, the breakdown products can actually promote plant growth.

Researchers at the Argonne National Laboratory (a center operated by the University of Chicago for the Department of Energy) have demonstrated that starchy, organic by-products can replace petrochemicals as the raw ingredients for making this plastic. Using potato scraps from French-fry processing plants, they manufactured a potato plastic made of long chains of lactic acid molecules strung together. The plastic degrades when exposed to water and can be modified to deteriorate when exposed to sunlight.

The scientists believe they can even regulate the time the plastic takes to degrade, from a few weeks to a few years.

There is still a long way to go before potato-plastic garbage bags and other products appear in the marketplace. The process has to be perfected and the cost reduced to a point where competitively priced products can be manufactured. The most optimistic forecast is 1994, but the year 2000 is more likely.

A patent is now pending on the process, and companies like Land-O-Lakes and Proctor and Gamble have expressed interest.

One thing for sure is that there will never be a shortage of raw materials. The food industry in the U.S. throws away about 10 billion pounds of potato scraps every year.

Another interesting property of potato plastic is that you can eat it. "It tastes terrible, but it is digestible," says Bob Schwabach, director of scientific communications at Argonne.

SALT-AND-WATER AIR CONDITIONER

ODDS: 90%

ETA: 1993

PRICE: $2,000 FOR "3 TON" AC

A realistic alternative to the big blast, environmentally unfriendly air conditioner is poised to enter the marketplace. The new appliance employs a process that dehumidifies and purifies air, using a strong saline solution, and then cools it with H_2O instead of ozone-harming chlorofluorocarbons.

This AC looks like any other AC: a rectangular box that's stuck in an open window and plugged into the wall. It runs on electricity with the addition of a small amount of gas fuel (oil or butane). The fuel is necessary to boil or clean the water so it can be reused continuously.

Although the salt-water air conditioner needs to be hooked up to an oil or gas line (unlike other ACs), it will only use about half as much electricity. That's because there are no fancy compressors, just some small pumps and fans.

The technology is fairly simple: The air conditioner takes fresh air, dehumidifies and cools it, and circulates it through the room. Incoming air is drawn by a fan and gets sprayed with a "desiccant" (a soluble salt such as lithium bromide) which absorbs the air's moisture. There's a "heat transfer" chamber inside the air conditioner that cools the air as it's being dried. The air then passes to another chamber where it's sprayed with water, which cools it to about 55 degrees Fahrenheit. The chilly blast is then delivered to your room.

The development of salt-and-water air conditioning was a happy accident. James Beckman, a chemical engineering professor at Arizona State University, and Walter Albers, a high-tech entrepreneur, were performing heat-mass transfer experiments in attempting to develop water purification and ethanol-production devices. When they added a saline solution into the equation, they discovered it had an air-cooling effect.

The salt-and-water air conditioners will be manufactured by Alessa Industries, a Saudi Arabian company; and Albers Air Conditioning Corporation of Tempe, Arizona, will be supplied with 20,000 units in 1992. Eventually they hope to market them to home owners everywhere through conventional distributors.

MANUAL GARBAGE COMPACTOR

ODDS: 100%

ETA: 1992

PRICE: $40

When historians write about trash in the years to come, Henry Massennet's name should have an honored place. The transplanted Frenchman's invention could change the way a nation handles its garbage.

Massennet's creation is the Manual Garbage Compactor. Like most enduring and successful inventions, it's simple. Imagine a standard, large-size kitchen garbage can. Inside, it uses a standard bag of 13-gallon capacity. Now, visualize a lever or plunger that goes into the can through a hole in the lid.

To work it, you open the top and dump in the garbage. When the top is closed, the bag is automatically secured to the can. Then pull the lever on the top to the right and push straight down. Your refuse is compacted; the bag is intact.

The polypropylene bin stores four to six times as much trash as a regular garbage can of the same size!

Michel Gauthier, head of Compac Manufacturing of Virginia Beach, Virginia, which is distributing the can, says, "Whereas other compactors are electric, this one is completely manual. A child can use it. It will crush beer cans, milk cartons, almost anything. It's also quite light—6.6 pounds.

"I have one under my desk. I use one bag for a week, crushing the accumulated trash five or six times during that period."

The manual compactor has already achieved some success on boats. Its first appearance for consumers will be in department stores in California.

POPCORN PACKING PELLETS

ODDS: 75%

ETA: 1993

PRICE: NA

Styrofoam peanuts, those little environmental scourges that protect stuff packed in boxes, are on their way out. Popcorn will soon be the new "in" packing material for cushioning everything from pottery to appliances. Popcorn is biodegradable, costs about a fifth less than Styrofoam, it's cling-free, and it tastes good.

Cork Foster, a Canadian businessman, is credited with starting the trend when he began using popcorn in the spring of 1990. His company, Berry-Hill Limited, of Saint Thomas, Ontario, specializes in goods for "hobby farmers and weekend gardeners." Foster had a feeling that sooner or later his customers were going to rebel against Styrofoam peanuts.

"In April of 1990, I had a meeting with our shipping supervisor and we agreed that our customers have a higher sense of environmental awareness than most other consumers. I said to him, 'The day will come when they will complain about Styrofoam.'

"Now, I'm not walking on water or anything," Foster continued, "but it was prophetic. The next day two cartons came back to us. The customers had taken out their merchandise, resealed the cartons, and sent the packing material back."

Foster went home that night, sat in front of the TV with a beer, and contemplated alternatives. "I looked at Styrofoam and said, 'Well, it kind of looks like popcorn.' So the next day we sent someone out to buy popcorn and decided to test the idea on the first six orders that came in that day.

"We asked the customers to call us collect and respond. We wanted to hear whatever complaints they would have. As it turns out, we got a great response. They were all happy with it. What's more, none of them called us collect! Now, if you can't read that kind of consumer message, you should get out of business."

Ever since, Berry-Hill has been packing in popcorn. "It's worked out great," says Foster. There have been no rodent or bug problems—although customers have been known to have a munch or two, despite the DO NOT EAT warning on the box.

Foster has had inquiries from General Motors, IBM, Xerox, and other corporations about the popcorn packing, and, at present, he's developing a popper that would yield large quantities specifically for packing.

As for a patent, Foster doesn't think so. First of all, he believes he heard about popcorn packing somewhere before he started doing it. Besides, he says, "It would be like copyrighting the Bible."

Oddly enough, Foster's company still has to use Styrofoam when shipping to his American customers. U.S. Customs has tight controls on agricultural products coming into the country.

ICE-POWERED VEHICLE

ODDS: 50%

ETA: 2001

PRICE: NA

In Northern Sweden, they know all about the power of ice: As water freezes it expands with a force that can crack metal pipes and burst rocks apart. Bo Nordell is a researcher at Lulea University of Technology in Sweden. He believes this force can be harnessed to provide a clean, inexpensive energy source in cold climates.

To prove his point to doubting colleagues, Nordell invented a cart called the Icy Rider, which can do an amazing 40 miles per hour, powered by the same substance academics use to keep their cocktails cold. True, Nordell's first cart only runs for a few hundred yards, but with modifications he can expand the range to several miles.

"The reason for building it was that my colleagues at the university did not believe I could construct such a cart," says Nordell. "The idea of the cart originated from the fact that cold climate and plenty of cold, clear water are natural resources in my province."

Icy Rider runs on a pressure tank filled with nine-tenths water and one-tenth oil. When the water in the tank freezes, it expands and pushes the oil into an accumulator, a small cylinder containing nitrogen gas. When a valve is opened the gas drives a hydraulic motor. Just leave the cart outside all night in the freezing northern winter, and energy produced by the freezing water will power the cart in the morning.

The prototype Icy Rider weighs 260 pounds and uses a 27-liter oxygen cylinder for a pressure tank. The tank holds enough water to power the cart the length of three or four football fields at a speed of 40 miles per hour. Nordell is certain that Icy Rider can be made to go farther and faster. For example, if the on-board pressure tank could be left at a base station to charge the accumulator between runs, the weight of the cart could be halved.

Nordell, at present, has no intention of developing the cart himself. "The prototype is simply a way of demonstrating the power of freezing water," he says.

Still, Icy Rider is an exciting concept. It runs on a new form of renewable energy that is quiet, clean, and practically unlimited in northern climates. Replace Icy Rider's wheels with runners and you have, in effect, a snowmobile, minus the noise and air pollution.

Nordell believes that by 2001 there will be a slew of ice-powered products on the market, of which Icy Rider may be one.

CAR PARTS MADE FROM RECYCLED SODA BOTTLES

• • • • •

ODDS: 90%

ETA: 1993

PRICE: 15–25% LESS THAN VIRGIN MATERIALS

• • • • •

The plastic soda bottle you pour from today may end up as part of the car you buy in 1993. And it should bring the price of that automobile down considerably.

A new material called Stanuloy has caught the attention of two of the three big U.S. car manufacturers. In addition to being less expensive than the resins it would replace, Stanuloy stretches and is said to be more temperature resistant. This makes it ideal for hubcaps, spoilers, body side moldings, and dashboards.

But the really good thing about Stanuloy is that it's made from recycled soft-drink bottles made of polyethylene terephthalate (PET).

This would seem to be an obvious plus when it comes to selling cars in the environmentally conscious nineties. The manufacturer of Stanuloy, MRC Polymers in Chicago, however, is not so sure.

According to George Staniulis, MRC's vice president of product development and marketing, the public perception of recycled materials for use in new products is still lukewarm. Especially in something as important and expensive as an automobile. "People want virgin material."

Still, Staniulis notes, "People are driven by economies and product performance." He claims Stanuloy is as good as the expensive resins now used in cars and costs 15 to 25 percent less.

"People's mind-set is that materials aren't as good once they're broken down and used again," he added. "But nobody ever said that about gold!"

SMART LIGHTING SYSTEMS

If you want to talk about wasting energy, just think about all the lights left on in American homes and office buildings (often for twenty-four hours) when there's no one around. Or equally bad, how light bulbs are kept blazing while sunlight comes streaming through the windows.

ODDS: 100%

ETA: 1993

PRICE: SLIGHTLY HIGHER THAN CURRENT SYSTEMS

All that is going to change. By the midnineties, automatic lighting systems will be as common as remote-control garage doors. Sensor systems will turn lights off when a room is empty and turn them back on at the first sensation of human movement.

These systems will dim the lights or turn them off completely when the sun is shining and turn them up as dusk approaches or a cloud passes.

Christian Scheder of Rising Sun Enterprises, a Colorado-based energy-efficient lighting consulting company, predicts that smart lighting controls of the near future will save us 20 to 40 percent on our electric lighting bills.

Coming soon is a versatile compact fluorescent light bulb that will last ten to thirteen times longer than incandescent bulbs yet produce the same quality of light and cut electricity use by up to 75 percent. The compact fluorescent technology exists now but is not universal in application, and prices are still high. Look for that price to come down.

Future lighting systems will also employ high-intensity discharge lights (HID), like those yellow-orange lights currently used in parking lots, but which produce appealing light comparable to that of regular light bulbs. They'll offer even more savings than the new fluorescent bulbs.

"People in general are slowly becoming more aware of the importance of lighting and its impact," says Scheder. Concern for the operating cost and the quality of light should make it a big field for lighting designers and lighting engineers of the future, he predicts.

REFRIGERATION BY SOUND

ODDS: 20%

ETA: 1995

PRICE: SAME AS REGULAR REFRIGERATORS

"Wow! Like the Grateful Dead can make ice cubes."

That might be one reaction to the news that the Navy has found a way to use sound, instead of environmentally unsafe chemical coolants, to power refrigerators.

Tom Hofler, a physicist at the Naval Postgraduate School in Monterey, California, was researching heat engines in the hope of developing a highly reliable cooler for the space program. "Very little fundamental new thinking has been done on classic gas cycle heat engines since the turn of the century," he explained.

While examining some earlier research, which showed how temperature change (heat) can be manipulated to create sound, Dr. John Wheatley and Dr. G. W. Swift of Los Alamos National Laboratory decided that the converse might be true—that sound could be used to create temperature change. Hofler, then working on his Ph.D.

thesis, invented the first large-temperature-span refrigerator based on these concepts.

Hofler, Wheatley, Swift, and another colleague, Albert Miglion, now hold a patent on exactly that—an acoustic cooling engine.

The technology uses a high-amplitude loudspeaker—similar to the one in your stereo—with a piston on it that moves slightly at a very high frequency. This piston is attached to a tube filled with a pressurized gas, such as helium, and a stack of parallel plates.

Electronically generated sound waves are sent through this device, causing it to "breathe" in and out, which pumps out the heat. This action, in turn, causes the tube to grow progressively colder. Voilà, refrigeration.

Current laboratory prototypes consist of an acoustic driver and a resonator. The driver is slightly bigger than a bread box and looks like "a fat pancake," about 9 inches in diameter and 4 inches wide, says Hofler. The resonator consists of a tubular section attached to a sphere and is about 14 inches long. The tubular section contains the thermal components.

The major advantage of an acoustic refrigerator is that it requires no Freon, a chlorofluorocarbon (CFC) that abuses the planet's ozone layer. For that reason, Hofler believes, his breakthrough invention has a fighting chance of making it to America's kitchens.

Durability is another plus: The acoustic fridge has only one moving part and no sliding seals, and the components, such as the resonator, will last a lifetime.

Whether we see sound-powered fridges or not will likely depend on whether other researchers can find a chemical replacement for Freon and other CFCs. Switching coolants will be easier than manufacturing a whole new type of refrigerator.

Still, the acoustic engine is a major breakthrough in refrigeration, which the space program, cryonic specialists, and computer technologists are all looking to for advances in their fields.

SUPER-FAST BATTERY CHARGER

ODDS: 50%

ETA: 1994

PRICE: $500 FOR CAR RECHARGER

In a single year, cars, trucks, planes, and buses burden our atmosphere with 41.2 million metric tons of carbon monoxide, 1.4 million metric tons of dust and soot, 1 million metric tons of sulphur dioxide, 8.1 million metric tons of nitrogen oxide, and 6.1 million metric tons of hydrocarbons.

That's a lot of burdening. And even though most of us can't imagine quantities as large as those numbers, we do understand that these air pollutants are ruining our health.

Which brings us to the Super-Fast Battery Charger developed by the Electronic Power Devices Corporation of Norcross, Georgia, outside of Atlanta.

Why? Because the ability to quickly and cheaply recharge a battery large enough to power a car will be a major factor in the ultimate decision to replace the internal combustion engine in vehicles with nonpolluting electric engines.

The Super-Fast Battery Charger was patented on May 9, 1989, and first used by Ted Turner's TBS-TV television station to recharge video camera batteries. It cuts the time for recharging a lead acid battery, large enough to power a car, from "overnight" to a mere hour or two. A nickel cadmium battery large enough for a TV camera could be recharged in fifteen minutes instead of eight hours.

So, imagine the service station of the future. While you have a bite to eat, play a video game, or otherwise amuse yourself (or in about half an hour), your car is recharged and ready to go for another 120 miles or so. Not perfect, but workable, and certainly much better than having to "dock" your car overnight.

This is the scenario as envisioned by Yury M. Podrazhansky, founder of EPDC and the man who invented a way to rapidly recharge a battery without doing it damage—which is what normally happens when recharging is accelerated by pumping in more electricity.

Podrazhansky's technique involves a special electronic controller that jolts the battery with high current for a few hundred milliseconds, then discharges it for two or three milliseconds. After a brief rest, so the battery can adjust, the cycle repeats. Podrazhansky claims that his method of recharging could keep a battery for electric cars alive long enough to power a car for 60,000 miles. Other methods have only been able to power a car for 20,000 miles and have been known to destroy batteries when recharged too fast.

The Super-Fast Battery Charger can recharge any type of battery. "Our method does not destroy the battery," promises Podrazhansky, a Russian immigrant who came to the United States in 1978. "Our version would extend the life cycle of the electric car battery to three times as much as other methods and you'd only need to buy a new battery every three years, instead of every year."

Which is good news for motorists and good news for the environment. "Anything that reduces air pollution, we're for," enthused David Ryan, a spokesman for the Environmental Protection Agency. "In principle, we're behind it."

HUMAN-POWERED FLASHLIGHT

ODDS: 80%
ETA: 1996
PRICE: $70

You know how it goes: You buy that sexy-looking flashlight, then it sits in the "junk" drawer with the blender warranty, the fondue forks, the miniature roulette wheel, New Year's Eve noisemakers, and loose string. Finally, a couple of years later, there's a power failure. Hurray! You finally get to use that fabulous flashlight. Boo. The batteries are dead.

Never again, says Charles Babboni, a 1990 graduate of the Milwaukee Institute of Art and Design, who has created a human-powered flashlight that will last as long as you do. Inspired by those old army telephones that a soldier cranked before they'd transmit, Babboni's flashlight contains a human-powered internal generator.

The body of the flashlight is cylindrical, 8 inches long and 2 inches in diameter. A collapsible crank is attached at one end. To operate, you unfold the crank and rotate it, like you would a fishing reel. The crank is connected to internal coils, which in turn are connected to a small generator.

The coils act as a magnetic field. The interaction of the winding with the coils creates an electrical charge, which is sent to the generator. The generator then charges a pair of nickel-cadmium batteries that store the electric current for use by a 6- to 9-volt light bulb. The batteries never have to be replaced.

The generator is "geared down," which means it has a series of gears that multiply the rotations of the crank. For every one wind you give it, the generator gives out five to ten rotations. Cranking the flashlight for thirty seconds will create ten to fifteen minutes of light.

Babboni's Human-Powered Flashlight took first prize as "most utilitarian" in a contest sponsored by the Wisconsin Industrial Designers Society. The inspiration for his invention came from Earth Day, says Babboni. "This is a flashlight you'd only need to buy one of in your whole life." Plus, there are no batteries to throw away.

EASY-OFF LABELS

ODDS: 30%
ETA: 1994
PRICE: NA

When I'm on the bus I see a lot of garbage on the side of the road, and I don't want it to be there," says ten-year-old Julie Dolly, winner of the environmental award in the 1990 Invent America contest, a contest for school kids nationwide.

Julie, like many other kids her age, is knowledgeable and upset about the neglect and damage that's been done to the world's ecology.

Her teachers have educated her about the environment in rural Washington State, close to the Pacific and nature where Julie lives. "It's really pretty out here. We saw four bear run across the road."

When the Invent America contest came to school, Julie, an avid recycler, came up with the idea of Easy-Off Labels. Anyone who has ever recycled a tin can knows how hard it is to scrape those labels off, which is a recycling requirement.

Like many good inventions, Julie's is simple. "There's a string underneath the label," she explained, "so you pull the string down and the label comes right off."

Julie and her mother used kite string and Campbell's soup cans to develop their first working prototype. The string, which is slightly longer than the length of the label, is placed on the can before the label is attached. By pulling the small piece of protruding string, a person can easily lift the paper label, and the can is ready for recycling.

Julie hopes this is just the first of many products she'll invent to help the environmental cause. "I think about all the trees that we're cutting down for paper, and that we need to recycle paper," she says. "The landfills are getting filled up. We need to find new places for them."

NONCHLORINE POOL CLEANER

ODDS: 90%
ETA: 1995
PRICE: $150

The idea of using metal ions to kill germs in water is not new. NASA used silver ions to purify the water on board the Apollo spacecraft. However, employing this method for something as seemingly mundane as cleaning a swimming pool appears to be scientific overkill. Until one remembers that chlorine evaporation damages the ozone layer and that there are millions of swimming pools. So anything that does away with chlorine is okay in this book.

Leonard L. Brown, a Greenville, South Carolina, inventor and burglar alarm specialist, realized that metal ions would keep a pool clear of algae and bacteria. Bacteria won't grow in the presence of tin, and copper stops the growth of algae.

Brown's device, called an Electrolytic Ion Generator (EIG), consists of mounting half-pound, tin-copper electrodes in the water return lines of the pool filtration system. When the current is applied, the electrodes react with the water, causing small metal particles to break off, which inhibits the growth of microorganisms. The EIG wastes away in about one year and has to be replaced.

The time it takes to clean a pool varies considerably from one part of the country to another, Brown explained. A pool in one area might take twelve to twenty hours to clean, while a pool of the same size someplace else can be cleaned in just two hours, due to different levels of bacteria and conductivity in the water.

Brown has a sense that his pool cleaner is going to catch on big. "A guy from California called and said that I'm going to make a hundred million dollars on it," Brown explained with a laugh. "So I asked him if he wanted to buy the patent from me for half that amount. He said he'd get back to me. I'm still waiting!"

RECYCLABLE CAR

ODDS: 95%
ETA: 2000
PRICE: $22,000

It's the year 2001 and that dream Chevy you bought back in '94 is just about ready for the junkyard. Except there is no more junkyard. Every bit of metal, plastic, chrome, and rubber is going to be recycled. So don't feel so bad. Your '94 dream car will be reincarnated as a gleaming new Chevy for the year 2002.

Actually it's BMW, Mercedes-Benz, and Volkswagen, the German car manufacturers, that are spearheading the drive to make environmentally correct vehicles. "Our objective is to have a car that's 100 percent recyclable by the year 2000," says Christoph Huss, BMW's product information manager for North America.

A pilot plant to research the best ways of completely recycling cars is in operation at Landshut, near Munich. It's operated by BMW and its partners involved in materials processing. A total of 1,500 cars is being disassembled in order to evaluate the materials that make up cars (especially plastics) and ways of recycling them. Researchers also hope that the disassembling process will show them how to construct future cars so that they can most easily be recycled when they wear out.

BMW expects to design the first car that can be totally recycled by 1996. However, it won't be until the turn of the century that BMW will be ready to mass-produce that car. When they do, it will happen at their production plants in Bavaria.

Volkswagen and Mercedes-Benz each have their own recycling research programs. Volkswagen has already opened a recycling technology facility in northern Germany. Mercedes-Benz, meanwhile, is manufacturing all of its glove compartments from waste products and using fabric scraps to manufacture sound insulation.

In the next recycling stage, the German auto companies plan a switch to plastics that can be easily reused, and they will demand that component suppliers utilize only born-again materials in their products. Farther down the line will come the compulsory recycling of batteries, fluids, and catalytic converters. Then, finally, the totally recyclable car.

VEGETARIAN VILLAGE

ODDS: 100%

ETA: 1995

PRICE: COMPARABLE TO SIMILAR HOUSING

The nuclear families of the nineties and the back-to-the-land communes of the sixties have met and fused in San Diego. The result is Vegetarian Village.

A thirty-unit town-house complex, Vegetarian Village is an outgrowth of the "lifestyle cluster" concept, which has been most successful in housing for singles and the elderly. In this case, units are intended for vegetarians and the health conscious.

To this end, sprouting racks and juicers—not microwave ovens—are standard equipment in kitchens. There's also a swimming pool (nonchlorinated, of course), a community room, play yard, and an organic garden area.

However, as happens in evolution, the results of this venture have not been totally predictable.

"I never realized there were so many kinds of vegetarians," says assistant manager Erika Larsen. "It's really been a lesson in lifestyles." Two vegetarians don't necessarily have any more in common than two senior citizens. In fact, there are even rumors of uninhibited backyard barbecues with hot dogs and hamburgers. "We just laugh," says Erika. "There aren't any rules against it."

While some behavior may differ, there is still a strong sense of common ground. "It feels safe here. We mind our own business, but we watch out for each other. It's great if you have kids. There's a real feeling of community."

Impromptu block parties are a regular event, as are shared trips to the local farmers' market. World Vegetation Day, October 1, is a major celebration with live music, speakers, and lots of vegetables. A residents' society has been formed to guide future developments of this sort.

Will your town have a Vegetarian Village sometime soon? Or perhaps an athletic village or an artists' village? Will this type of grouping be the next wave in residential trends?

Some deep thinkers might say that Vegetarian Village is simultaneously an ingenious marketing concept and a utopian vision. That it reconciles idealism and economics, change and tradition, isolation and interdependence, the nuclear family and the tribalhood of yore.

Or it might just be a bunch of vegetarians living together in the 'burbs. Time will tell.

CHAPTER 4

looking good, feeling good

ANTI-AGING SUBSTANCE

This is not about the fountain of youth, nor the picture of Dorian Gray, but in the battle against aging, this is a significant breakthrough. Doctors have isolated a growth hormone that appears to keep our bodies younger longer.

> **ODDS:** 50%
>
> **ETA:** 2001
>
> **PRICE:** $14,000 A YEAR FOR 3 DOSES PER WEEK

By the time most of us reach our forties, it's apparent that our bodies are changing no matter how much wheat germ and exercise we get. Even if you've maintained the same body weight since you were twenty (a miracle), there has been "shifting" of composition. Fat gains a larger share while muscle deteriorates.

A substance called "growth hormone," emitted by the pituitary gland in the brain, looks after the development of muscle and bone. At middle age, the pituitary gland slows down its production of this hormone, and body composition changes.

Since 1985, genetic engineering has been able to produce growth hormone outside of the body. And scientists have begun trying to use the hormone to forestall muscle deterioration.

Much research still needs to be done. However, in a recent study conducted by Dr. Daniel Rudman at the Medical College of Wisconsin, twelve men in their sixties, seventies, and eighties who received growth hormone for six months gained 9 percent muscle and lost 14 percent of their body fat.

What scientists don't know yet is whether or not these new muscles are functional. "Before we can say that giving growth hormone is truly beneficial, we have to demonstrate an increase in muscle strength, muscle endurance, and mobility," says Dr. Mary Lee Vance, a leading endocrine specialist in this area, at the University of Virginia.

If the hormone is proven effective and safe, people at middle age would take it in injection form, daily or three times a week, in order to keep their bodies muscular. Growth hormone might even ease some skin wrinkling, though "it's not going to replace face lifts," says Dr. Vance.

An important note of caution: Some athletes and bodybuilders have obtained growth hormone on the black market and use it in large doses to force muscle growth. Unusually large doses can lead to disfigurement and even death from a disease called acromegaly.

Should all go well in the testing of growth hormone, it may enable us to look and feel younger in middle age and beyond. However, we repeat, it is not a panacea. Hair will still turn gray, memory will fade, and skin will wrinkle. So don't give up the wheat germ and exercise quite yet.

HAIR-GROWTH STIMULATOR

Is this the cure that bald men and women all over the world have been waiting for? Sort of.

ODDS: 90%

ETA: 1993

PRICE: $50 PER SESSION

First the good news. This baldness treatment has been developed with the assistance of a leading Canadian university, so there's no quackery involved. It has demonstrated astounding success. The treatment is simple and there appear to be no side effects. On the downside, it's expensive; it requires lifelong treatments; and it only works on those who have recently lost their hair.

The treatment involves the use of electricity and a hooded device that looks like a beauty salon hair dryer. The hood has four pairs of positively and negatively charged electrodes, which are powered by a 12-volt battery. While the patient sits under the hood for twelve minutes, his/her head is surrounded by an electrostatic field of positive and negative charges which stimulate hair growth. The truth is that no one knows exactly why the treatment works. But when a patient takes the treatment once a week for a period of one to two years, hair comes back.

How successful is the treatment? According to an abstract in the *International Journal of Dermatology* (vol. 29, no. 6, July/August 1990), a thirty-six-week controlled study showed the following results: "Mean hair count comparisons within the group significantly favor the treatment group, which exhibited a 66.1% hair count increase over baseline. The control group increase over baseline was 25.6%. It is notable also that 29 of the 30 treatment subjects (97.6%) exhibited regrowth or no further hair loss. The process is without side effects and untoward reactions."

When the study was extended from thirty-six weeks to a full year, the hair count increase rose from 66.1 percent to 94 percent.

The hair stimulator treatment was developed at the University of British Columbia under the direction of dermatologist Dr. Stuart Maddin and by Current Technology Corporation, a Vancouver, British Columbia, company.

According to Anne Kramer, president of Current Technology, "The idea is to catch the balding before it gets too bad. If someone has a shiny dome, this suggests that the follicles are dead. If someone has a smaller area of balding or is receding at the temples, that probably means that the follicles are simply dormant, not dead, in which case we can probably restimulate the follicles to produce mature hair again."

For those recently bald or presently losing hair the outlook is good. But, says Kramer, "This is a treatment, not a cure."

After hair has been regrown to optimum capacity, treatment sessions must be continued for life, though only once a month.

In Canada, treatments will become available to the public in 1991. In the U.S., Current Technology Corporation is waiting for FDA approval.

PEANUT-OIL BREAST IMPLANT

ODDS: 95%
ETA: 1994
PRICE: NA

Women who want to enlarge the size of their breasts or who require breast reconstruction after a mastectomy may soon have a safer option in the form of an implant filled with peanut oil.

Why peanut oil?

Dr. Judy Destouet, head of mammography at the Mallinckrodt Institute of Radiology at Washington University Medical Center in St. Louis, is one of the developers of the new implant. One of the special properties of peanut oil is that it's radiolucent, meaning that X rays will pass through it, she explains. Silicone gel and saline, the most commonly used fillers for breast implants, are more radiopaque, preventing X rays from passing through.

Because X-ray photography—mammography—is such an important tool in the early detection of breast cancer, an implant that allows its full use could well be lifesaving.

Breast cancer occurs in one of every ten women. Breast implants themselves are not considered carcinogenic, but with so many women opting to have them (2½ million in the U.S. so far), a significant number are at risk because the implants interfere with the mammography. And early detection is crucial to successful treatment.

The peanut-oil-filled implant must still undergo clinical testing and receive FDA approval. Then, the amazingly versatile peanut will have found yet another use: enhancing self-esteem.

MENTAL FITNESS GEAR

ODDS: 90%

ETA: 1992

PRICE: $599 PER BASIC MODEL

If you believe that mind power can cure anything from a bad habit to a deadly disease, then you're going to be intrigued by a product called I.R.I.S.

I.R.I.S. stands for Information Relaxation Imagination System. It's a product of Light and Sound Research of Scottsdale, Arizona, a leading conveyor of products designed to alter the state of your mind.

Where your mind should be with these products, according to David Trepas of Light and Sound, is in a place called theta. And the best way to describe that state, says Trepas, is to think of that time just before you fall asleep.

Light and Sound, using I.R.I.S., will be able to put you in that peaceful, creative, and receptive place easily for whatever purpose you desire. "Physically, I.R.I.S. is a 3-ounce, wireless pair of goggles, with everything—including ten improvement programs—'on board' in one slick piece," says Trepas. There are no wires, battery packs, or headphones. Just a wide strip that covers your eyes and adjusts snugly over your ears. It's compact, it runs on solar energy, and you can use it anywhere.

Now, what makes I.R.I.S. really interesting is that you can change the on-board programs by using an external pack about the size of a cigarette box. The external pack plugs into I.R.I.S. and downloads the programs. While the ten basic programs deal with relaxation and energy, the subject matter of the additional programs varies widely—from weight loss, to pain management, to customized messages prepared for you.

Each program will be accompanied by specific patterns of light and sound, which, the manufacturer claims, have proven effective with each condition.

An introductory version of I.R.I.S. is already available but without the interchangeable disk capacity. Today's model can only get you to the theta state. What you do once you're there is up to you.

NEW, IMPROVED DEODORANT (REALLY!)

ODDS: 80%

ETA: 1993

PRICE: COMPETITIVE

This time it's not an advertising claim nor the result of some ridiculous comparison test. This time it's for real. Scientists have identified the specific chemicals that make sweat smell bad. The result will be new deodorants that actually eliminate odor while letting you sweat freely.

Body odor is caused by harmless bacteria that live on the skin's surface and thrive on numerous chemical compounds found in our sweat. However, only those compounds in apocrine gland sweat, when exposed to the action of these bacteria, produce the unmistakable locker-room aroma.

To date, the personal hygiene industry has used two approaches to cope with this problem: deodorants that reduce and mask odor, and antiperspirants, which reduce sweating. Both contain antibacterial agents as well. But neither offers an ideal solution because sweat serves many healthy functions and many people are allergic to perfumed products.

So it was a big day for perspirers (all of us) when biochemical researchers identified the specific chemical compound in sweat that is responsible for the objectionable odor. Led by Dr. George Preti, a team of scientists at the Monell Chemical Senses Center in Philadelphia collected sweat samples from volunteers' armpits over a period of weeks. Samples were analyzed via chemical extraction, gas chromatography, mass spectrometry, and other sophisticated techniques. The culprit? A compound called 3-methyl-2-hexenoic acid.

Now someone has to come up with a way to prevent this compound from being produced from apocrine gland secretion and market a product.

One question, though: How, after years of exaggerated hype, will hygiene companies ever convince the public that there is a "new, improved" deodorant that really works?

Incidentally, further research may lead to new forms of birth control. There appears to be a link between underarm perspiration and hormone secretion in reproductive cycles.

FEMININE HYGIENE PADETTE

ODDS: 98%

ETA: 1992

PRICE: $2.50 FOR 24

The first real innovation in feminine hygiene since the tampon should be on drugstore shelves in the very near future.

Called a padette, it is narrower than a tampon, but about the same length and made of the same absorbent material. The innovation is that it's not exactly worn externally, like a regular pad. Nor is it worn internally, like a tampon. The padette is worn interlabially, between the vaginal

folds, where it's held in place by the gentle pressure of the body.

The padette, ladies, is for those certain days when you don't want to put in a tampon or wear a bulky pad. It is also most effective in dealing with stress-induced incontinence.

In Florida, where some initial testing was conducted, women had the same questions you're probably wondering about right now: "Won't it fall out?" (answer: no), "Is it comfortable?" (yes), and "How much will it hold?" (It holds as much as a regular-size tampon.)

Dr. Solomon Hirschman, a specialist in infectious diseases and an authority on toxic shock syndrome, is the creator of the padette. After he and his wife played tennis against another couple, their female opponent complained of weak muscles, which permitted a slight flow of urine to escape whenever she would exert herself. This condition, known as stress incontinence, often begins after childbirth and worsens with age.

The woman friend suggested to Dr. Hirschman that he might want to find a solution to the problem. That solution is the padette.

A company called Xtramedics of Deerfield, Illinois, is handling the further developing and marketing of the padette. According to Xtramedics president Dennis Treu, it has already received FDA approval, and additional financial backing is being negotiated. "A large regional rollout in the West will probably be the first target," he predicts.

Asked how users rated the padette in test marketing, Treu responded, "Women love this product."

VITAMIN A FOR ACNE

ODDS: 95%

ETA: 1995

PRICE: NA

High school can be cruel. And if you have acne, it can be worse. No "cool" friends. No date on Saturday night. The chess club. Total death.

High schools in the latter nineties will be kinder and gentler places to be, thanks to RBG, a new drug based on vitamin A for those who can't tolerate the side effects of Retin-A and Accutane, the two current acne champs.

The new compound, retinoyl-beta-glucuronide (RBG) is a topical creme that's applied once a day. Accutane is a highly effective acne treatment, but it's ingested and can produce severe side effects, including birth defects in pregnant women and an increase in triglycerides in the blood. Retin-A, a much safer though less powerful treatment, can cause rashes, burning sensations, and peeling, according to Dr. Arun Barua, an Iowa State University researcher who is testing RBG.

"Clinical trials found RBG as effective at reducing acne as Retin-A," said Barua, who noted that both treatments take about six months. The difference is that RBG has not produced any side effects in preliminary tests.

RBG is also being tested to see if it can rejuvenate skin. Retin-A received tremendous publicity for its alleged ability to make wrinkles fade away. "It's too early in the testing to say anything about wrinkles," admitted Barua.

However, members of a small preliminary test group concluded that the general condition of their skin improved after they'd used RBG. In particular, those with darker complexions said that RBG seemed to fade scars left by acne.

Where was this stuff when we were in high school?

ANTI-AGING THERAPY

"It takes a long time to become young."
—Pablo Picasso

•••••

ODDS: 90%

ETA: 1993

PRICE: $500 PER MONTH

•••••

Remember when you thought everything revolved around sex? And if you weren't getting any or doing it right, there were hordes of books, magazines, talk shows, and therapists you could turn to for advice. As the American population grays, the interest in orgasms is slowly giving way to concern about energy, elasticity, skin tone, and peace of mind.

Which has led at least one forward-thinking woman to the notion that millions of baby boomers will soon need therapy to deal with the accumulating decades. Hattie Wiener, fiftyish, platinum haired, cellulite free, a former dance teacher and psychotherapist, winner of the Roseland Over-Fifty Bathing Beauty Contest and a woman of unbridled optimism, claims to be the first of what will undoubtedly be many anti-aging consultants.

The idea is to change the *me* generation into the *re*generation. Her mission is to give her clients a whole new life, or at least a new lifestyle. To do this, she has to first change her clients' general attitudes about growing older. "Every day that you age is another twenty-four hours of opportunity to create youth" is one of many "Hattietudes" her clients learn.

The actual program is akin to training for an Olympic event. Hattie changes your eating habits. She shows you the exercises (mostly stretches) that will make your body as supple and posture-perfect as hers. She'll advise on skin care, hair care, and every other kind of care that will make you look and feel good. And she'll instill in you the attitude that you really are becoming younger in so many important ways.

"With anti-aging therapy, you will become a truly ageless human being," Hattie promises . . . as she dials her daughter to make plans for an afternoon of skydiving.

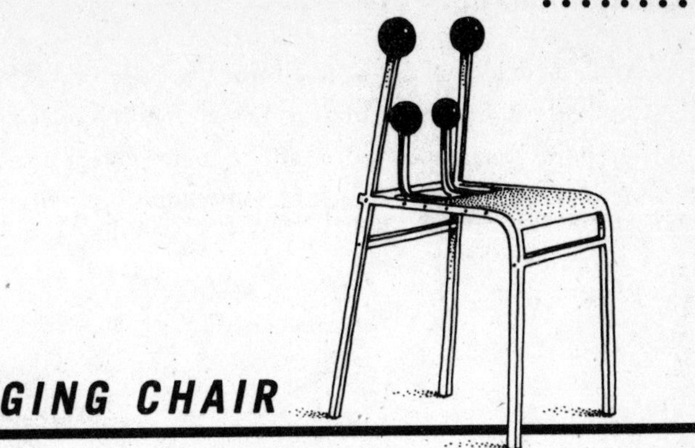

ANTI-AGING CHAIR

• • • • •

ODDS: 75%

ETA: 1992

PRICE: $600

• • • • •

If you're desperate about losing the battle with your bulge . . . and you know you should exercise more . . . but half of every day is spent sitting in a chair that's turning your middle into mush . . . don't give up. Hattie Wiener, the anti-aging consultant (see page 64) has invented a chair that will actually improve your body while you do other stuff.

In a normal, everyday chair, you sit on your gluteus maximus, the fleshy part of your rump. Your back slumps, your pelvis is cramped, and all the musculature is flaccid. "It's as if you were dropped onto a surface like a blob of flesh," says Wiener.

Proper seating would have you resting on your ischial tuberosities (*sitz* bones), with the pelvis held high and the back arching like a swan's.

For those mortals who can't hold that position for extended periods of time, Wiener, a former dancer who can, has designed the anti-aging chair. With no effort, she says, anyone can maintain an erect and proper sitting position that will improve the way you look and eliminate that sagged-out feeling.

The chair has two long outer prongs and two shorter inner prongs that make up the back. The prongs are topped with 3-inch-thick rubber balls that hold you on either side of your thoracic spine (above the waist) and on either side of your sacrum (below the waist).

The seat is shallower than a regular chair's, so the hamstrings are relaxed and "not squeezing the veins and arteries, which can cause bad circulation and varicose veins," says Wiener. A 3-inch open space at the back of the seat allows the base of the user's spine to rest unobstructed, rather than to be jammed against a surface.

The chair looks good, too. Made of metal and rubber, it could pass for one of Marcel Duchamps's famous "found objects."

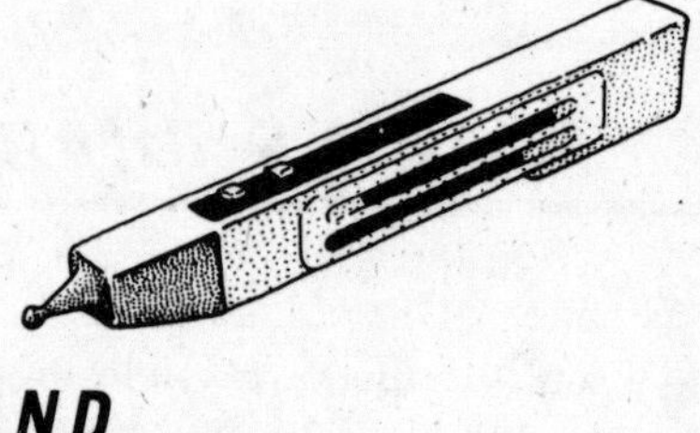

DO-IT-YOURSELF ACUPUNCTURE WAND

For people intrigued by acupuncture yet squeamish about needles, Chinese scientists have invented a do-it-yourself acupuncture wand that does away with scary skin punctures.

ODDS: 50%

ETA: 1994

PRICE: $120

Researchers at the Jinghua Technology Institute of Shanghai, China, teamed up with acupuncture specialists from the famous Long Hua Hospital of Shanghai. Together they developed this battery-powered wand that should soon be available in Sharper Image catalogues.

The wand has two basic functions. First, it can determine the exact location of an acupuncture point anywhere on the body. Second, it can—without penetrating the skin—administer a predetermined electrical charge that has the same pain-relieving effect as the insertion of acupuncture needles.

The tip of the wand is a ball point, a little larger than the ballpoint on a pen. Passed slowly over the body, it will detect the highly sensitized acupuncture points. A light signals the exact location of each point. The user then selects the strength of the electrical charge that the wand will administer. There are four settings—strong, high, medium, and weak.

The user must also decide the frequency of the charge. There're two settings—fast and slow. The final step is to push the CURE button.

What results is a zap of electrical current that can be fairly severe.

The Chinese don't claim that acupuncture provides instant relief from whatever ails you. But they do believe that it is capable of curing some diseases, relieving pain, and bringing about partial anesthesia by manipulating the body's energy.

Wang Tie Ying, chief of the science and technology business department at the Shanghai Trading Company (which started the Jinghua Institute in 1989), says the Do-It-Yourself Acupuncture Wand comes with explicit instructions, a detailed map of the body's acupuncture points, and information as to what they heal.

When asked if he would ever use the wand, Wang replied, "I already have. I used it on a toothache and on a stomachache. It works!"

THERAPEUTIC EARRINGS

ODDS: 25%

ETA: 1995

PRICE: $35 PER PAIR

From the people who brought us acupuncture and ginseng comes another treatment that can help us feel better without costly pills or appointments: magnets.

That's right. Those same metal pieces that we use to attach messages to our refrigerators can, according to the Chinese, heal headaches, backaches, stomachaches . . . whatever-aches, just by being placed at key points on the body.

In the Orient, people believe that when a magnet is placed over a particular part of the body, it causes energy to flow to that spot. And if that spot is an acupuncture point, the gush of energy will heal whatever ailment corresponds to that point.

The human ear is a hotbed of acupuncture points. So it was probably just a matter of time before some enterprising healer decided to put magnets in jewelry. The tiny magnetic cubes—smaller than breadcrumbs—fit in the back of earrings—either pierced or clip-on.

The Tianjin Technical Renovation Investment & Service Corporation is planning to sell its own line of earrings but will custom make a pair to a customer's special taste and requirements. Larger magnets will also be available for severe ailments.

The magnetic treatment takes a week or two to work. According to Wei Zhi Qiang, a Chinese marketer who is trying to sell the earrings to a U.S. distributor, the user wears the earrings for two to four hours a day for the first two days. After that, the earrings are worn continuously for a week or more.

The earrings have been tested at a number of hospitals in China, including the General Hospital of Beijing Military Command and the Beijing College of Chinese Medicine.

Men, who might not want to wear earrings, "can wear a necklace," says Wei, "with a magnet resting on the spine or on the base of the neck." There are plenty of acupuncture points in these areas.

NEW, SAFER ANTIWRINKLE CREAM

ODDS: 70%

ETA: 1994

PRICE: NA

We've known for years that vitamin C is a very good thing to put into our bodies. Now it turns out that vitamin C is a good thing for outside our bodies as well.

Ascorbic acid (vitamin C) is the principal ingredient in a new skin cream developed by two medical researchers, Dr. Lorraine F. Meisner, an associate professor of preventive medicine at the University of Wisconsin at Madison, and Dr. Michael R. Schinitsky, a pathologist. They explain that vitamin C fights wrinkles by stimulating the growth of fibroblast cells, which are vital to the health of gums, skin, and other connective tissues.

In the cream, vitamin C is used in conjunction with zinc and tyrosine, an amino acid. Together, these substances help replenish the undernourished layer of the skin responsible for wrinkles. The result is that skin formerly wrinkled by aging and sun exposure is renourished and revitalized.

"In our research we addressed the basic pathogenesis [how disease develops] of the skin," explained Dr. Meisner. "We put the cream together, tested it on our friends and relatives, and it appeared to work. Still, we weren't serious about it until we read about Retin-A [the acne medicine that supposedly fights wrinkles], which is not the answer.

"Our cream addresses the premise that wrinkles have a basis in the dermis, and it supplies ingredients that are needed by it. It appears to work, and it is less toxic than Retin-A."

The two doctors have obtained a patent for their wrinkle-fighting cream and are moving towards having it commercialized as a cosmetic (since it nourishes the dermis) rather than a drug.

NO MORE COKE-BOTTLE EYEGLASSES

ODDS: 100%

ETA: 1993

PRICE: 10% MORE THAN REGULAR LENSES

There's a revolution going on in the eyeglass industry that should forever do away with those horrible Coke-bottle lenses.

For centuries, not much has really changed in the way lenses are made. Basically, a lens is one piece of glass ground only on the surface. And if your eyesight is bad enough, you get stuck with a very thick piece of glass.

History. That's what heavy eyeglasses will become with the introduction of GRIN lenses. GRIN stands for gradient refractive index, the measure of the degree to which light can be bent. For three hundred years, the making of eyeglasses required light to be bent only one time. With GRIN, several quarter-of-a-millimeter-thin lenses

are fused together, allowing light to be gradually bent many thousands of times.

What this means for people who wear glasses is that many light rays will be focused on the retina at one time. Your present glasses focus only one ray of light on the eye. But with GRIN, no matter how bad your eyesight, your lenses will be no thicker than anyone else's.

"It's taken me a couple of years to understand the physics involved," admits Paul Dempewolf, the marketing director of Isotec, the Tucson, Arizona, firm that is selling GRIN to optical companies. "If you speak to the physicists, this technology is beyond beyond!"

MAGNETIC RAZOR BLADE CONDITIONER

ODDS: 100%

ETA: 1992

PRICE: $15

One morning a decade ago, John Hastie got a smooth, close shave from a five-day-old razor blade that he was planning to discard after one last use. "It felt like a brand-new blade!" he remembers. "It really did."

A lucky blade? That's what most other men might have thought. But not Hastie, a particularly inquisitive sort with a background in science and engineering.

After much thought and investigation, Hastie concluded that he had inadvertently left his razor on the bathroom vanity the day before at such an angle that the earth's magnetic field was pulled across the blade by the iron material under the ceramic finish of the basin.

"It took me a year to figure it out," he admits.

If it all sounds a bit farfetched, keep in mind that Hastie is a former engineer for Rockwell International and that he has, since he made his discovery, patented his Acusharpe Razor Conditioner, which can do for any single- or double-blade razor or cartridge what the earth's magnetic field did for his that amazing morning.

Hastie explains that a perfectly straight blade is what gives a smooth shave, and that magnetic energy will keep a razor blade from getting rippled or bent. Razor blade edges don't go "dull," he says, until after many shaves. "It's the rough edge that is the problem."

The Acusharpe (as in "acutely sharp") is about the size of a TV remote-control unit. When you rest your razor on it, the blade sits in a magnetic slot.

"You'll get as many as ten times the number of shaves out of your blade," says Hastie, who lives in Ellijay, Georgia. And each one will be smooth and irritation free.

LITMUS TEST FOR HAIR

ODDS: 95%

ETA: 1993

PRICE: UNDER $10 FOR KIT OF 12

Modern life is tough on hair. Air pollution and acid rain are the new enemies of healthy hair. The old foes—permanent hair coloring, straightening, and perms—are still around. So what's a girl (or a guy) to do?

Nasser Norman Tehrani, an independent cosmetic chemist who used to toil for biggies like Shulton and Clairol, believes that knowledge is the first step toward healing. So he has patented the first litmus test for hair.

According to Tehrani, a healthy pH means there is a balance between the acidity and alkalinity of the hair. The pH for normal, healthy hair is about 6.4. However, because hair is porous and absorbs all pollutants in the shaft (everything from car emissions to hair dye), the pH can drop to a very unhealthy 2 to 3 or rise to 9 or 10.

Tehrani's test will allow us to diagnose our own hair's condition. The procedure is simple. Each package will hold a dozen premeasured test tubes containing two chemicals: bromthymol blue and methyl red. Take a few strands of hair and insert them into the test tube. Cap and shake vigorously. If the liquid turns green, it means your hair is healthy. If it turns blue, it means your hair has been damaged by permanent hair color, straightening, or perms. And if the liquid becomes yellow, your hair is suffering from the effects of air pollution and acid rain.

What will you do with this information once you've acquired it? Tehrani's company, Iso-Tech, Inc., of Stamford, Connecticut, plans on having a line of remedies on the market—shampoos and conditioners—to deal with each of the problems.

If you don't do anything, Tehrani warns, your hair will become dull and lifeless, resistant to combing, and likely to break.

CHAPTER

5

house stuff

THE HANDYMAN ROBOT

ODDS: 70%

ETA: 1997

PRICE: $15,000

Now here's the robot we've all been waiting for ever since robotics and artificial intelligence became modern-day buzz words. This cute little R2D2 look-alike will prepare meals, mow the lawn, vacuum floors, fetch the newspaper, and pour drinks—all without pay, complaint, or commitment.

It's voice activated (and you only have to ask once), knows dozens of tasks, and can be "taught" to learn more, like making your favorite pasta sauce. And while you sleep, this robot will roam your abode, serving as an all-night sentry.

Droid Genesis I is the name, and for $15,000, he/she/it is a bargain.

"Simplifying people's lives," is what it's all about, according to Robert Danial, president of Droid Systems, the New York City company that is developing this household robot. And while there may be a few robots already on the market, they're mere "toys," says Danial. "They can carry a drink around on a tray—but they have no intelligence and no strength."

What constitutes intelligence in a machine is still open to debate, but Danial feels Droid Genesis I will come closer to replicating human behavior than any robot so far. "We really take for granted complex and numerous steps that happen, for example, between feeling a hot stove and removing our hand. In that action a lot of information is transmitted from the hand to the brain.

"With artificial intelligence, we model, simplify and replicate how the human mind goes about performing tasks—from vision to speech to hearing to sensing, even to smelling. Then we process that information and obtain 'intelligent' results."

The present state of Droid Genesis I is partly in the workshop and partly on the drawing board. Danial admits that while the body is set to go, the brain (i.e., the software) is still being developed.

The body is 4 feet, 6 inches tall, weighs 180 pounds, and can lift up to 15 pounds.

By the turn of the century, Droids could be as much at home in our homes as we are. "A robot will start out as a novelty," says Danial, "then it will become something we can't live without."

HOT/COOL WALLS

Walls and ceilings haven't changed much through the centuries. They still provide structure, solidarity, and shelter, just like they always have. But walls and ceilings will do more in the years ahead by actively heating and cooling your home.

ODDS: 90%
ETA: 1999
PRICE: EXPENSIVE

According to David K. Benson, the principal scientist at the Solar Energy Research Institute, the introduction of "phase-change materials" into ordinary wallboard, plywood, and ceiling tiles will forever change ceilings and walls. The changes will come from polyalcohols, ordinary hydrocarbons that can be designed to absorb or release heat when an environment reaches a certain temperature.

What this will mean to the average consumer is a bundle saved on utility bills.

Imagine your home on a blazing summer day. The rooms fill with heat that naturally rises to the ceiling. When the temperature reaches 80 degrees, the polyalcohols in the ceiling tiles spring into action, absorbing heat. It works well enough that you can delay turning on the air-conditioning for hours. Or you may not need the AC at all. The temperature range is adjusted before the walls are installed. Any further heating or cooling is up to you.

Why does this happen? "It happens," says Benson, "because of the way in which the molecules bind together. It's similar to the way ice cubes absorb heat and begin to melt. Except instead of falling down and melting on your head, the polyalcohols go through a crystalline change—that is, from one crystal to another—as they take in the heat."

Benson estimates that on an average summer day, polyalcohol walls and ceilings can delay air conditioning use from four to eight hours. However, it depends on where you are. In Death Valley, well . . . polyalcohols can do only so much.

At night, the heat stored in the tiles *must* be released. "You've got the option to turn on your air conditioning when it's cheaper at night," explained Benson. "Or in places where it's cool at night, you can let outside air into the building to cool off the ceiling tiles."

In cold climates, the technology works basically the same way. Heat absorbed during the day is released at night when outside temperatures drop.

These "phase-change" materials will be expensive when they come on the market near the end of the century. "But over time, they will be worth it," says Benson.

Worth it for the individual home owner, and for the environment, as well, by reducing energy needs.

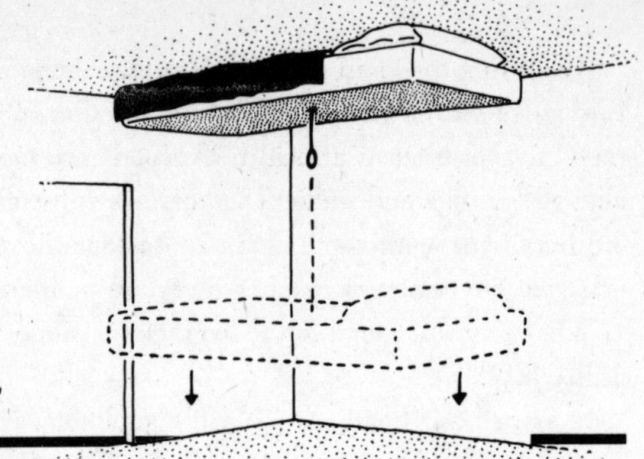

FLOATING FURNITURE

Hang onto your hats! At first thought, lighter-than-air furniture sounds a little wacko. But think again, and there is a certain bizarre practicality about sofas, beds, and chairs that disappear when not in use.

ODDS: 60%

ETA: 2001

PRICE: NA

The concept comes from a perfectly reasonable man—a doctor, in fact—William Calderwood, a family practitioner from Sun City, Arizona.

The idea of floating furniture, like many strange and wonderful ideas, was hit on during the solution of a minor problem. Dr. Calderwood's ten-year-old son wouldn't make his bed in the mornings. "I thought that if there was a bed that would just disappear when he got out of it, we could avoid the interminable daily arguments."

So Dr. Calderwood checked out his local camping and party-favor stores to see what they had. Then he began experimenting with air mattresses, balloons, and helium tanks. Within a few months, he had developed a prototype bed that stayed aloft for six weeks in his patent attorney's office.

The advantages of floating furniture are obvious to anyone in a small apartment or house. You can keep that guest bed on the ceiling until you have overnight visitors. Need extra chairs for company? Just pull them down. And cleaning floors becomes a snap when furniture is on the ceiling.

The floating bed has a bladder that's filled with helium or any other lighter-than-air gas. The bladder is designed to stay stable when the bed is in use. A tether is used to raise and lower the furniture.

There appears to be an additional benefit to lighter-than-air beds. Another of Dr. Calderwood's sons is handicapped. Because the mattress is softer than a normal one and allows for a more even weight distribution, it can prevent the pressure sores that afflict people who, like Dr. Calderwood's son, are confined to bed for long periods of time.

"Lighter-than-air furniture is 100 years ahead of its time," says Dr. Calderwood. But we can expect it in stores in about ten.

VOICE-ACTIVATED MICROWAVE OVEN

ODDS: 80%

ETA: 1992

PRICE: $500

The microwave oven, so indispensible to the modern-day kitchen, is about to get even less dispensible with the introduction of the voice-activated microwave oven. You may be thinking, "Who needs a voice-activated microwave? It's already so easy to use."

The answer is that the microwave of the future does a lot more than just follow your oral commands. It comes programmed with 250 recipes and the ability to give step-by-step cooking instructions customized for the number of diners. You can also add your own recipes. The voice-activated microwave will even help you choose which dish to prepare by showing, on its display screen, appetite-enhancing pictures of any of the 250 recipes.

If your dinner guest has high blood pressure or diabetes, the oven will suggest meals that meet the dietary restrictions of these or other illnesses.

The oven also comes with a remote-control device. In fact, you never actually have to touch the oven. You preprogram it to open on a set command, such as "Open sesame," and it will, extending a tray on which to place the food. Say, "Close sesame," and the tray retracts and the door closes.

The Voice-Activated Microwave Oven is the brainchild of Myun W. Lee, Ph.D., of the Research Institute of Engineering Science at Seoul National University in South Korea. It is being manufactured by the Daewoo Electronics Company, also of Seoul.

MICROWAVE FRYER

ODDS: 20%
ETA: 2000
PRICE: $250

Don't try this with your regular microwave oven—it could be dangerous—but Toshiba of Japan has a microwave that can fry food.

Manufacturers generally discourage consumers from trying to deep-fry in their microwaves because existing models can't do the job properly. And there's been at least one disaster when a cook was badly burned trying. Toshiba's "Ero" microwave, however, is specifically made to deep-fry.

What's special about Ero is that it can reach very high temperatures, up to 572° Fahrenheit, and that it's built to withstand those temperatures. In addition, the oven walls feature an easy-to-clean coating to ensure that spatters of oil don't stick to the inside surfaces.

With Ero, you don't immerse food in a pan of oil. Instead you simply brush a little oil onto the food and push the FRY button. The food comes out crispy and with a deep-fried flavor, without a lot of the fat and calories.

The microwave is safer than regular frying because it eliminates the possibility of oil catching fire on the stove. There's also no used oil to dispose of afterwards.

The bad news is that for economic reasons Toshiba has no immediate plans to sell Ero in America. Times, of course, change. A shift in the dollar-to-yen exchange rate might have Americans frying in their microwaves before you know it.

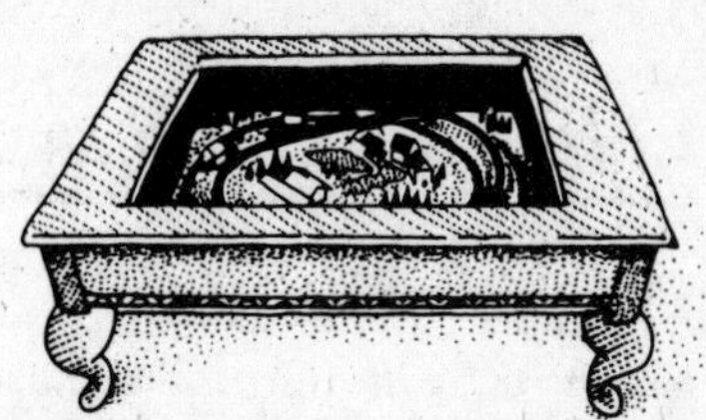

TRAIN IN A COFFEE TABLE

So the Joneses bought a marble coffee table for their living room. Big deal. You can have a complete Bavarian village, with little trees, cows, buildings, and people under the glass of your coffee table. Not only that, but push a button and a tiny steam engine with three cars behind it will come chugging through. Lift your chin in the air and say "Harumph" to the Joneses.

• • • • •

ODDS: 100%

ETA: 1992

PRICE: $1,950

• • • • •

The table is standard coffee-table size—32 inches by 48 inches by 18 inches. The train is Z gauge, the smallest scale made. Each car is less than an inch long. The whole kit and caboose'll fit in the palm of your hand.

But there's no need to handle anything, although a drawer under the table does provide access. Switches on the table control speed and direction.

Klaus Koch, of Europacific Horizons in Hoffman Estates, Illinois, creator of the train in a coffee table, believes it is most likely to catch on as a diversion in lobbies and waiting rooms. But we think it will be just great right in the living room.

BATHTUB WITH A DOOR

ODDS: 90%

ETA: 1995

PRICE: $1,500

Who of you out there has never slipped and hurt yourself getting in or out of the bathtub?

Hopefully whatever happened to you wasn't serious. Still, with 270,000 Americans injuring themselves in the tub every year, anything that makes bathing safer (especially with the population aging) is welcome news.

Richard Johnson of White Bear Lake, Minnesota, is the man with the patent on the bathtub with the door. He and his now-deceased father came up with the idea five years ago after a casual conversation with some older people. "Dad was speaking to some elderly relatives who live in a nursing home and he was surprised to hear that one of the things they missed most was the ability to take a bath," Johnson recalls. "In some cases, nursing homes have a device, much like a pulley, that can hoist an individual in the air and place him in the tub. However, the fear of falling, combined with the indignity of the procedure, means that many elderly prefer to forego their baths altogether."

With the elderly in mind, Johnson invented a hinged door with double magnetic seals that's mounted in the side of the tub or whirlpool. Drain holes between the two seals eliminate the possibility of leakage past the outer seal. In addition, the door swings in, so water pressure also helps maintain the seal.

Johnson, who suffers from back pain, believes his design is also of value to people with arthritis, pregnant women, and those who have had surgery or a recent injury. "It's ironic," he notes, "when you consider that many physicians will recommend a long, hot bath for individuals suffering from back pain, arthritis, or sore muscles, and yet it's those very injuries that can make it impossible to get in and out of the bathtub."

Naturally, you must be seated in the tub with the door closed before you begin filling it with water. Likewise, the water must be drained before you can open the door to leave. For those concerned about getting a chill while waiting, Johnson suggests installing heat lamps over the tub.

Johnson now has a prototype of his tub, which he is showing to manufacturers. With the growing population of elderly and the increase in sports-related injuries, he believes that his bathtub with a door could become a standard feature in the bathrooms of the future.

HOT CARPET

ODDS: 10%

ETA: 1994

PRICE: $1,400

With electric blankets so popular in America and Europe, it's surprising that the concept hasn't spread to other products. In Japan, on the other hand, electric carpets, electric floorboards, and even heated chairs are not unusual.

Toshiba is the major manufacturer of these "hot" luxuries, and, according to Kazue Noguchi, a public communications officer in Tokyo, Toshiba is considering marketing "hot carpets" in the U.S.

The rugs come with a removable, electrically charged power pack that channels electricity into hidden wires inside the carpet. The 6-by-2-inch pack has several heat settings and simply snaps onto the edge of the carpet. A cord runs from the pack to an electrical outlet.

The prices of the carpets vary in accordance with quality and size. But many are Belgian made and 100 percent wool.

The carpets keep feet warm and provide a cozy atmosphere in Japanese living rooms and around the TV.

If the hot carpet finds its way to the U.S., Americans might even start removing their shoes after a hard day at the office.

GUTTER CLEANING MACHINE

Cleaning gutters is no fun. It means ladders, hoses, heights, and a mess. Either that, or you pay someone to do it for you.

ODDS: 75%

ETA: 1993

PRICE: UNDER $20

William Putnam, a machinist from Portland, Oregon, and a reluctant gutter cleaner for most of his twenty-two years, decided he'd had enough. There had to be a better way, he said to himself.

After months of backyard experimentation, Putnam developed a water-powered gutter tool which he hopes to mass-produce.

You don't need a ladder with Putnam's tool, so the risk of injury is eliminated, and the job takes a fraction of the time to do. You just walk along beneath the gutter—one pass, Putnam says, will do the trick—while his gutter cleaner gets the job done.

The tool looks like an old-fashioned edger. Two aluminum or plastic tubes (one fitting inside the other) are connected by a clamp. The length of the tool can be adjusted to the height of the gutter by loosening the clamp and extending or reducing the inner tube.

A water hose is connected to the bottom end of the tube. At the other end, there's a rolling spray head which the operator runs along the lip of the gutter.

So, as you walk along holding Putnam's tool against the edge of the gutter, the spray nozzle is shooting water inside the gutter.

The nozzle is designed to rotate 180 degrees to the right or left, according to the direction the operator is moving. The nozzle can also be adjusted downward into the mouth of the downspout if clogging occurs.

One of the major advantages of Putnam's device is that it can't get stuck in the gutter. Because it rides on the rim above the gutter, even nails and branches won't stop it.

STAR NAILS

The first artisan's nails (from Mesopotamia) date back to 3500 B.C. And since the eighteenth century, nails have been mass-produced by machine in basically the same form as today. One would assume that the design, having stood the test of time, is the most logical and efficient for holding wooden things together. Well, maybe it is and maybe it isn't.

ODDS: 90%

ETA: 1994

PRICE: SAME PRICE AS REGULAR NAILS

Casting doubt on the traditional cylindrical nail's record is Frank R. Potucek, a design engineer from Palmetto, Florida. He makes a convincing argument that his invention, the Star Nail, is, in fact, far superior—that it has 85 percent more friction surface to hold the wood, and that it is less likely to cause a split.

The Star Nail has five flutes rolled into its body and barbs within each flute. A cross section of the nail does indeed look like a star. The purpose of all these flutes is to increase the surface area of the nail, thus providing more friction when it's hammered into wood. The barbs act like fishhooks. The end result is that it should hold better.

"I played around with other shapes, trying to find the best configuration before I decided on this one," Potucek said. "I tried nails with 2 sides, 3 sides, and 4 sides, until I made one with 5 sides, and that one worked the best."

The shape also works well with nail guns. The Star Nails interlock so that no binding material is necessary to hold them lined up in the gun.

The five flutes significantly reduce the amount of metal required to make each nail, so Star Nails weigh about half as much as regular nails. A 27-pound box containing approximately 5,650 nails will cost about $18.

In limited industrial tests, the nails have done well, reports Potucek. "Foremen who have used Star Nails say they've saved so much on split wood that they'd pay twice as much for them."

REMOTE-CONTROL VACUUM CLEANER

If Junior can make his remote-control car zoom in and out of the living room furniture while he sits on the couch, why can't you do the same with the vacuum cleaner? If any home appliance was meant to be operated by remote control, this is the one.

ODDS: 60%

ETA: 1993

PRICE: $500

Besides, nobody likes vacuuming.

The Koreans will probably be the first out with a remote-control vacuum cleaner. Daewoo Electronics is developing a whole line of products called High-Touch (see "Walking, Talking TV," page 101) that will keep us in our seats.

The vacuum cleaner is called the Power Brush. Its futuristic mushroom-shaped base has a standard long hose and handle with a head attached at the end. A control box is attached to the handle—at waist level, so you don't have to bend.

Turn the Power Brush on and roll it back and forth. All pretty normal. Now turn the machine off, detach the hose and handle, and put them away. But first, take the head off and attach it directly to the mushroom-shaped base. Snap off the control box from the handle and take a seat on the couch.

Housecleaning heaven. You can send the little machine scurrying around the room—back and forth, left, right—without ever getting up. You control the direction, speed, and power from the remote unit.

The Power Brush head has several detachable pieces, including a comb for lint and a separate container that collects screws and pins. The base has a flip-top lid for easy emptying.

The Power Brush should be extremely useful for the handicapped and the elderly.

Dr. Myun Lee of Seoul National University is the inventor of the Power Brush and other High-Touch products. Sometimes, he says, "designers seem to forget about consumer convenience."

MOTORIZED SHELVES

If you are short, disabled, or have trouble stretching, the Liftshelf can help you get at that long-abandoned pickle jar at the very back of the highest shelf over the kitchen counter.

ODDS: 85%

ETA: 1993

PRICE: $450 PER UNIT

Invented by Dale Owens and Mike Kingsborough of Owens Design in Bellevue, Ohio, these are motorized shelf units that fit inside standard kitchen cabinets. A flick of a switch activates the motor, which moves the unit out then lowers it until it

rests on the countertop. Remove the pickle jar, hit the switch again, and the shelves return to their place inside the cabinet.

Kingsborough's wife, Judy, provided the inspiration for the Liftshelf. A childhood polio victim, Judy has little upper-body strength, which makes it difficult for her to stretch. Mike asked his friend Dale, an engineer, to help him design shelves to help her.

They soon realized that there are a lot of people out there like Judy who could use a hand in reaching high places. "There are 40 million people in the U.S. who are either over fifty-five, or handicapped, or both," says Dale, "and many of them find it hard to reach that top shelf, so we think there could be a big market for the Liftshelf.

"We've designed the units in three standard sizes," he explained, "so that they fit into most people's existing kitchen cabinets. Talking to disabled people, we've found that they want their homes to look like everybody else's. They don't want special equipment lying around."

Designed for easy installation, a handyman/woman should be able to get the job done in about forty-five minutes, plus time for the wiring. The switches are usually placed in the lower cabinet, just inside the door, but could be located anywhere that's convenient for the user.

Mike and Dale have been selling their homemade units locally. But the big-time is just around the corner. They've joined forces with a manufacturer that can turn out 4,000 to 5,000 units a year.

"Because disabled and elderly people often live on limited incomes, we hope we can keep the price low," says Dale. "We're hoping that by the year 2001, Liftshelf will be a household word—at least in households with disabled people."

HOLOGRAPHIC WINDOWS

If you are an office worker, a home owner, or hopelessly romantic, holograhic windows will make your life better.

Now, it may seem a stretch to say that a mere window will change the way we work, live, and love, but the holographic window is not just another pane of glass.

ODDS: 70%

ETA: 1993

PRICE: $4 PER SQUARE FOOT

Technically called a "holographic diffractive structure" (HDS), it will cast natural sunlight to the farthest corner of a room. A complex microscopic diffraction pattern of ridges and valleys in a single layer on the glass bends the light, redirecting it wherever you choose. Under development at the Advanced Environmental Research Group (AERG) in Providence, Rhode Island, holographic windows are only a few years away.

When they do arrive, they'll make your workplace a far better place. According to Elizabeth King of AERG, "The use of natural full-spectrum sunlight instead of fluorescent lighting makes for a more gentle and peaceful environment than the harsh light from fluorescent bulbs. It definitely will improve worker morale and productivity. It's a very good light for seeing, and gives you the best possible resolution of what you're looking at."

In office buildings, sunlight will be able to penetrate up to 80 feet within a room and increase the light level by 200 percent, without glare.

Holographic windows will also be able to funnel light into windowless bathrooms, storage rooms, conference rooms, and dark corridors. By being focused into a narrow beam and directed through a light duct, natural sunlight could reach these interior spaces. Upon leaving the duct, the light beam would redirect off a mirror at a 45-degree angle, bouncing down through a port into the ceiling of the windowless room.

At home, the holographic window will not only give you better light, it will conserve energy and save you money. The cost of light bulbs is the obvious, but not the only, savings. "At the hottest time of the day—that's when you really want to turn the lights off," explained King, "because even the best electric lighting produces more heat than light. The cost savings will be felt most in the sunbelt states. Up to 50 percent of the total energy costs [air conditioning, etc.] of a building could be saved by using holographic windows."

Now here comes the sexy part. When light rays hit a hologram, those of a specific wavelength or color are diverted from their original path and redirected. If many holograms are overlaid in the holographic window, light rays can be thrown in different directions in a room, producing a spectacular array of colors. You'll be able to choose the colors and patterns to set the desired mood for your room.

The idea of holographic windows belongs to Sally Weber, a holographic artist and principal of AERG, whose 1980 thesis for her degree at the Massachusetts Institute of Technology dealt with light defraction. One day while she watched the brilliant display of colors produced by her hologram, the thought hit that there must be a practical application for all this energy. "Why not use it to illuminate the interior of buildings," Weber decided.

A sealed, double-pane sandwich structure with stick-on film is what the AERG people devised. Both are easy to install and maintain, using the same installation procedure as ordinary double-pane glass. The holographic window can also be inexpensively mass-produced. "And it won't need any maintenance at all," explained King. "It will never need to be adjusted, and there are no mechanical parts to go wrong."

The HDS windows work with sunlight from many different angles, though deepest penetration is during summer afternoons when the sun angles are highest.

Holographic windows, says King, can make sunlight travel "where sunlight wouldn't ordinarily go."

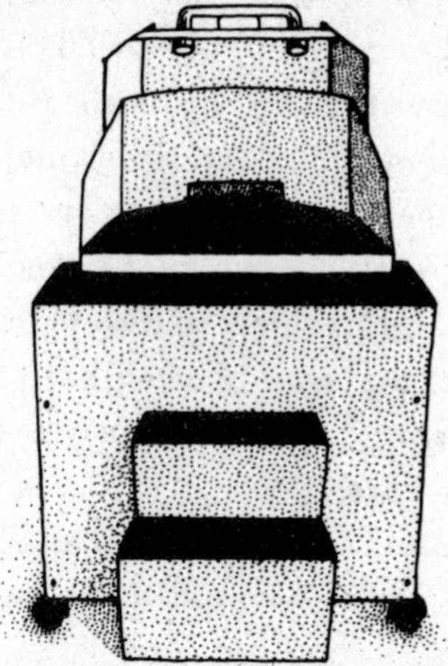

DOG TOILET

ODDS: 65%

ETA: 1993

PRICE: $150

It was a dark and stormy night. A cold rain beat down. The wind shook the trees. The ferocity of the thunder and lightning frightened grown men. But you were fine, curled up on the living-room couch, safe and warm, watching your favorite video. Suddenly, a bark rang out. Then another. Then some pathetic whining.

"Oh, no! *No!* It's Snoopy. And he needs to be walked."

Every dog owner knows this scenario. It's the price you pay for the companionship of a pet. Still, you'd think if they can put a man on the moon, they can surely put a dog on a toilet.

A similar thought crossed the mind of Richard R. Wooten, a young American foreign service officer stationed in Paris, one morning in 1984. "A lady came into the embassy and went off about her dog getting her up at 4 A.M. while it was raining and she had to walk him," Wooten recalls. The woman's exasperation with her pet made quite an impression on the young Wooten. He said to himself, "What if . . . ?"

Six years later, in Mitchellville, Maryland, where he makes his home, Wooten invented his doggie toilet. A mobile apparatus, it is rolled into position so that the "dog" seat is directly above the "human" seat. Three inches separate the two platforms. A cylindrical chute extends from the hole in the dog seat down through the hole in the human seat and into the bowl below. This way, nothing touches the human seat. When the dog has finished its business, a sensor automatically flushes the toilet and rinses the chute.

By the way, the dog reaches his seat by way of four little steps. According to Wooten, in two weeks even a dumb dog can learn to climb the stairs, do its thing, and step down.

Walk-Me-Not, the name Wooten has picked for his invention, is made of lightweight, easy-to-clean polyethylene. It weighs 15 pounds and folds up for travel.

How does Wooten's dog like it? "I'm allergic to dogs, though I do love them," he replies, unruffled. "I have fish. Sixteen Japanese goldfish."

CLEAN AIR MACHINE

ODDS: 90%
ETA: 1995
PRICE: $500

Ozone. It's a charged word. The ozone layer way up high in the atmosphere protects us, but ozone in breathing vicinity is toxic.

Larry McMurray, a mechanical engineer in Seattle, has worked with ozone since 1982. He learned that odor in the air can actually be killed by ozone.

So McMurray developed a machine that takes the oxygen in a room, churns it through the machine, converts it into ozone, and then blows it around the room with a built-in fan. The unit weighs 15 pounds and fits into a carrying case the size of a woman's cosmetic luggage case (7 inches by 7 inches by 15 inches).

Once the room is full of ozone, it gets to work scrubbing out any smoke, mildew, germs, or pet odors it comes across. It then calmly reverts back to oxygen.

Since you can't judge exactly how much ozone would be needed, and since any leftover ozone is hazardous, McMurray has added a safety feature. After the ozone has been dispersed in the room, a water-based rinsing solution is sent into the air so that any remaining ozone will have particles to break down into oxygen. The rinsing solution can be scented with whatever fragrance you like. When you reenter the room, all the odors—and the ozone—will be gone.

After a room full of poker players' cigar smoke, the machine needs to be turned on for twenty minutes. For mildew from a flood, it can be used for twenty-four hours. The room is to be evacuated when the machine is on, no matter what the quantity of odor. And the room has to be sealed.

DIVERSIFIED FURNITURE UNIT

ODDS: 65%

ETA: 1995

PRICE: NA

Bridgette Holley, a Colorado nurse, looked around her small studio apartment one day and came up with an idea that could change the shape of the furniture world. "What if you could have a whole houseful of furniture in just a few modular, multifunctional pieces?" she pondered. "You could make the most of small living spaces and save money."

So to all of you out there living in tiny abodes on tight budgets, Holley says, "You don't have to sacrifice the luxuries and benefits of a large home just because you're living in a small apartment."

To prove her point, Holley designed a modular set of furniture pieces that can fit into a space just 13 feet by 14 feet and can be arranged in sixteen different configurations, including a U-shaped pattern for use as a single unit. In that space you will have a china cabinet, bookcase, bar, wine cabinet, dresser, sleeper sofa, bed, dining table, and entertainment center.

The modular furniture will be made of wood and plastic, with glass, leather, and plastic trim. Although no prices have been set yet, the modules will cost the buyer far less than the equivalent amount of functions in regular furniture of the same quality.

The Invention Submission Corporation of Pittsburgh, Pennsylvania, is promoting the Diversified Comfort Unit. Key marketing targets will be students, retirees, and anyone who lives in a studio apartment.

MACHINE-WASHABLE WOOL

Good news for us. Bad news for the dry cleaners. Soon you'll be able to toss your fine wool sweaters into the automatic washer and dryer without a worry.

ODDS: 95%

ETA: 1993

PRICE: 20% MORE THAN REGULAR WOOL

This breakthrough comes to us from a "down under" company called Brandella, which has kept Australian kids in school uniforms for the past 60 years. Three years ago, when the company decided to enter the worldwide professional uniform market, it also began research on a washable, dryable wool. What they came up with is now called the "Brandella Process," and it involves submerging the knitted garment into a chemical compound that renders the garment totally washable and dryable in domestic laundries.

"You can wash and dry with no shrinkage, no piling, no stretching, and no color loss," says Glen Stinebaugh, the company's North American director. "Brandella is coming into this marketplace putting a two-year guarantee on the garments."

Brandella plans to launch a high-profile advertising campaign to publicize the new easy-to-care-for wool. Also in the works are plans to open a manufacturing plant in the U.S. to more effectively service the needs of the North American market.

But perhaps most exciting for those of us who like wool but don't wear uniforms, Brandella plans to license its technology to other manufacturers. "We've already had initial conversations with several companies interested in our technology," Stinebaugh revealed.

BLUE ROSES

ODDS: 90%

ETA: 1995

PRICE: $100 PER STEM

The gift of a dozen red roses is a statement of passionate love. What a bouquet of blue roses will represent is up for grabs, because they're still on the genetic drawing board.

Perhaps blue roses will signify sadness. When you have the "blues," send them to the man or woman who broke your heart. More likely, blue roses will stand for "broke," as in $100 apiece or $1,200 a dozen.

That's the anticipated selling price in today's dollars when blue roses turn up for sale at your neighborhood florist shop. "In flowers, novelty has value," explained Michael Dalling, president of Calgene Pacific, the Melbourne, Australia, company that's developing the new roses in a joint venture with a Japanese firm, Suntory.

Nationalism is another reason Calgene Pacific expects to get top dollar for blue roses. The American flag, the Australian flag, the British flag—they're all red, white, and blue. Just imagine the rose decorations on the Fourth of July or the twenty-fourth of May (Queen Victoria's Birthday).

Ahhh, but the roses aren't here yet. In Melbourne, genetic engineers are working to purify an enzyme that is missing in roses but accounts for blue color in other flowers, such as petunias. Once the enzyme is purified, the gene to produce it will be cloned and inserted into rose plants. The altered plant will pass on its blue color to its progeny, ensuring future blue generations.

The roses will not only be beautiful, we're assured, but they will last longer. Calgene Pacific is developing a technique to block the production of ethylene, a substance naturally produced by flowers that leads to wilting after they're cut.

THE INDESTRUCTIBLE LAWN

ODDS: 95%

ETA: 1995

PRICE: $5–$8 PER POUND PLUS COST OF PLANTING

A vibrantly green, meticulously manicured front lawn is as much a part of the American mentality as Thanksgiving, baseball, and Old Glory. Yet for many suburbanites, and especially those in severe climates, the perfect lawn is a time-consuming and elusive thing.

The U.S. Department of Agriculture is about to change that with a grass from the Far East called zoysia.

True grass aficionados know all about this stuff. It makes a beautiful lawn, and it's impervious to heat, cold, drought, insects, and disease. The downside is that zoysia has to be planted plug by plug, a painstaking and expensive process ($20 a pound).

Researchers at the USDA's National Turfgrass Evaluation Program are hard at work evaluating a new breed of zoysia that maintains all of the advantages while being easier to plant and therefore less costly.

Already, the USDA team in Beltsville, Maryland, has come up with a fast-seeding variety that's able to grow and spread into a lawn within three months. And they have the cost down to about $5 per pound, for a coverage of 1,000 square feet.

What's more, as a result of cross-pollination of different varieties of zoysia seed, the new lawn will require 50 percent less watering. And although zoysia needs to be mowed weekly during the growing season, if left unmowed for several weeks it will only grow 6 to 8 inches.

Weeds rarely creep into zoysia grass, because it's so thick they have no place to grow. "We're trying to reduce the consumer's dependence on weed killers," says Kevin Morris, head of the USDA's program.

There is still one major drawback to the grass that has not been remedied: It turns brown in winter. The USDA researchers are testing a mix of zoysia seed with tall fescue, a type of winter grass, in an effort to keep lawns green year-round.

Even if you are not a lawn lover, there's another advantage that may come out of this research. Zoysia could replace artificial turf on baseball and football fields. As any sports purist knows, fake turf alters the game, causes injuries, and shortens careers.

CHAPTER 6

entertainment stuff

PERSONALIZED TV

Television services are going to change radically and improve dramatically by the end of the century. The big difference is that technology will permit you to truly personalize your viewing habits.

• • • • •

ODDS: 70%

ETA: 2000

PRICE: NA

• • • • •

Here are the major improvements you can expect by the year 2000.

- When you open your TV-listing magazine, don't expect to find shows categorized by day and time. Instead, they'll be listed by subject matter, such as science fiction, comedy, adventure, etc. You'll be able to watch any show you want at any time you want.

- Channels will disappear, except for a few local broadcast stations. You will have access to an almost limitless set of programs and be able to order up as many as four at a time.
- Your home will become a live TV studio. Using the telephone network, you'll have the capability to send live or recorded video footage from one subscriber to another. "If a family has a birthday party for a six-year-old and Grandma can't come, they could turn on their video camera, use the remote controller to dial, and send signals over to Grandma, who simply pushes a button to receive the signal," explains Walter M. Carleton of GTE Laboratories in Waltham, Massachusetts, the company spearheading this new technology.

If these innovations seem impossibly futuristic, consider that tests are about to begin in the town of Cerritos, California. The technology behind it is a "broadband switch," which will be installed in your local telephone central office. It is capable of carrying more and higher-frequency signals than the type of cable that now connects to your television box. The switch is designed to control video signals on coaxial or fiber telephone networks.

The subscriber will be able to choose any show he or she wants for instant viewing because the system will be hooked up to several video libraries. Simply pick a title from the on-screen menus and the signal will be transmitted across the phone wire onto your video screen, while allowing features such as fast forward and freeze frame.

Perfecting this technology will be the first of three hurdles GTE will face in the coming years. The second is the U.S. Congress, which is debating the concept of sending video programming via telephone systems. The Federal Communications Commission has given GTE until 1994 to show what they can do in test towns like Cerritos.

The final judge is the public, says Carleton. "A lot depends on consumer acceptance."

And consumer acceptance depends a lot on the price—which has yet to be determined.

TINY TV

At 1 square inch, this television screen is so small that it makes a Watchman look big. In fact, the entire set is half the size of a cigarette pack and weighs only 1½ ounces, yet the picture is as large as that of a 14-inch living-room model.

ODDS: 85%

ETA: 1995

PRICE: $150

Is this double-talk or what?

What. The tiny TV hooks onto your eyeglasses or is worn with a headset. The hardware will occupy only about one-tenth of your field of vision. When you look through its 1-inch-square lens, you will see a transparent, 14-inch-size picture that will appear to be floating in front of you.

"It's sort of like bifocals," says Allen Becker, president of Reflection Technology, the Waltham, Massachusetts, company that's developed the tiny TV. "You can look through them or not, as you wish. And if you do, you'll see everything in your field of vision, plus a TV show." Without any hardware interfering with your movement you'll be able to shop, walk, jog, bike, sail, whatever, and still watch your favorite TV show.

Becker, who studied electrical engineering at MIT but never graduated, admits he "stumbled across the technology and then brought in some guys I knew who could make it work."

The set is called the Private Eye TV. Becker and company also developed the Private Eye computer, an identically sized screen hooked up to a pocket keyboard. This "floating screen" allows doctors and engineers, and others who need to work and see a computer at the same time, to be more efficient.

The Private Eye TV should help you do two things at once as well. The unit picks up signals just like a regular set and runs on two AA batteries. Although you won't get cable, videotapes are a real possibility via a minideck for 8mm cassettes that would be worn on a belt.

"REAL 3-D" LASER DISPLAY

In 1990, Texas Instruments unveiled a laser display system that offered three-dimensional images when viewed from any angle, by any number of people, and the viewers didn't need to wear colored eyeglasses.

ODDS: 90%

ETA: 1995

PRICE: NA

The system is called OmniView, and Texas Instruments claims it's the first system to create an image with real depth rather than a flat image that tricks the eye into seeing three dimensions.

Don Williams, a human factors engineer in the company's computer systems laboratory, and Felix Garcia, an opto/mechanical technician, are behind OmniView. They wanted to create a 3-D display that had "true volume, with all the visual cues real objects have."

They figured that the problems could be solved by using a rotating surface rather than a flat one. What they came up with is a large double helical (spiral) disc made of translucent material. This disc rotates on the end of a drive shaft, allowing viewers to look at it from any angle. As the double helix rotates, it presents a screen area which continually varies in depth. (Compare it to the threads on a large, moving screw.)

A laser beam scans the disc as it turns, similar to the way the electron beam inside a TV tube scans the screen surface. And, just like the electron beam in your TV, the brightness of the laser beam varies to create an image.

As the laser beam scans onto the turning disc surface, points of light are projected into the space swept out by the disc. In this way,

Williams explained, "the eye fuses the 2-D slices of light into 3-D."

When OmniView reaches our homes, it will probably take the form of a dome that will sit on a table in the middle of the room. The viewer will be able to walk around the dome, observing the image from all sides. Broadcast TV in 3-D would be extremely complex and expensive, although Williams predicts that it may someday happen.

Texas Instruments is seeking a partner to jointly develop OmniView. The company already has customers, including the U.S. military. Williams foresees many other uses for OmniView including 3-D CAT scans to diagnose disease and plot surgery, screens to view "giant" DNA molecules, and 3-D radar screens for air-traffic controllers.

WALKING, TALKING TV

With all the power our society attributes to television, the set itself is rather boring. It's inert, unmoving, uninteresting—until it gets turned on. One company is about to change all that by instilling the TV set with more lifelike qualities.

ODDS: 50%

ETA: 1993

PRICE: $2,500

The High-Touch TV from Daewoo Electronics of Korea won't just sit there in the corner. Using your remote-control box, you can move it around the room without ever leaving the couch. You can even adjust the angle of the set, tilting it right or left, until it's just right.

Ah, but High-Touch TV does more than just move around like a remote-control toy. You can "reserve," or automatically videotape a TV program, simply by talking to the tube. Just press the key for "program reservation" and a soft , feminine voice will ask you a series of questions. "What date do you want to tape this program? What channel? What time do you want to start? What time do you want to end?" Your answers are programmed into the remote-control box.

Reservations can be made on a daily or weekly basis. You can even set the TV to automatically switch on when the program is about to begin.

"High-Touch is a concept which emphasizes human dignity in product design and new functions," says Myun Lee, the Seoul National University professor who developed the technology for Daewoo. "The product is intended to emphasize the consumer's point of view. You don't have to refer to a thick manual."

High-Touch does a bunch of other stuff besides talk, listen, and move. For example, the viewer can play cinematographer by selecting "screen types." A viewer might choose a soft screen for a romantic movie, a dark screen for a mystery, or a bright screen for sports events.

High-Touch also has a number of computerlike functions: It can store important telephone numbers and Christmas card lists.

For your birthday, High-Touch does something a little extra. It remembers the date by showing your name on the screen, accompanied by the appropriate zodiac graphic. Then it hums "Happy Birthday."

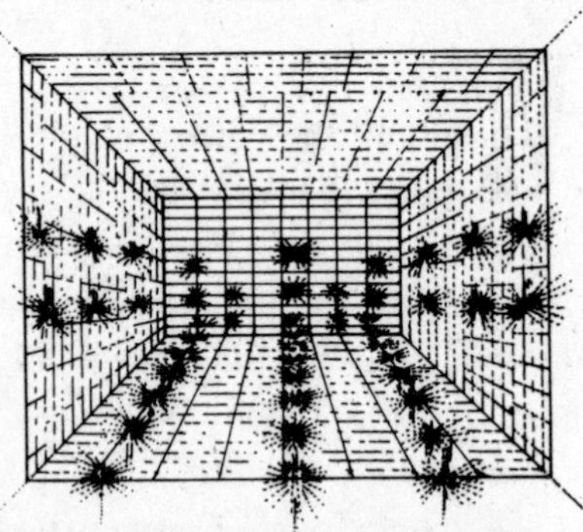

DESIGNER SOUND

ODDS: 95%

ETA: 1999

PRICE: $1,000

Imagine looking at your living room reproduced on a 3-D computer screen. On the screen a simulated note is sounded from the stereo in the room's center. Suddenly, brightly colored clusters of spikes, cones, and rectangles burst forth on the screen, where they're superimposed over the image of your couches, chairs, tables, ceiling, and walls. This is the language of sound.

According to Adam Stettner, developer of the computer program Sound Tracer, this "tool" will help architects predict the quality of sound in a room even before a single brick is laid. Naturally, its first applications will be in rooms—like concert halls and theaters—where the quality of sound is of paramount importance.

Until now, acousticians and architects have made design judgments based on complicated scale models, using light waves to simulate sound travel—a tedious, imprecise, and expensive method, according to Stettner. Because Sound Tracer is less costly and more accurate, it will not only help build great concert halls and auditoriums, but down the road it will also make noise control more of a reality in the design of factories, restaurants, train stations—anyplace humans and machines congregate.

"There have been studies that show noise can severely affect someone's well-being," says Stettner. "If you're working in a space that has a lot of residual noise, it can affect your sleep cycle, your metabolism, and your psychological state. There's no reason why a lot of these factories have to be so noisy. We'd all be better off with the sound of crickets and cows lowing."

Sound Tracer works by measuring three aspects of simulated sound: loudness, clarity, and spatial impression (the extent that one feels "immersed" in sound). On the computer screen, Sound Tracer uses colorful icons to represent visually the varying degree of these elements in a room. For example, the length and color of a line next to the far windows would show the strength of a sound received at that point. The architect of a proposed room could tell the computer to heighten a ceiling or change the walls from wood to tile and the icons would then show the resulting change in sound quality.

"The product will start for large spaces, but by the end of the century the ultimate goal is that anyone could use it for any space they wanted to," says Stettner, who first worked on the technology at Cornell University with Prof. Donald Greenberg. "On a personal computer at home you will be able to put in the dimensions and materials of your room, and the program would suggest where to put the speakers for your stereo depending on the type of sound you desire."

It will be a few years before the program gets down to the design of living rooms, however. "The physical phenomenon of sound is more complex to simulate in small spaces," says Stettner.

ARTIFICIAL PIANIST

We're not talking player piano. We're not talking robots that play music. We're not talking the standard, computerized, metronome-perfect plunking of piano keys. Above all, we're not talking synthesized, electronic, computer-generated sounds.

ODDS: 90%

ETA: 1995

PRICE: NA

What we are talking about is a computer program that plays a piano as well as a human being can and is capable of accompanying singers or other musicians. The artificial pianist is sensitive to the lead performer's style, tempo, and mood. If he/she holds a note an extra millisecond or scurries through a Chopin étude, the artificial pianist will be able to follow with as much finesse as a live accompanist.

The artificial pianist is the creation of Dr. Barry Vercoe of the MIT Media Lab, that remarkable place in Cambridge, Massachusetts, where the future is advanced daily. Dr. Vercoe calls his invention the Synthetic Performer.

When it's actually playing, you don't see much. The keys on your wired-up Steinway or Yamaha go up and down, but there's no one there.

How does it work? "You need a fast computer," says Dr. Vercoe, "and then you have to give it a pair of electronic ears." Each key on the piano needs to be wired with an electronic switch or "fake fingers" so the Synthetic Performer can actually play the keyboard. And the live performer needs a mike linked to the computer.

Just like a real accompanist, Synthetic Performer has to warm up to your personal style by hearing you play. A few run-throughs, though, and it's show time. Synthetic Performer will match you, rubato for rubato.

At the Media Lab scientists have been having lots of fun figuring out all the things Synthetic Performer can do. They've even played a piece for four hands—two human and two artificial.

What are the career prospects for the Synthetic Performer? It has no desire to put performing musicians out of work. But as a practice or rehearsal accompanist, hey, Synthetic Performer is "cool" and can play all day without ever taking five!

VIDEOHARP

When Bob Dylan first used an electric guitar back in the sixties, it was considered by purists to be musical treason. Wonder what those critics would think of the Videoharp?

• • • • •

ODDS: 100%

ETA: 1993

PRICE: $9,500

• • • • •

How times have changed, indeed. The Videoharp is the newest incredible computer contribution to the field of music. Looking somewhat like a harp (that's how it got its name), the trapezoidal-shaped instrument can make almost any sound, from a single violin to a complete orchestra. And all you do is run your hands up and down its length.

"It all depends on how the thing is programmed," explains Paul MacAvinney, its creator. A computer whiz since 1965 (around the time Dylan switched), MacAvinney first invented a touch screen which he called Sensor Frame, now the name of his Pittsburgh, Pennsylvania, company. The frame fit over a monitor and helped the computer to understand hand gestures. Then he realized, "Maybe I could make a musical instrument out of this."

The 11½-pound Videoharp senses the vertical and horizontal position of all the fingers of the hand as they move across its surface. "Touch screens are already around," says MacAvinney, "but the difference between me and the others is, mine is first to be able to detect more than one finger in a plane."

Imagine this configuration: On one side of the harp, on the spot programmed for pitch, you move your finger up and down like on a keyboard. On the other side, you use one or more fingers from your other hand, spaced closely or wide, to change the volume and the modulation to "bend" the sound sharp or flat, just like on a violin.

Or you can try this: Move three fingers spaced widely apart over one quadrant of the harp and get a series of three-part chords played by saxophones. Place one finger from the other hand on another quadrant and play a sober bass fiddle.

How does the Videoharp work? A sensor in the middle of the instrument monitors how much light is entering. Where your finger casts a shadow, the harp knows to transmit a signal to the computer. The computer, similar to a Macintosh, then transmits a code to a synthesizer that emits the specified sound.

Although not a musician, MacAvinney is a classical music lover who is more excited by the prospect of others playing his instrument than in using it himself. "Probably Antonio Stradivari was not a great musician, but people remember him more than the violinists who used his famous violins."

CAMCORDER ZOOM SOUND

ODDS: 30%

ETA: 1993

PRICE: ADD $75 TO COST OF CAMCORDER

With all the video innovations of the past decade and all the major electronics companies that make camcorders, it's incredible that no one ever developed this one: zoom sound to match the images produced by the zoom lens.

The zoom sound moves in tandem with the zoom lens. If the camera is focused in tight, say on one person, then the zoom sound microphone would pick up sound only from directly in front of the camera. If the lens is zoomed "out" to a wide-angle view of a pasture and horses, the microphone would automatically pick up sounds from all directions.

In the irony of ironies, video zoom sound was invented by a scientist at Eastman-Kodak, a camera company that does not manufacture camcorders.

Lynn Dann of Rochester, New York, came up with the idea by combining work on 8mm projects at Kodak with personal camcorder experiences. "The best part of this device is that the person can get to the center of interest with both audio and video," says Dann. "This way when you're taping something far away, you won't just get the noise around you, you'll get only the sound that goes with the picture."

On those occasions when you are shooting tight but want "wider" sound or vice versa, the simultaneous sound focus can be disengaged.

The key to zoom sound is a retractable sound baffle that surrounds the microphone. The baffle moves in tandem with the camera's zoom lens so that when the lens is focused wide, the microphone extends out, exposing the entire surface. When the lens is focused close in, the microphone retreats almost entirely inside the baffle.

SUPER LIGHTWEIGHT BATTERY

ODDS: 100%

ETA: 1993

PRICE: SLIGHTLY LESS THAN RECHARGEABLE BATTERIES

With all the portable electronic stuff we now carry around, from laptop computers to video cameras, the weight of batteries can make a significant difference to the comfort level. Cut the weight of the batteries in half and everything gets a little easier to carry and use.

Scientists at the Lawrence Berkeley Laboratories at the University of California at Berkeley are effectively doing that, plus their new battery is almost entirely biodegradable.

The Berkeley battery is made up of three layers: A thin first layer of lithium metal, like aluminum foil; then the liquid-free solid-state separator, similar in appearance to plastic wrap; next a sulphur polymer, like a plastic garbage bag; finally, the battery is heat sealed together.

Tiny and light, the whole thing is about 4/1,000 of an inch thick, or the thickness of bond paper. However, one of these batteries does not have enough strength to power a flashlight. So what the Berkeley scientists have done, in effect, is stack a bunch of these batteries together to form one larger battery about the thickness of a deck of cards.

Still, it's 50 percent lighter than a traditional rechargeable battery with the same power and energy. And, according to Steven Visco, one of its inventors, "Most of the basic ingredients used to make the battery are biodegradable. Other rechargeables contain highly toxic materials." Also, once charged, Visco's batteries will stay charged almost forever.

Clearly, this lightweight, solid-state, no-liquid, no-leak, mostly biodegradable battery is superior to the rechargeables we use now. The first applications will be in the consumer market. But the hope is to eventually make batteries for the first practical, electronic, non-polluting cars.

VCR LOCK

ODDS: 80%

ETA: 1992

PRICE: $15

Like many young children, Catherine Filipow's two-year-old son, Anthony, liked to feed the family VCR. First he gave it raisins. Then, for a real treat, he fed it crackers and a Popsicle. Another day, by Godzilla, the VCR ate a toy car.

VCR repairs were costly, but more than that Catherine was afraid that Anthony's little fingers or arm might disappear next into the machinery's dark slot. She feared that an electrical shock or burn might result.

When Catherine couldn't find anything in the stores to childproof VCRs, she decided to conduct her own survey. She developed a questionnaire and knocked on nearly 500 doors in her Ottawa, Canada, neighborhood. Her research revealed that one out of every three families either had a child or knew of a child who put stuff in the VCR.

"VCRs have been fed everything from dog biscuits to bubble gum, nickels, and peanut butter sandwiches," she says.

Catherine, a registered nurse, decided to turn inventor and solve this problem herself. The result is the VCR-LOC, a plastic block that fits into the VCR slot, like a tape, only the LOC's outer edge is slightly longer and wider than a tape and blocks the outside of the slot.

"You can't even put a piece of paper or a paper clip inside because the entire opening is completely sealed," Catherine explains.

There's a steel, key-lock mechanism in the center of the block, so the VCR-LOC can't be removed by prying fingers.

Catherine and her husband, Bernard, a government lawyer, have started their own marketing company called Global Community Traders, Inc. They hope to introduce the VCR-LOC in the U.S. Already, they have the VCR-LOC on sale in some Canadian electronics stores.

PHOTO CDs

ODDS: 100%

ETA: 1992

PRICE: $450 FOR PLAYER, $20 FOR DISC

Soon you will be able to "play" your photo albums in the same format and on the same unit as your favorite music—the compact disc.

Kodak is about to introduce a new system that allows you to use your present 35mm camera, yet show your photographs on a TV screen. As usual, when you've finished a roll, take the film to your neighborhood photofinisher. Normally, you would get back negatives and prints or slides. But now you'll also be able to have images converted to digital data and recorded on a compact disc.

You'll need to buy a new dual-purpose CD player so you can display

your pictures on TV. Using the same machine, you'll be able to play audio recordings on your player.

As with the audio CDs, you'll have programming control when you play your photographs. You'll be able to alter the sequence, skip images, change from vertical to horizontal, and zoom in for close-ups.

Each CD will hold up to a hundred pictures; you'll be able to take it back to your photo store and add rolls of film until it's filled up.

Kodak also plans to offer print-scanning capabilities, so you'll be able to create custom "albums" from that shoe box–full of slides, snaps, yearbook portraits, and prom pix of years gone by.

How does this all differ from the Japanese electronic still cameras introduced a couple of years ago? First, the Kodak system gives you a choice: print, slide, or disc. Secondly, for less than the price of an electronic still camera you buy the disc player, which also accepts audio discs. And finally, the Kodak picture, shot on regular 35mm film, surpasses any picture taken by the electronic still camera.

Film offers superior qualities of depth, clarity, and detail that electronic images cannot, says Mike Sullivan, of Kodak's editorial services department. Electronic still cameras are limited in the amount of data that they can read and transmit. By using regular film as the source of the image, the Kodak system is actually capable of transmitting a far clearer image than you can see on your TV—or even on the forthcoming High-Definition TV.

In addition, more and more computers are capable of reading information from CDs. So someday in the very near future you'll be able to treat your photos as part of a data base, add text, use them in desktop publishing. . . . The possibilities are practically endless.

DISPOSABLE VIDEO CASSETTES

Look out, world. A new kind of junk mail is coming your way!

ODDS: 95%

ETA: 1993

PRICE: NA

And unlike most of the stuff that clogs up your mailbox now, this promotion is less likely to be dumped in the circular file. At least not right way. A free disposable video cassette is bound to make you a little curious.

These VHS cassettes are being developed by Philmax of Owings Mills, Maryland. "The basic difference between disposable and regular cassettes is that these are made out of cardboard," explains Philip Brecher, Philmax's vice president of sales and marketing. "They have a self-mailer that wraps around and is perforated along one side. You take off the mailer and the cassette is ready to be put into the VCR."

They play clearly but they don't last long. "They wear out after a few [5–10] plays," admits Brecher. "Theoretically people can reuse them, but that's not what they've been designed for. They're designed for companies to introduce products in a new form of direct mail."

Disposable cassettes were actually created unintentionally. "We were approached by clients who wanted to have video cassettes made that cost less than one dollar," Brecher remembers. "We laughed and said the only way to do that was to make them out of cardboard. Then we found out it was possible."

Since the cassettes can be played only a few times, they are inevitably going to add to the nation's trash. And although the cardboard shell is biodegradable, the reels and tape are not.

Still, corporate America is excited. "Right now I'm holding orders for more than 8 million copies," says Brecher. "The response has been overwhelming."

3-D ADVERTISING

If advertising can be made to be entertaining, there's no problem holding on to an audience. Some predict 3-D advertising will be so hot, people will stand in line to see it.

ODDS: 95%
ETA: 1993
PRICE: NA

When you visit a mall circa 1993, you'll find a kiosk called a Micro Theatre. Look inside and what you will see are lifelike, full-motion 3-D images, about 6 inches high, that spin out of thin air. Imagine a talking head making a sales spiel; or a petite dancer tapping around a tiny sports car, pointing out its best features. Anything is possible in the world of the Micro Theatre.

The kiosk is about 7 feet high and 40 inches by 40 inches. The actual stage is only 20 inches by 12 inches, while the image area, the "sweet spot," is only 10 inches by 10 inches. The rest of the kiosk houses the hidden projection equipment.

How does it all work? The folks at With Design in Mind in Chatsworth, California, who manufacture the technology, aren't talking. However this much is known: Live talent, computer graphics, and animation are all employed. For example, the tap dancer is real, and her routine has been videotaped. The image is reduced to 6 inches and transferred to a laser disc (looks like a record or compact disc). A laser beam reads signals from the laser disc and converts them to video signals, which are then processed through With Design in Mind's patented optical system.

According to Michael Levin, vice president of marketing, calling it 3-D doesn't really do justice to this technology. It could be called "video holography," he suggests. Actual holography is static, like a photograph on film. What With Design in Mind has come up with has true motion, color, and sound.

Imagine the video game possibilities!

CHAPTER 7

phone stuff

TELESKETCH

Imagine this scenario:

••••

ODDS: 85%

ETA: 1994

PRICE: $300

••••

CLIENT (sketching): "I'm interested in a sectional sofa something like this . . . with doohickeys on the back, like this."

DESIGNER: "Okay, what if we narrowed it here [drawing over the first drawing in a different color] and added a fringe over here, like so?"

CLIENT: "Doesn't look right. Needs softer edges."

DESIGNER (sketching over original drawing): "How about like this?"

CLIENT: "Perfect."

Now imagine the same scenario taking place over the telephone.

With the advent of Telesketch, this may soon be a common way of working. Paul Lanna, a student at the Art Center College of Design in Pasadena, California, created this special telephone so that designers and clients could "brainstorm visually."

As the above conversation demonstrates, Telesketch is an "audiographic telecommunication system"—meaning it integrates written and spoken messages.

Two common technologies—liquid crystal display (LCD) and a digitizing system—are integrated in this phone, Lanna explains. The LCD is a vertical screen that functions as a sketch pad, while the digitization resides in a special pencil that converts your sketching gestures into electronic impulses which are transmitted in real time.

Telesketch has a rectangular base unit with an LCD screen and an armrest. To dial, you just touch the digits on the heat-sensitive screen. To draw, just run your pencil over the glass that protects the LCD screen. All verbal communication is conducted over a speakerphone.

With Telesketch, says Lanna, designer and client can work more closely through all the developmental stages of a project, not to mention the savings in time, paper, and faxes.

Lanna, who won a Sony Design Vision '90 award for Telesketch, believes it has "endless applications" as a business, entertainment, and teaching tool.

SMART TELEPHONE

ODDS: 75%

ETA: 1993

PRICE: $250

For more than a decade, experts have been saying that personal computers will take over American homes, becoming as commonplace and beloved as television sets. Yet always, the computerized household seems to be just around the next suburban bend. The problem, apparently, is that PCs are perceived to be too complicated and expensive. So most of us continue to write checks the way our parents did. We're still buying groceries the old-fashioned way. And we're still folding our laundry one towel at a time.

Now AT&T may have come up with the ultimate weapon to get even the most computer-phobic homemaker into the twenty-first century. Their plan is to make a computer that looks like a telephone (and who doesn't love a telephone?).

The Smart Phone is a computer that links households to a range of services through a subscription-based system. The machine looks like a telephone with a 4½-by-6-inch screen displaying ten autodial buttons. The user can program each of these buttons to obey a different command.

For example, you could press one button that would automatically order tickets for basketball games. Another button might be used to buy and sell stocks. Yet another would transfer bank funds. Others could do anything from ordering groceries to making travel arrangements.

"It makes it easier to get even very routine information because it not only makes the phone call, it asks the questions for you," says Mike Grisham, the AT&T inventor who spent four years putting together this system.

Essentially, the Smart Phone is a computer with a modem and software similar to Prodigy or other informational networks that people currently subscribe to on their personal computers. "What's really different," says Grisham, "is this idea of being able to create your own buttons."

For each button, the user must enter instructions into the computer using a touch-sensitive keyboard that appears on the phone's screen. For example, you might dial the travel agency and input instructions that you always want an aisle seat and the lowest possible rate whenever you fly.

The intention of the Smart Phone is to be unintimidating and inexpensive compared with a computer.

The Smart Phone can also be programmed to offer a menu of choices on a single button. You might designate one button as the emergency line. When you press it, a choice will appear: POLICE, FIRE, HOSPITAL, DOCTOR.

According to AT&T, the first Smart Phones will be offered only by banks and other service providers. Then as production increases, they'll be available in phone stores, department stores, and computer stores, circa 1995.

THE FEELING PHONE

ODDS: 60%
ETA: 1996
PRICE: $750

Here's a phone that makes the slogan "Reach out and touch someone" take on new meaning. Called the TAK-tile Communicator, it merges voice, image, and touch technologies so that lovers can look into each others' eyes and caress; working mothers can comfort latchkey kids; and business-people can shake hands—all over the phone.

"We felt touch was a form of communication that had never been looked at; it's interesting and sincere," explains Albert Shum, a student at the University of Waterloo in Ontario, Canada. He and fellow student Wilson Tang invented the TAK-tile Communicator for the Sony Design Vision '90 contest.

Their phone has a thin, flip-up video screen, much like a computer monitor. A pad with sensors is employed like a keyboard. To use the phone, you first select the desired mode. You can choose audio, audio/video, audio/touch, or audio/video/touch. Next you dial by pressing the numbered areas of the pad.

When your party answers, if you select all modes, you'll see him on the color video screen, and he'll see you, because both phones are equipped with small video cameras.

The phone's most novel feature, touch, is accomplished using a grid of pins, which the inventors call the "force transducers." When you press down on your pad, the pins come up on the pad at the other end of the line. Wherever you press or however you move your fingers, that exact pressure and design will be transmitted to the other pad. In this way your party can feel your movement, and, of course, it works both ways, so you can feel movement back.

The technology does not attempt to mimic the warmth or texture of skin, explains Shum, but it does let you feel a general sense of touch.

Shum and Tang feel their tactile invention will "warm up" a "cold" technology. Sony apparently agrees. The Japanese giant has expressed interest in manufacturing the TAK-tile Communicator.

TELEPHONE FOR THE DEAF

ODDS: 70%

ETA: 1998

PRICE: $1,200

After decades of being a rather benign communications device, telephone technology exploded in the eighties. Suddenly everyone had an answering machine, two lines (at least), a cordless at home, a cellular in the car, and a charge card. You could get in touch with anyone from anywhere—on a train, on a plane, or even the fourteenth hole. Yet with all these advances, there was one group disenfranchised from the telephone revolution: the deaf.

Imagine not being able to use the telephone. Well, that may be about to change. British Telecom has devised an ingenious video telephone system that transmits an animated black-and-white outline, or cartoon, of the individual's face and his sign language hand movements. The "listener" can identify the "speaker" and "read" what he/she has to say.

The "sign language" phone is a spin-off of the long-awaited videophone, which promises to bring us clear color pictures of the party on the other end of the line. The problem with the videophone is that it requires a digital system, since its picture content is too high for a single phone line.

British Telecom, however, working with the University of Essex, has managed to reduce the picture content of the sign language phone to a level enabling its information to be sent over a regular analogue phone line.

The unit that hooks up to a normal telephone is about the size of a small VCR. It contains a miniature video camera and a black-and-white TV screen that's 6 centimeters square. Instead of there being a ring signal, bright lights blink to indicate an incoming call.

The first tests of the system were conducted using two members of the Suffolk Deaf Association in England. Next up is a larger trial involving twenty people.

Commercial use of the system is still a few years away. "Picture quality needs to be improved, and we need to make wider use of cheaper components to help keep down the price," Ian Corbett, British Telecom's project team leader, explained. "If such a system does become a commercial proposition, we would hope it would cost no more than an upmarket video recorder."

REMOTE CONTROL CALL FORWARDING

ODDS: 90%

ETA: 1992

PRICE: $120 PER UNIT

You're having one of those soap-opera days when you're expecting the "call that can change your life," but you still have five business appointments to make. Sure, you have call forwarding, but that only transfers your phone calls to the first meeting. And if you miss that big call, your life could be destroyed forever, or worse. What's a guy or gal to do?

In the future, he/she would purchase a remote control call forwarding device (in conjunction with the phone company call forwarding service) that will let you reprogram your phone from afar. You'll be able to change the destination of your calls as often as you like as you move from place to place.

Elliot Rais, a former computer engineer and now a real estate developer, along with fellow inventor Dan Fogel, have patented this beeper-free way to stay in touch while on the move.

When you purchase the product, a module about half the size of a standard answering machine is plugged into your wall jack. A microchip inside the module makes it possible to call home anytime thereafter, punching in a privacy code and the number where you can be reached. Your calls will be sent there until you tell the machine to send them elsewhere. You will do that by calling home again, punching in the privacy code again, and entering the new number.

You can even let your home phone know how long you will be available at a particular number. When that time expires, say in three hours, call forwarding will terminate and your home answering machine will automatically be activated.

HANDS-FREE PHONE

ODDS: 85%

ETA: 1997

PRICE: $130

A voice-activated, clip-to-your-clothes phone makes communicating a totally hands-free operation for people with physical disabilities or those who need to perform manual tasks while talking. Called Speakeasy, it really does live up to its name.

Like a traditional cordless phone, it has a touch-tone format keyboard. However, it also has a small, plastic, donut-shaped microphone-and-speaker piece that clips onto clothing. "It's almost like a piece of jewelry," says Speakeasy co-inventor Donna Cohn.

Cohn, a graduate student, and Mark Atkinson, a 1990 graduate of the Rhode Island School of Design, wanted to create a phone for disabled people and anyone else who frequently has their hands occupied. The "noninvasive" aspect of Speakeasy makes it much easier for the user to move and talk simultaneously. And it's less cumbersome than the headgear usually used by quadriplegics.

Speakeasy also allows the user to make calls without summoning an operator. You simply talk to it, like so:

YOU: "Speakeasy."
IT: "Yes."
YOU: "Call Uncle Harry [or a series of digits]."

It may be programmed with frequently dialed numbers. Speakeasy also has a built-in answering machine to take messages or record conversations.

And in a real emergency, Speakeasy could save the life of a disabled person. It can not only dial the police or fire department on demand; a programmed outgoing message can announce, "Send help to 34 Menin Road."

All of the technology now exists to produce Speakeasy but it will be a few years before it can be manufactured at an affordable price.

CHAPTER 8

for those who have everything

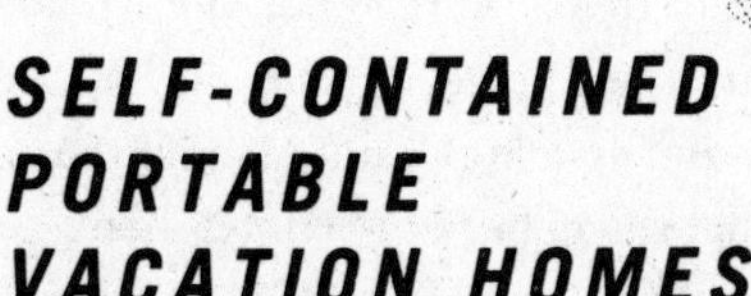

SELF-CONTAINED PORTABLE VACATION HOMES

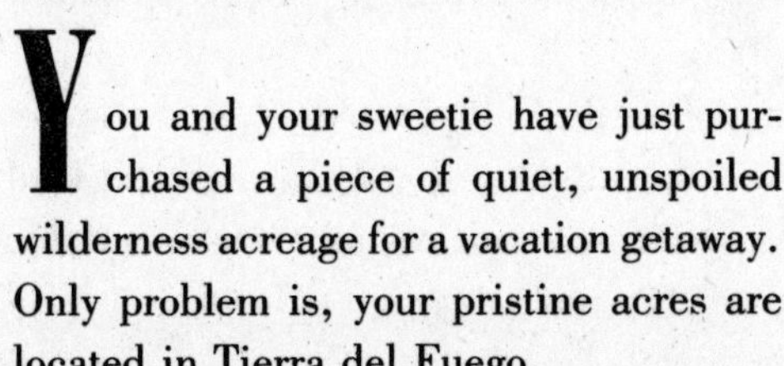

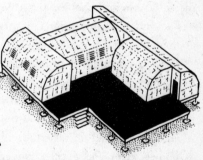

You and your sweetie have just purchased a piece of quiet, unspoiled wilderness acreage for a vacation getaway. Only problem is, your pristine acres are located in Tierra del Fuego.

It's awfully pretty in Tierra del Fuego, but the weather can be ghastly. It gets

• • • • •

ODDS: 90%

ETA: 1994

PRICE: $50 PER SQUARE FOOT

• • • • •

extremely hot, extremely cold, and extremely windy . . . not a good place to pitch a tent. Oh, and there aren't any water, gas, or electrical hookups for many, many miles. Forget about building a house.

No problem, though. You and your sweetie have Hypertat, the high-performance, self-contained, modular habitat developed by Mike Jantzen and Ted Bakewell III of Saint Louis, Missouri, and produced by Hypertat Corporation.

It arrives at your site in a standard shipping container. In less than a day, using simple tools, you and your sweetie construct sturdy, well-insulated, roomy living quarters. Soon thereafter you install solar panels, wind generators, water condensers, and satellite communications. You are now able to live quite comfortably—and autonomously.

Should you decide to pack up and try Sri Lanka for a while, you can disassemble Hypertat as quickly as you put it up. And you will be leaving Tierra del Fuego as pristine as you found it.

Hypertat is the result of a lot of experimentation and research by Jantzen and Bakewell. Although they noodled with the idea for over a decade, only recently have developments in materials and energy technology caught up with their vision, making mass production of the self-sufficient shelters possible. In fact, their work with Hypertat has stimulated innovations in insulation, cladding, and structural components that are filtering down to more general applications.

There are a number of ingenious aspects to the design, including the self-leveling foundation, which requires no site preparation. Walls and roof are formed of identical arch segments, which are easy to handle individually but form strong and spacious vault-shaped rooms when clipped together. The individual segments can be interchanged. Windows, doors, skylights, louvers, or solar heating panels replace each other to suit the requirements of the user. The price of Hypertat homes begins at about $25,000.

"We're offering a combination of flexibility, mobility, and comfort that's never been seen before," says Bakewell. "We're doing for land areas what yachts did for the ocean—making remote areas accessible while preserving their integrity. We want Hypertat to have a minimal ecological impact."

Besides being the material for vacation homes, Hypertat has many other applications: remote field research stations, emergency housing, temporary hospitals, and facilities for events like the Olympics. But it's the opportunity to live well in spectacular, remote locations that's so exciting.

PERSONAL HOVERVEHICLE

I'm flying. I'm flyyyyinnngggg . . . even if I'm only 8 inches off the ground.

ODDS: 100%
ETA: 1993
PRICE: UNDER $10,000

And so what if it is a Hovervehicle. Don't knock it. You don't need a pilot's license, you can store it in your backyard, and it costs less than most cars. Try finding an airplane to fit that bill.

Hovercraft™ are not new. In fact, the idea has been around for more than a century. And huge Hovercraft have been carrying people across the English Channel for years.

But we're talking about a snappy little personal Hovervehicle built for two. It's called the RX2000 and comes in colors like Ferrari Red and Sunshine Yellow.

The RX2000's manufacturer, HoverDynamics of Cumming, Georgia, wants you to think in terms of recreational vehicles, not ferryboats. New materials and engine technology have made the personal Hovervehicle—small, low cost, stylish, and reliable—a reality.

The RX2000 has an impressive range of capabilities. It can zoom over land, water, ice, or snow with equanimity because it's supported on a cushion of air while moving, never touching a surface. However, if you land on water, it floats. Great for fishing!

Actually a small Hovervehicle is good for a lot of things, from wave jumping to search-and-rescue missions. In this latter capacity, nothing can navigate marshy wetlands, broken ice, and deep snow like a Hovervehicle.

The RX2000 is easy to drive, flies for three hours on six gallons of gas, does up to 48 miles per hour, and can climb a 35-degree incline. It's 13 feet long, 7.25 feet wide, and weighs 520 pounds. It carries two adults or a payload of 450 pounds.

In a few years, personal Hovervehicles should be as common as speedboats. HoverDynamics is already working on a five-passenger model so you can take the kids.

BULLETPROOF CLOTHING

When the day comes that there's ever a widespread need for these items, we're all in deep trouble. But when a security consultant and a fashion designer in New York City got together after a spate of violent crimes, you can easily imagine how the idea of high-fashion bulletproof clothing emerged from the conversation.

• • • • •

ODDS: 50%

ETA: 1995

PRICE: FROM $95 FOR A CAP TO $80,000 FOR A FUR COAT

• • • • •

Stephen D'Andrilli, a former police officer, was looking to buy his wife a fur coat. Tom Zizzo, a designer, wanted a pistol permit. What came out of their acquaintance is this: two separate companies making bulletproof clothes and accessories.

Zizzo's company, Zizzo Bullet Proof Apparel in Manhattan, will custom make almost any apparel, including fur coats. At the bottom of the price range is a silk taffeta windbreaker for $900, while at the summit is an $80,000 Russian sable. The clientele? All high-profile, wealthy, international travelers, says Zizzo.

To make a garment bulletproof, both Zizzo and D'Andrilli use Kevlar, a fiber manufactured by DuPont, which also protects our men in blue. Five times as strong as its equal weight in steel, Kevlar has a high stretch resistance and is flame retardant. Once inserted in the lining, it is undetectable, though it does add about 3 pounds (depending on the level of protection) to the weight of a full-length fur coat.

After a customer picks the fur and style of his garment, the final decision is the "threat level." Explains Zizzo, there are a number of different levels of protection you can buy depending on how powerful you perceive your potential attacker to be. Is the customer talking mugger with a handgun or terrorist with an Uzi?

Over at D'Andrilli's Guardian Group International there's more of a concern about random violence in our cities. D'Andrilli sells a complete line of bullet-resistant clothing for everyone from executives to children. In addition to clothes, his kids' line includes schoolbags, umbrellas, clipboards, and knapsacks. A cap sells for $95; a clipboard, $225; kids' jackets, $300 to $600, adult T-shirt, $400 to $500; and an executive dress vest, $650 to $2,100.

HOT PINK MINI-EXCAVATOR

ODDS: 35%

ETA: 1996

PRICE: $15,000

Okay, so everybody has a VCR, camcorder, car and RV, power mower and snow blower, bigscreen TV, lots of cable and a condo in Florida—what's the next big suburban status symbol? Keeping up with the Joneses just might mean getting your own excavator.

Not any excavator, mind you. A cute little excavator that comes in colors like hot pink and baby blue. As construction machinery goes, this is the Mighty Mouse of excavators.

A product of the Komatsu company of Japan, the PC02—that's its real name—weighs 1,047 pounds and can lift 1,200. Just 27 inches wide, it has a hydraulic gear system, a diesel engine, and a speed of 1 mile per hour. It has a 7-inch-tall front blade and an 11-inch-wide bucket. The bucket extends from the boom arm and can swing left or right up to 90 degrees.

The PC02 has been designed for use by any professional or nonprofessional construction worker (a promotion picture features a young woman at the controls) who needs to scoop, dig, or clear land. Komatsu envisions this mini–power shovel mainly doing home landscaping or yard work and other small excavations.

The PC02 is now being test-marketed in Japan. While there are no firm plans to bring it to America, you can bet your new sprinkler system that hot pink mini-excavators will make it to suburbia in the nineties.

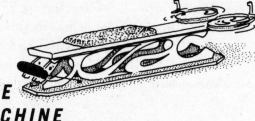

THE ULTIMATE EXERCISE MACHINE

This is the exercise machine for people who are bored to tears with every other exercise machine. It is different, exciting, inspiring, and beautiful—so don't be deterred by the name Gyrotonic Expansion Unit.

ODDS: 100%
ETA: 1992
PRICE: $7,000

First, picture a fitness machine made of polished rosewood and aluminum, one that's as graceful looking as you hope to be. Then imagine it will put you through 130 variations of 50 different sets of exercises inspired by yoga, swimming, and ballet. Finally, believe that it will do all of this in such a smooth and fluid way that you won't strain or cause yourself pain.

The Gyrotonic Expansion Unit is the creation of Juliu Horvath, now a yoga instructor in New York City, formerly a soloist with the Romanian Ballet. The principle behind the machine is that major muscle groups should be worked in a coordinated fashion through circular leg and arm movements, exercises that lead to precision strengthening in a natural way. Unlike conventional exercise machines, which are designed for weight lifting that develops one set of muscles at a time, the Gyrotonic helps you work many muscles in a circular motion. The tension of the machine helps build strength.

"I love turns," says Horvath, "and I was a very good turner when

I danced ballet. One day I was playing in the sand and noticed how naturally the energy moved through my arms and legs while I tried to make Leonardo da Vinci's circle. I felt particular centers in my body open up.

"Soon after that, I was standing on a ballet turning machine used for pirouettes. When I placed my hands instead of my feet on it, I got an instant revelation. That's when I decided to create this machine."

Why the clunky-sounding name? "*Gyro* is short for 'gyrates,' " Horvath explains, "and *tonic* stands for 'tones.' " (As in "tones your body.")

The machine looks graceful, but the results are powerful. For example, lie down, put your feet in the stirrups, and move your legs in a frog kick. The upper body can execute the arm movements of a breaststroke. "Internal organs are stimulated and massaged inside and the glandular and nervous system is also awakened," he says. Dancers who come off the machine marvel at the buttery, creamy feel of the lift.

The Gyrotonic Expansion Unit is 7½ feet long, 5 feet wide, and 8 feet tall. The rosewood and aluminum model costs $7,000. Smaller plywood machines sell for $1,800 to $4,500. The unit has a double-tension pulley with weights and a ball-bearing plate that reduces unnecessary stress. It can be adjusted to any height, length, or breadth of movement and to individual strength.

So far, Horvath has sold about thirty machines worldwide, mostly to spas and studios. Dancers from the American Ballet Theatre, the Dance Theatre of Harlem, the Joffrey Ballet, the New York City Ballet, the School of American Ballet, and the Martha Graham and Merce Cunningham troupes, as well as many Broadway, jazz, and ballroom dancers, use the machines.

The good word is bound to get out. Horvath should be selling many, many machines in the years to come.

SHOOTER MAKER

ODDS: 98%

ETA: 1992

PRICE: $10

In drinks as in dress, fashions go in cycles. Tie-dyed clothes are trendy again, and so are elaborate, multicolored cocktails. Once they were known as *pousse-cafés* and had names like the Angel's Kiss and the Pousse l'Amour (literally, the Push of Love). Now they're called shooters and have names like B-52 and the Cuban Flamethrower.

However, the basic premise remains the same. Several different types of liquids—cordials, liqueurs, cream, grenadine, or whatever—are carefully poured, one at a time, into a glass. Thanks to the same law of physics that explains why oil and water don't mix (it has to do with a quality called specific gravity, or density), each liquid will form a separate, distinct layer.

The result is a drink with stripes. It's very impressive.

And, until now, fairly hard to achieve. You must pour each layer *verrry* slowly over the back of a spoon or down a stirring rod, so as not to disturb the previous layer. One slip of the wrist and all you'll have is a muddled muck. Even experienced bartenders find it difficult.

That's why Mark Boissoneault of Winnipeg, Manitoba, invented a special shooter pourer. The patented design is based on an asymmetrical spout that causes the liquid to trickle down the side of the glass no matter how fast or clumsily your pour it.

And if you're actually drinking these things, you can get clumsy awfully fast. They're potent.

Boissoneault's pourer is not just for the show-off-at-home crowd. He expects that professional bartenders will appreciate the increased ease and speed of shooter pouring with his device. Already available in Canada at Den for Men gift stores, the shooter pourer's a hit.

CHÂTEAU BOW WOW

While some experts see the human condition declining as we enter the twenty-first century, others predict that the lives of our pets will get better.

• • • • •

ODDS: 100%

ETA: 1993

PRICE: $25 TO $2,950

• • • • •

For example, take the forward-thinking folks at Hammacher Schlemmer, the department store where for fifty years consumer appetites have been anticipated (they were the first store to sell coffee makers and personal computers)—their catalogue now offers a French Château Doghouse.

Described in the following fashion, the place is definitely for FiFi and not for Fido:

"This exceptional late French renaissance–style palace for your pet is authentic in every detail from its removable Mansard roof and faux marble floor, to its tapestry-covered bed cushion. The château . . . offers countless optional features such as tapestried walls, a marble floor or goosedown-filled cushions."

The doghouse is 28 inches square and 46 inches tall, weighs 293 pounds, and can be used indoors or out (it's weatherproofed with five coats of oil enamel).

The château is the top-of-the-line maison of Animal Manors, Inc., a Connecticut–based company that specializes in custom dwellings

for cats and dogs. The philosophy of the company was explained by its president, Ms. Cannon Garber. "When we design these houses we keep in mind two things—an aesthetic design that will appeal to humans, and the needs and scale that appeal to the animal.

"Typically," Ms. Garber continued, "we wouldn't recommend the French Château for everyone. It's for any dog that likes a space to pull away from it all."

Animal Manors is developing simpler homes for simpler pets and owners with more limited pocketbooks. For example, there is a $25 cardboard cat house designed as an Italian villa.

Garber welcomes questions about the morality of making expensive pet homes while the streets are full of homeless humans. "We live in a country where people feel comfortable wearing $5,000 Rolex watches," she says. "When people spend money on themselves, we tend not to notice. When people spend money on pets, it is much more noticeable. This highlights an attitude that animals are not important."

Ms. Garber says her high-quality homes are good for pets even if they aren't aware of the aesthetics because animals sense when their owners value something.

PARKING SPACE DOUBLER

ODDS: 90%
ETA: 1993
PRICE: $5,000

New Yorkers and Europeans already know about these weird-looking contraptions that park cars one on top of another. Commercial parking garages in the Big Apple and across the Atlantic have been using them for years to create extra spots in tight lots. Now, however, the price of buying a parking spot in a co-op or condominium is getting so high, the $5,000 for a parking space doubler looks reasonable even for individual consumers.

Phil Harding, vice president of HARDING-AFG, Inc., which

makes the Car-Lift, believes that many urbanites will want to maximize their "parking real estate" because they are now or will shortly be paying over $100,000 to buy a parking space near their condos.

The Car-Lift has one solid parking platform and a pair of electro-hydraulic arms that slowly raise the first car above the ground. In thirty seconds, the car reaches its optimum height, at which time two sets of locks automatically grip it in place. The second vehicle can then be parked on the platform underneath. The two full-size cars require only 9 feet of clearance.

The unit is charged from a 110-volt, 12-foot-long, industrial-gauge cord that plugs into any standard outlet.

For safety's sake, the Car-Lift is "key locked," which means that if you take your hand away from the key, the unit automatically stops and freezes in place.

And, in case you're wondering, the car on top can't roll off: The front tires sink into a wheel gulley carved in the platform. For extra protection, the platform is slightly bent, causing the front and rear ends of the car to lean in opposite directions, so that it can't slide forward or back.

The top platform will hold up to 4,850 pounds, enough to accommodate any car, except those heavy Caddys of the late '50s and '60s.

PERSONAL SUBMARINE

ODDS: 75%

ETA: 1995

PRICE: INITIAL: $100,000; WHEN MASS-PRODUCED: $25,000

Like every other boy who followed the exploits of Jacques Cousteau, Tommy Fury fantasized about having great underwater adventures. He even imagined building his own personal submarine in which to explore the oceans.

For some boys, dreams die hard. Fury never let go of his, and now, at the age of forty-seven, he has U.S. Patent #4,841,896 on the SSSV two-person submarine.

"SSSV stands for Shallow Sightseeing Submerged Vehicle," Fury explained. "It's unique in its design. The main complaint with other small submarines has always been the six-inch porthole. So my SSSV has a transparent top and bottom, giving full visibility above and below."

And, unlike other small submarines, the SSSV has its own air supply, just like the "big boys." You don't wear an oxygen mask inside the cabin.

The egg-shaped craft is 18 feet long and 8 feet wide and weighs 10,000 pounds. It's easy to operate and can be transported on a regular boat trailer.

Built for two, the SSSV will dive to 100 feet, perfect for fish and fauna sightseeing in clear waters. The vehicle's six battery-powered electric engines, similar to those used on small fishing boats, will keep it moving for nine hours. According to Fury, the sub will carry enough air to last for two full days.

Fury's novel ballast system is one of the key features covered by his patent. The ballast tanks are at the end of two sets of struts. To submerge, extend the struts. They unfold like wings from the sub's midsection, and the tanks fill with water. To surface, you swing the struts down so that the tanks are positioned directly below the craft. The tanks are then emptied and their position pushes the sub straight up to the surface.

The craft is steered by a joystick, which directs the four rear engines (the other two are in front). Although the sub is easier to drive than a car with a manual transmission, operators will have to qualify for a license.

Fury, a former farmer and now a full-time inventor in Clovis, New Mexico, is putting the finishing touches on his SSSV prototype. "This has been my dream since I was a kid watching Jacques Cousteau shows."

CHAPTER 9

travel stuff

AIRPLANE CONVENIENCE MODULES

For all of us who've missed connecting flights, had our luggage end up in Montserrat instead of Montreal, or generally been disgusted with the incivility of air travel, Albert A. Lupinetti offers hope. There *is* a better way!

• • • • •

ODDS: 50%

ETA: 2000

PRICE: NA

• • • • •

Lupinetti, a chief scientist at the Federal Aviation Administration's Technical Center in Atlantic City, New Jersey, says most of the troubles can be traced to one root cause: "Airports are overloaded, both with people and with airplanes." A completely new way of doing things is needed, and Lupinetti has the solution. It will eliminate delays, air congestion, scheduling hassles, and even lost luggage.

Central to his system is a self-contained travel module that holds ten to twenty passengers, a small kitchen, a bathroom, and a luggage compartment. Passengers will board these modules at outposts miles away from the airport.

Imagine—you're a Connecticut resident who plans to catch a plane at New York's J.F.K. Airport. Your destination is Seattle. You have to change planes in Chicago. With Lupinetti's plan, you'll go to the local train station, where you'll board the Seattle module.

As you sit back and enjoy a drink, the module is transported by train to the New York airport. There it is loaded onto a conveyor track and moved directly to the Chicago-bound plane.

Your module is snapped in place with a number of other modules, which have arrived from New Jersey, Westchester County, Long Island, and upstate New York. When all modules are on board, the plane takes off.

In Chicago, your module is disconnected and transported to the Seattle-bound plane. Other modules on your original flight are dispersed to various other connecting flights. When you arrive in Seattle several hours later, your luggage is placed right by your side as you depart. It's been in the luggage compartment of the module, with you for the entire trip.

"The whole objective is to make the system more efficient and able to handle a larger capacity than it does now," says Lupinetti.

It would even encourage cooperation among the airlines. "One airplane could hold modules from many travel companies. Each airline or travel company could have a module on an airplane, making air travel very efficient. Several companies could make money on one flight." Departures can be scheduled in a more reasonable way. Even more important is the idea of eliminating half-full (or less) planes that crowd runways and cause delays.

And if a plane isn't full with passenger modules, it could carry cargo modules as well. "One hundred percent load factor makes it more profitable and practical for the airlines," says Lupinetti.

There's no question that this system, implemented over time, would cost a great deal. Lupinetti won't even guess as to how much, though full planes and greater efficiency would eventually earn the money back.

On a lighter note, Lupinetti can see the day when specialized modules would appeal to our every traveler's whim. "You could have a module with a spa, modules that serve Italian food, modules decorated in Early American, and company modules rather than company planes."

JET-LAG PILL

ODDS: 90%

ETA: 1993

PRICE: A BIT MORE THAN ASPIRIN

If you'e a frequent flyer who can't fall asleep in L.A. and can't stay awake in New York, there may once and for all be a jet-lag cure on the horizon.

Scientists are now testing a pill made of melatonin, a hormone secreted by the brain's pineal gland, which helps regulate the body's internal clock. An extra dose of melatonin seems to adjust that clock, putting travelers in sync with their new time zone.

The good thing about melatonin is that it's natural. "It's not like introducing a foreign substance into the body," says Dr. Russel J. Reiter, professor of neuroendocrinology at the University of Texas Health Sciences Center in San Antonio, where the pill is being tested.

The bad part is that there are side effects. While most of melatonin's uses are positive—inhibiting the growth of tumors and benefitting some types of depression—it can cause fertility problems if used on a regular basis. So a stewardess planning a pregnancy should not use the jet-lag pill.

Researchers in the United States and Europe have now tested the hormone on about two dozen subjects. Dr. Reiter has taken melatonin himself and reports that the drug reduced all of his jet-lag symptoms except for red eyes.

A half-dozen pharmaceutical companies and the FDA are now taking a hard look at melatonin. Dr. Reiter expects it will pass scrutiny and be on your drugstore shelf by about 1993.

A LA CARTE HOTELS

Check into a Studio Plus Hotel without knowing the score and you might lose your cool. There's no TV, no maid service, no towels, no sheets. Boo.

But wait a minute. Check the room rate on the back of the door—$175 per *week!* That's the price for *one night* in Manhattan. Hey, this place isn't so bad after all.

ODDS: 90%

ETA: 1994

PRICE: $175 PER WEEK (BASIC)

For the basic rate of $25 a day, business travelers get a pretty nice room, a double bed, couch, chair, desk, and a "breakfast bar" kitchenette. Everything else is extra.

Studio Pluses are a la carte hotels for business travelers. Right now, they exist only in Kentucky, Ohio, Indiana, and Tennessee. But you can bet your next vacation that Studio Pluses for tourists will soon be springing up like dandelions all over America.

Here's why, according to Rick Bubenhofer, director of public relations for the hotel company. "Our guests determine how expensive or inexpensive their stay is. We have everything a hotel has, yet we eliminate the responsibility for paying for unnecessary services. For example, maid service at Studio Plus is optional. Why should a guest pay for something he doesn't want?"

If you do want maid service, it'll cost you $15 per visit. "Most people who are staying for awhile only want the maid to come by once a week," says Bubenhofer.

A TV set can be rented for $10 a week. Guests can even bring their own sheets and towels, or they can rent the ones available with the Studio Plus "Comfort Kit."

Telephone use is $10 a week for unlimited local calls.

Companies can save fortunes. "If a company is sending employees to another city for training, or if a salesperson is going to be in town for several days, staying here is a really cost-effective alternative to a hotel or renting a short-term apartment," says Bubenhofer.

Norwood Cowgill Jr. is the president of Studio Plus of America and the man who came up with the concept. Expansion to more cities and the vacation market are next on the Studio Plus agenda. "We're wide open in terms of guests," says Bubenhofer. "We aren't in any major resort areas yet, but we think we'd go over well in Florida."

Or anywhere. Americans like to be treated fairly and to save money. So far, the Studio Plus occupancy rate is an excellent 88 percent. Says Bubenhofer, "So many of our guests ask themselves, 'Why hasn't someone else done this before?' "

ROBOTIC LUGGAGE CARRIER

ODDS: 65%

ETA: 1995

PRICE: $200

Mark Woehrer, a student at the University of Nebraska, remembers how and when he came up with the idea of his Tag-A-Long Luggage Carrier. "I was on my way home from a high school science contest in Seattle and delayed for two hours in Denver. As I was lugging my bags from gate to gate I started thinking how wonderful it would be if my luggage could simply follow me." Later that year, "on December 24, 1989, at 11:05 P.M.," it hit him.

Tag-A-Long is a motorized platform, or carrier, on which you put your luggage. It will then follow you around. The carrier tracks an infrared transmitter that you strap to your ankle. This transmitter emits a continuous beam that enables the carrier to "know" where you are at all times.

The present prototype, displayed at science fairs and contests, does just that. And if it does lose track of Mark in a crowd, it makes tight circles in an attempt to find him again. If unsuccessful, it sets off a siren to call him back. The siren also sounds in the case of theft or stairs.

Woehrer made the prototype in his bedroom-laboratory while still a high school student in Wahoo, Nebraska. Test runs were conducted in the family living room with the consent of his mother. His father, a deputy sheriff, made regular runs to Lincoln to pick up obscure electrical parts.

Woehrer believes Tag-A-Long will eliminate the most aggravating element of travel—lugging suitcases through airports.

Ah, but won't things get just as frustrating and confusing when everybody has one? What happens if your suitcase starts tailing someone else and ends up at Gate A instead of Gate Z? Not to worry, says Woehrer. Each transmitter sends out a completely individual beacon.

Woehrer's not finished with Tag-A-Long. In future models the whole thing will be built right into the suitcase, occupying about 3 inches at the bottom. "Eventually, I believe that each suitcase will have retractable wheels, eliminating the need for the motorized platform. When the owner places the bag on the ground the wheels will automatically release and the bag will be ready to roll."

Woehrer is researching a method to replace the beacon in the infrared transmitter and use the individual's body as the tracking target. "Everybody has a unique and individual infrared body signal much like a fingerprint," he explains. "This would serve as a way for the transporter to track its owner."

A student of electrical engineering, Woehrer wants to work in the field of artificial intelligence. "I want to make machines that think just like you and I."

COOLING COIL

That heating coil frequent travelers take along to make a cup of coffee on the go will someday have a traveling companion. A cooling coil, which works in the cup just like its cousin, will make warm soda cold in just a few minutes.

ODDS: 70%

ETA: 1999

PRICE: $20

Dr. B. Mathiprakasam of the Midwest Research Institute in Kansas City, Missouri, has conceptually designed the coil using thermoelectric technology (electricity to produce cooling).

The palm-size unit has a cord at one end and an 8-inch rod at the other. Plug it into any electrical socket, insert the rod into your beverage, and stir. The longer you leave it in and stir, the colder your beverage gets, says Dr. Mathiprakasam.

At the moment, his company is not planning to produce the cooling coil. "If I wanted to make the coil today, it would cost $200. But if someone came along with the financing to develop the idea, it could be produced very cheaply," explains Dr. Mathiprakasam.

TRAILER/HOUSEBOAT

ODDS: 50%

ETA: 1994

PRICE: $7,500

There's something that excites the imagination about a gadget that can do more than one thing. So a big gadget that doubles as a houseboat and camper is sure to cause a stir among outdoorsmen and women when it arrives in the U.S.

Australian Ian Cummins is the creator of the Cummins Craft, which has become quite the rage "down under." Twenty-two feet long and 8 feet wide in the water, the craft can sleep six and comes complete with a stove, oven, refrigerator, shower, toilet, stowaway dining table, and storage space. Powered by an ordinary outboard motor, the craft cruises at about 8 knots. It has a molded fiberglass hull designed for stability and shallow draft—the Cummins can navigate in water only a foot deep.

The real neat part about the vehicle, however, is that it can be folded up when you take it on the road. Folding reduces its length from 22 feet to 13 feet. The folding action, operated by pulleys, draws up the bow so it's perpendicular and flush to the enclosed cabin of the boat.

On land, it's easily towed behind a car, and even when it's in the folded position travelers have access to the interior galley and toilet facilities. The main cabin sleeps two, while the bow, folded down at night, provides an additional sleeping area for four more.

JET-LAG WATCH

Think of this watch as a mind-altering magic trick designed to make time fly or to move more slowly. What it does is automatically spread the time change over the course of a traveler's airplane ride as he or she moves through time zones.

• • • • •

ODDS: 85%

ETA: 1992

PRICE: $350 ANALOG
$75 DIGITAL

• • • • •

For the frequent flier who hates jet lag, the watch can provide a psychologically smooth transition. "It's a seamless means of traveling through the world's time zones," says inventor Ross Mitchell, an international systems consultant from Newtonville, Massachusetts. "Instead of that jolt—asking your body and mind to believe the new time—you can gradually make the change over the trip."

For example, if you board an 8 P.M. Eastern Standard Time flight from New York, it will land in Los Angeles at 11 P.M. Pacific Coast Time. Only three hours' difference. But the flight takes six hours, so when you land, it's really 2 A.M. in New York. You reset your watch to L.A. time. Your mind and your body have to suddenly adjust to an extra three hours.

Now, with the jet-lag watch, you would program in the number of time zones from point of departure to destination before leaving New York. The watch would gradually add three hours of time over the course of the six-hour flight.

Mitchell, a frequent traveler to Europe, used to play this game using a regular watch. "I would increment my time over the course of the trip, trying to trick myself. This worked fairly well, but it was still pretty primitive," he explained. "I believe the jet-lag watch will change forever the way people travel through time zones."

Well, at the very least, it will make an interesting in-flight conversation piece or gift for the traveler who has everything.

AIR TRAVEL SAFETY COURSE

Former airline flight attendant Linda Pearson made a rather startling discovery while training flight attendants for Braniff Airlines. In her research she found that attendants are incapacitated or killed on impact in over 40 percent of crash cases.

• • • • •

ODDS: 70%

ETA: 1992

PRICE: $50 FOR 90-MINUTE PROGRAM

• • • • •

"What this told me," says Pearson, "is that passengers often have to evacuate the plane themselves, so why not educate people ahead of time." Which is exactly the business that she is now in—running crash safety seminars, called Traveling With Confidence, for corporate frequent flyers.

There's a surprising amount of information to learn. For example, did you know that you should use the restroom often because a full bladder can burst on crash impact? Or that you shouldn't wear clothes made of synthetics, because they could melt? Instead, wear cotton or wool. Also, don't carry pens on your person because they have a way of shooting up into the face. And, above all, believe it when they tell you to fasten your seatbelt *securely*. If it's loose, you can get sucked right out from under the belt.

Pearson likes to simulate flight emergencies in her seminars. The lecture room is set up so that the seats are close together (with no legroom), in rows of three across. She turns out the lights, turns on sound effects, and puts her students through mock evacuation drills.

One would think the airlines would be supportive of this kind of educational program. Not so, says Pearson. "The airlines don't want anyone to think that their planes aren't safe to fly on. But most of the airlines have had crashes."

SafeAir Services, Pearson's Dallas-based company, plans to begin offering their crash survival courses to the general public in 1992.

CHAPTER 10

sun, sand, & surf

SHARK REPELLENT BELT AND CUFFS

ODDS: 95%
ETA: 1993
PRICE: NA

You're having *that* dream. You know, the one where the boat gets blown apart by dynamite, leaving you clinging, bleeding and desperate, to the rapidly deflating life preserver. Suddenly you *hear* sharks . . . den, den, den, den . . . then you see shark fins. And look, who's that over there in the water? Why, it's Roy Scheider! And over there, *agggghhhhh*, Richard

Dreyfuss! "Oh, no, no," you scream, "this must be my *JAWS I* Nightmare."

Hey, relax. Chill out. Don't worry about those crazy sharks. Just remember what you read on page 144 of *More Future Stuff:* This time in the dream you have on your shark belt, complemented by the matching ankle and wrist cuffs. Each contains a number of refillable mesh pockets holding cubes of sodium lauryl sulfate—a chemical that sharks hate. So tell those sharks with the big teeth to just get out of your dream, or you'll get really mad!

David Schneider, a twenty-eight-year-old psychologist and marine biologist from Falmouth, Massachusetts, is the creator of the shark belt. Ten years ago, he and his father watched a television program about the Moses sole, a fish that emits a rare chemical capable of fending off sharks. It seems this chemical attacks the shark's nervous system, sending it into convulsions. So when the shark gets his first whiff of the stuff, he swims away.

A great chemical if you can get it! Well, you can't, but some university professors found that it closely resembles sodium lauryl sulfate, an ingredient frequently found in shampoos and shaving creams.

The Schneiders decided there were products worth developing here. They came up with a belt for scuba divers and a series of snap-on straps for life jackets. They expect the latter to be more popular than the former. "A growing number of scuba divers aren't that afraid of sharks," David explained. "A common attitude today is that if you stay out of their way, they stay out of yours." Among non–scuba divers, most are scared to death of sharks.

The entire shark repellent system weighs about 2 pounds. The straps run from the life jacket down both sides of the body to a pair of ankle cuffs. Mesh pockets every few inches along the strap and around the cuffs contain 1-inch-square-by-½-inch-thick cubes of the repellent.

The cubes are time released so that a few go off every hour, giving forty-eight-hour protection—the known limit for human survival in salt water. Simple treading or kicking in the water will spread a chemical cloud around the swimmer, keeping sharks at a safe distance.

By the way, in your dream, should you survive longer than the forty-eight-hour record, more good news. An extra emergency repellent cube comes with the system. This epoxy-coated reserve will release only when the user breaks it—offering you more time to be rescued . . . or to wake up.

FINSURFER

It's fun, it's fast, it's safe, it doesn't pollute, and it's coming soon to a body of water near you. It's the finsurfer!

• • • • •

ODDS: 90%

ETA: 1993

PRICE: $1,150, BUT WILL DROP WITH MASS PRODUCTION

• • • • •

Gosh, can't you just feel the excitement? Surfboarders and windsurfers probably can—this new toy is going to put millions of new people on the water next to them. Because finsurfing is easy. "If you can walk, you can finsurf," says its inventor, Adam Momot, of Vancouver, British Columbia, Canada.

The finsurfer looks an awful lot like a regular surfboard in shape and size (12 feet long and 3 feet wide). The difference is that you don't need surf or wind to get it going. You just need you. And "you" don't even have to be strong, well coordinated, or agile.

The board, which is lightweight and unsinkable, provides a stable platform. Standing upright, you rock the board by shifting your weight from leg to leg, which activates the underwater fin. Put into motion, the fin swishes up and down like a fish's tail and propels you forward. Even an adult can do it!

"It's an almost perfect form of exercise," boasts Momot. "It's gentle and relaxing if you want it to be, but you can also make it more challenging by going faster, farther, or into rougher water, where you can use the wave action to increase your speed."

Momot has personally finsurfed 50 miles in two days in the cold and breezy Pacific off the coast of British Columbia. "It was great," he says. (What else is he going to say?) "In fact, I think it could be a new form of touring. One could finsurf from inn to inn, much as one might hike or bike."

Grand Canal, here we come.

INSTANT-RESPONSE SUNGLASSES

ODDS: 50%
ETA: 1993
PRICE: $200

From Miami to Malibu, sunglasses that darken or lighten instantly at the flick of a switch will be the new status shades for all cool, hip, and trendy sun lovers.

"Wait a minute," you're probably thinking, "aren't there already sunglasses that *automatically* adjust to light and darkness?"

Yes, there are. But the lenses take up to sixty seconds to adjust. In the interim, blinded by bright light, you could stumble, fall, or bump into a Calypso drum and spill your Margarita.

Instant-Response Electroshades will prevent such catastrophes.

"You won't have to wait around for that minute when you have no control over the darkness and light," says Bob Saxe, president of Research Frontiers Inc., the Woodbury, New York, company that's developing these futuristic shades. You'll just flick the tiny switch on the side of the frames to adjust the tint.

The key to the technology is a less-than-one-thousandth-of-an-inch-thick liquid suspension of needle-shaped, light-absorbing, randomly positioned particles. The particles are sandwiched in layers of glass and can be positioned to make the sunglasses lighter or darker.

When the Electroshades are switched on at the side of the frame, the tiny AC voltage is applied through an indium-tin-oxide conductor lining the glass, causing the particles to align in uniform fashion. The wearer instantly and consistently sees the world more clearly.

There's no catchy name yet for these innovative shades. But the price tag should read around $200. So don't leave them lying on a chaise longue.

BEACH BRUSH

ODDS: 100%

ETA: 1992

PRICE: $6

There's no high-tech anything here. Just a simple idea for a simple product that will make our lives just a bit less annoying.

When you get sand on your clothes, towel, blanket, food, radio, swimming goggles, bathing cap, dog, or yourself, you brush the stuff off with the Beach Brush.

Right now you are either thinking, "This is a product?" or, "Why didn't I think of this?"

Yes, it is, and the person who did think of it is Jill Olson, president and owner of Sun Products. "I got the idea around Thanksgiving of 1986 and toyed with it until last year, when I figured, why not go for it?"

Why not. The brush has one row of sand-colored, coarse hair bristles (apparently ideal for getting at sand) and a handle, which will come in six neon colors, including pink and yellow. "It's about 7 inches long and about the shape of a fat comb," says Olson. And oh, yes, "It feels good to hold," she adds.

Already available in some parts of California, it has found an unintended use in parks and playgrounds. "Kids love playing in sandboxes and moms like it because they can just brush the kids off," says Olson.

TANNING UMBRELLA

Ah, remember those hot, languid summer afternoons when we would offer our bodies to the blazing sun, bare skin shining with baby oil and sweat? Today we wouldn't be caught dead at midday exposing ourselves to the sun's rays without the most sophisticated sunscreens on every inch of our susceptible bodies. We've learned about wrinkles and skin cancer.

ODDS: 90%
ETA: 1992
PRICE: $40 LARGE
$10 SMALL

A new form of protection will soon be here in the form of a beach umbrella with sunscreen "built" right into the plastic fabric. This way you can sit in the shade, out of the glare and heat of the direct sun, and still receive the UVA rays, which tan, while blocking out the harmful UVB rays. The plastic fabric is impregnated with UV absorbers that selectively block bad UVB rays and pass through healthy, tanning UVA rays.

"This is the first alternative to sunscreens applied to your skin," says Jim Bowie, president of Decent Exposure, Inc., the Columbus, Georgia, company that will sell the tanning umbrellas, as well as other "tan-through" products, such as sunvisors.

The umbrellas will be available in two styles—a small one that clamps onto a beach chair and a family-sized umbrella that you plant in the sand.

SOLAR BEACH-UMBRELLA FAN

ODDS: 50%

ETA: 2001

PRICE: $30

If a day at the beach circa 2001 is cooler and therefore more enjoyable, a young lady of twenty-one will be able to take the credit. Her name is Emily Peters, and she is the inventor of the solar beach-umbrella fan.

Right now Emily is still in elementary school in Richmond, Virginia. And her solar fan is part-reality, part-fantasy.

As a precocious fifth-grader in a class for the talented and gifted, Emily decided she would enter the Invent America contest. Except she didn't know what to invent. Methodically, she asked people she knew if they had any problems she could solve. "I asked my teacher, and she said one of the problems about going to the beach is that it's so hot."

Emily's solution is an umbrella that uses solar panels to power the blades of a fan attached to the umbrella pole. "The model I entered in the competition used cardboard blades," Emily explained. "Then my stepfather, who works for a plastic company, was able to get blades made out of plastic."

Emily's idea was good enough to win an Invent America award in her grade division. But, she admits, even with plastic blades, the darn thing isn't working.

"None of our fans have worked yet," she says, without a trace of pessimism. "We are still trying to get solar panels that will work."

The idea is sound, the inventor's determined, and it does get hot under those beach umbrellas. By the time she's twenty-one, Emily could be a very successful young lady.

ARTIFICIAL SURFING

For sure, the Beach Boys didn't have this in mind when they sang "Surfing U.S.A." But soon surfer wannabes from Memphis to Muskegon will be able to experience the ultimate surfing high far from any ocean.

ODDS: 90%

ETA: 1992

PRICE: $1 PER RIDE

Thomas J. Lochtefeld, thirty-eight, who's been riding real waves since the '60s, is the inventor of the Sheet Flow Generator (you'll know it as Man-O-Wave in amusement parks). Like, one day, *wow*, it hit Lochtefeld that the surfing action all takes place on the surface, therefore you don't need most of the water underneath. What a concept! Lochtefeld took it to the patent office and came away with #4,954,014 for an artificial surfing machine.

A surface approximately 40 feet long and 40 feet wide with an asymmetrical, upwardly inclined bottom rises in the shape of a wave to a height of 6 feet. When not in use it lies flat on the bottom of the water area. When it's time to surf, water, only 3 to 5 inches deep, rushes over it to form the wave. The type of wave—unbroken, spilling, or tubing—can be determined by adjusting the force of the water and the angle of the incline.

The surfer is carried up with the wall by the force of the water. Then gravity takes over and the fun begins as he/she surfs down the "wave." How you interact with the wave, using hands, edge of board, positioning—all known as "drag forces"—will determine how you come up the flow.

Lochtefeld, once a tax real estate lawyer, changed careers in 1982 to create water theme parks. "You can make money at that [lawyering], but life's short, and it's wisest to choose interesting things to do and go at them with a passion."

Calling his latest invention "the ultimate three-dimensional arcade game," he says the hardest part of real surfing is timing, judgment, paddling, and catching the wave. "The beauty of this thing is you just hop on, and you just slide down, and you're there. Minimal skill. Maximum fun. It's the future."

DIVERS' RATE OF ASCENT METER

ODDS: 90%

ETA: 1992

PRICE: $50

Even if you know nothing else about scuba diving, you know this: Ascend to the surface too quickly and you get the bends, a condition that hurts and can even kill. Considering the consequences, it's surprising that no one actually knows what the right rate of ascent is. Also surprising is the lack of an instrument that accurately measures how quickly a diver surfaces.

After thirty years of believing the proper rate of ascent was 60 feet per minute, doctors are now saying it should be 30 and recommending 20 feet per minute near the surface. Divers have long used a pressure gauge and a watch to measure their speed. If you were 60 feet down, under the new guidelines, you should take two minutes to surface.

When the computer age came upon us, an expensive ($400 to $800) gadget materialized. It tells the diver if he is coming up too fast. But it doesn't tell the speed.

Now comes the rate of ascent meter, which, for about $50, at least gives you some idea of how fast you are rising.

Half the size of a cigarette pack, the meter can hook onto equipment or be worn like a watch. Three LED lights (like those red ones on your office phone) serve as indicators on the meter. When you enter the water, the first light automatically goes on. Later, when you start ascending, if you reach a rate of 40 feet per minute, the second light comes on and the first goes off. This is a warning: You are rising too fast. Slow down, and the two lights blink in tandem, meaning you're okay. If your rate ever reaches 60 feet per minute, the third light comes on, indicating danger.

What makes the meter work is a transducer—an inexpensive little mechanism found in many household appliances. It's a small brass disc that creates an electrical charge when it's deflected. In this application, as the diver rises against the water, pressure causes the disc to bend, and that creates an electrical signal. The faster the diver rises, the faster it bends, because the pressure is changing more rapidly.

"It's a very unique tool," says Bill Stephens, CEO of Princeton Tectonics of Bordentown, New Jersey, the company that plans to manufacture the meter. "Because we're using a device [the transducer] that sells for 20 to 30 cents, it allows us to build a relatively inexpensive piece of equipment. It should be something that every diver can afford rather than spending $400 to $800 on a diving computer—although both instruments can be used together."

The rate of ascent meter was invented and patented by three Canadian engineers—Malcolm Saubolle, Italo De Blasi, and Stanley Livshitz. Princeton Tectonics worked for two years to develop the prototype.

DEEP-SEA WALKIE-TALKIE

ODDS: 95%

ETA: 1994

PRICE: $650 FOR HEADSETS
$1,700 FOR SURFACE COMMUNICATOR

Scuba divers must be thinking that it's about time something like this surfaced—a simple walkie-talkie that allows divers to talk to one another underwater. In the age of cellular telephones and communication dishes that search the heavens for extraterrestrial life, it's hard to believe divers have been so ignored.

Billed as "the world's first affordable ultrasonic underwater headphone transceiver" by its maker, ASTI Pacific Corporation of Hamamatsu, Japan, the battery-operated headsets and mouth masks can keep two divers in touch across 50 meters of water. The headsets are great looking (in yellow and baby blue) and lightweight, and they operate by means of a push-and-talk button on the right earphone.

What does indeed make the unit special is a built-in ultrasonic electronic device that transmits the speaker's voice "as clear as a bellfish," say ASTI officials.

A surface device sold separately links the underwater divers to their ship. Compact and portable (about the size of a school lunch box), the surface communicator is also battery operated and can communicate with divers up to 100 meters away.

Loquacious divers can talk for twenty hours, while those more prone to listening can expect batteries to last for thirty hours. A buzzing sound in the headset lets divers know when the voltage is fading.

SUN-SAFETY WATCH

ODDS: 100%

ETA: 1992

PRICE: $40

By now everyone knows the danger of staying in the sun too long. This high-tech multifunctional watch takes the guesswork out of how much is too much of the sun's harmful ultraviolet rays.

First the wearer programs into the watch his or her skin type (one of the six standard types identified by the FDA) and whether a sunscreen—and of what SPF (sun protection factor)—has been applied. The watch is then pointed at the sun so that its sensors can measure the UV rays.

The watch's computer evaluates all of this information and calculates how long the wearer can remain in the sun without burning. Like a stopwatch, the device counts down to 0 then beeps a warning when it's time to head for the shade.

Developed at the Elexis Corporation in Miami, Florida, the watch is called Sundial. It's about the size of a standard digital watch, only its face is in the shape of a D.

In an effort to make it precise, its developers gave the watch a couple of other key functions. If the weather changes (say, it clouds over), you simply point the watch at the sun again and it will recalculate the UVB effects, taking into account how long you've already been exposed under the previous conditions. Also, if you decide to go indoors for a while, you can put the Sundial on hold. When you go back outside, the watch will pick up all calculations where it left off.

According to Chuck Owen, vice president of operations at Elexis, it took two and a half years to develop Sundial. The challenge, he explained, was to create a sensor that would measure only the ultraviolet rays and to find a way to include the sophisticated measurements while keeping the cost down to about $40.

Sundial also does more mundane stuff, like telling the time and date.

SUPER "TIDE" TELLER

• • • • •

ODDS: 100%

ETA: 1992

PRICE: $1,500 TO $2,000

• • • • •

With a name like Super Professional Tidal Chronometer and a four-figure price tag, this watch had better do some terrific stuff besides tell time.

According to Ira Krieger, president of the Krieger Watch Corporation in Miami, Florida, the watch delivers. In addition to providing information on the state of the ocean's tides, the Super Professional Tidal Chronometer gives you the depth of water beneath your boat.

Is this a sailor's dream, or what?

To make the "tide" teller fully functional, you need to set the tidal monitor according to standard tide information that is available in charts and books. In each twelve-hour period, there is one high tide and one low tide, separated by about six hours and thirteen minutes.

After you input this information, the watch's automatic tidal chronometer takes over, showing—on a small dial inset on the larger time dial—the phases of the tides for each twelve-hour period.

"Besides telling you high and low tides, it will also tell you the rates of speed of the tide as it is coming," says Krieger, noting that the intensity of the incoming tide varies, with the earlier phase of the onset being fastest.

What makes the Krieger watch unique, however, is that the wearer can determine the depth of the water beneath his or her boat. Around the crystal of the watch are two dials, an outer and an inner one. They carry out this function.

The wearer first reads the tide indicator and sets one dial to reflect the tide at that given moment. Then he sets the other dial to indicate what is known to be the general depth in the vicinity of the boat (this information is available from charts and maps). The watch then uses these two pieces of information to calibrate the depth of the water beneath the boat at that moment. "It's like using a slide rule," says Krieger.

The normal procedure for serious boaters is to use radar equipment to calculate the depth of the water through sound waves. The watch is smaller and easier to use, particularly for divers.

"People will also use the watch for fishing," adds Krieger. "It will become an indispensable tool for commercial and professional fishermen."

LIQUID SUNGLASSES

ODDS: 95%
ETA: 1993
PRICE: NA

Forget the sunglasses. Lose the visor. Pass up the hat. Special eyedrops will soon be the best defense against dangerous ultraviolet rays.

Dr. Neville A. Baron, a Secaucus, New Jersey, ophthalmologist, has developed drops that will screen out up to 98 percent of ultraviolet light. With the continuing depletion of the ozone layer and the increasing amount of ultraviolet light passing through it, this is no small invention.

Sunglasses block out 60 to 95 percent of ultraviolet A rays, which some doctors believe cause blindness by destroying retinal cells; and 60 to 95 percent of ultraviolet B, which contributes to the formation of cataracts.

The idea for the eyedrops came while Dr. Baron was doing research on chromophores—chemical compounds that can be adjusted to absorb specific wavelengths of light. He and other researchers were studying the compounds in relation to laser treatments of cataracts, retinopathy, and disorders of the vitreous humor. However, it eventually became apparent that the chromophores could serve as liquid sunglasses if they were adjusted to absorb ultraviolet radiation.

"Ophthalmology is an innovative specialty," notes Dr. Baron, "and often breaks ground for ideas and techniques that are later used more broadly."

Another advantage of eyedrops over dark glasses is that you see better indoors. Since 40 percent of our exposure to ultraviolet rays happens inside—from television sets, computer screens, and fluorescent lighting—some people will choose to use the drops even when they aren't in the sun.

The drops are clear, colorless, nonirritating, and effective for two to four hours. As soon as clinical testing is completed and FDA approval obtained, they should become as widely available as suntan lotion.

CHAPTER 11

high-tech matchmaking & other essential services

HIGH-TECH MATCHMAKING

Meeting, greeting, dating, and mating are going high tech.

So smile and say hi to IntroVision.

IntroVision is the yenta of the nineties. And the chutzpa behind IntroVision belongs to Harvard M.B.A.er David Hilger

• • • • •

ODDS: 75%

ETA: 1993

PRICE: $100 TO $250 PLUS MONTHLY FEE

• • • • •

and marketer Sheldon Smith, who have combined optical scanners, electronic cameras, video digitizers, and voice mail to offer what they say is the most convenient and discreet method of finding that special someone for Saturday night—or forever.

One of IntroVision's features is that it's portable. It goes to nightclubs, trade shows, office building lobbies . . . anywhere a target audience might gather. You fill out a questionnaire and pose for a photo. Both are then fed into a computer. The computer compares your answers to answers from the opposite sex and prints out eight names with profiles whose responses most closely match yours—plus you get their photos.

There hasn't been an icebreaker like this since the *Titanic*.

Actually, this isn't just another party game. Hilger and Smith have done their homework. "We worked with a group of psychologists to develop a set of questions on values, demographics, life-style, and personality," Smith explains. "We emphasize values because that's what we found was most important in terms of success in long-term relationships. You can still use your intuition—you do have a photo—but you also know that you're apt to be talking to someone who has a lot in common with you."

If you are shy or embarrassed about using "one of those dating services," you can do the whole thing by mail and phone. You receive the same printouts and pictures, with monthly updates, but you'll contact any potential dates through the firm's voice-mail network.

IntroVision has even broader potential than just mates, Smith points out. "You can get matched up with all kinds of special interest groups—people who like winter sailing or macrobiotic food or swing dancing."

Look for IntroVision at a singles hangout near you. Hilger and Smith will be moving it from big city to big city starting anytime soon.

ON-TIME DELIVERY SYSTEM

•••••

ODDS: 95%

ETA: 1992

PRICE: NA

•••••

You know the story: Take a whole day off work to wait for the new sofa (carpet, TV, bed, dining-room set, cable installation, telephone repairman). Leave the house once for ten minutes to fetch a loaf of bread at the corner store. At 6 P.M., still no sofa. Sinking feeling in pit of stomach. Anger at the way the world works (i.e., doesn't work). Find out later what you already knew. Delivery van came while you went to store.

Some people call it Murphy's Law—if anything can go wrong, it will. Others call it life.

The solution is called C-ARDS, which stands for Computer-Aided Radio Dispatch System. It was developed by Consolidated Natural Gas in Pittsburgh and has already been bought by several big utility and cable television companies.

A computer system that links the driver through to the company computer and to your home, C-ARDS removes delivery inefficiencies. Companies that use it will be able to promise a delivery window of just two hours. No more "anytime between 9 A.M. and 6 P.M." Drivers with the C-ARDS system notify the central computer when they arrive in your neighborhood. You receive a call five to ten minutes before delivery, so you don't run out for bread.

According to Martin Gareau, manager of the technical products division of Consolidated Natural Gas, "A company using the C-ARDS system can give their customer a specific delivery time, say between the hours of 8 A.M. and 10 A.M., because the dispatch can communicate directly with the delivery person.

"For example," Gareau continues, "if we fall behind schedule, we can change the route and send the next customer a representative who is closest to their home, because we can communicate directly with the driver.

"The unit in the truck is about 8 inches by 15 inches and is more cost-effective than using a cellular phone, where you are charged by the amount of calls you make. With C-ARDS, you pay for the system once and can transmit as much data as you need. And using a computer means there are no interference problems—which is often the case with radio systems."

There are a number of other ways that C-ARDS can help companies become more efficient. For the consumer, just getting the stuff there on time is plenty.

SOLAR-POWERED PARKING METERS

ODDS: 100%

ETA: 1992

PRICE: NA

In the next ten years, solar parking meters will be introduced on city streets all over the world.

Contain your excitement. You'll go to park your car one day, and the familiar meter—the kind that's been around for fifty years—won't be there anymore. In its place will be a futuristic-looking, solar-powered meter.

It will still take your money and let you stay for an allotted time. But that's about where the similarity ends.

This Advanced Parking Meter (APM) will also take tokens. And if you have a special credit card, you can punch it in as well.

The APM is run by a number of interior circuit boards that contain soldered lines, so they never corrode or rust. Which means you won't lose a quarter or get a ticket because of a faulty meter.

Inspectors using a remote-control device can just aim it at the meter to get a record of all activity. The remote-control reading unit is then downloaded into an IBM computer that audits each meter.

Now, this next bit of information is really scary. These solar meters have memory and can recognize cars. They can tell when the same car has been parked in the same spot for too long. The meter has been programmed to stop accepting coins after a certain amount of time. The driver either has to move his vehicle or risk getting a ticket.

With computerized meters, it'll be a snap for municipalities to change rates from weekdays to weekends or even to raise the rates. No more costly and time consuming rebuilding of meters.

POM, the company that's developed the Advanced Parking Meter, is a direct descendent of the company that installed the world's first parking meter in Oklahoma City in 1935 (amaze your friends with this bit of trivia).

According to Bobra Wilbanks, technical sales manager at POM in Russelville, Arizona, all of the nation's 1.2 million parking meters will be solar powered within the next twenty years.

COMPUTER JOB INTERVIEWER

ODDS: 100%

ETA: 1993

PRICE: NA

Only a decade ago, the idea that a machine would have a say in the destiny of a human being was the fodder of science-fiction horror. Today we are so accustomed to computers in our lives that to apply for a job and find the recruiter is a computer screen and a keyboard would be only momentarily disorienting.

The program that interviews people for employment is called the Greentree Interview. It was developed by Dr. Brooks Mitchell, a University of Wyoming professor of management studies, who is careful to point out that the computer does not replace people. A traditional human face-to-face conversation follows the Greentree "icebreaker."

After filling out an application, a potential employee takes a seat at the computer. He is then subjected to a series of questions.

So why is this test so different from a pencil-and-paper objective test? With the computer, the answer given to any question will determine subsequent questions. So the path of each computer interview is based on the interviewee's responses. The computer also suggests questions for the live interview.

"The computer does not decide on the applicant before the interviewer meets him, rather it gives the interviewer a more detailed description of the applicant's background and experience and makes for a better face-to-face interview," says Mitchell.

The computer guards against the human mistakes a live interviewer might make. "The hardest problem is getting interviewers to ask the right questions during the interview. Since the computer asks questions triggered by the applicant's responses, no two interviews are alike. The computer turns out thorough, consistent descriptions of each applicant. It never forgets to ask a question."

There are two other advantages to the system, Mitchell contends. People like to be interviewed this way. "It removes the need for socially desired responses. People are more honest since they aren't afraid of any negative feedback."

And companies like the interview because it gives them access to all sorts of measurable information about their employees. "The information collected over time provides the company with statistical information as to what types of people had a successful live interview and stayed with the company," explained Mitchell.

A few large companies, like Marriott Hotels, are already using the interview program. It is manufactured by Mitchell's own DES-Aspentree System Company of Laramie, Wyoming.

FASHION TRY-ON SIMULATION

ODDS: 95%
ETA: 1992
PRICE: FREE

Buying clothes is great; trying them on is not. Buckles, belts, zippers, laces, cramped dressing rooms, clothes that don't fit, those awful plastic clips—it all adds up to department store torture.

Laurence G. Maloomian of Needham,

Massachusetts, is the man who will deliver us from all this. Maloomian is the inventor of the Fashion Screen System, which makes trying on clothes as easy as watching TV.

The shopper's image is captured by video camera and recorded in the system's computer memory. The image can then be interfaced with any of the clothes stored in the computer's memory (and almost all will be), so that the shopper's body in the chosen outfit will appear on the screen. The picture, says Maloomian, is a very clear, high-resolution image. "It is virtually a mirror image of the person."

Maloomian came up with the idea for the Fashion Screen System when he was in the bridal business. Wedding dress samples usually come only in size 8 or 10. Women who don't fit in those sizes have to buy without ever really seeing themselves in the dress. And even in the right size, wedding dresses are cumbersome and time-consuming to try on.

"I set out to find a way to allow women to 'preview' dresses very quickly, narrow down the dresses they would really like to try on, and give them the opportunity to know quickly and easily what a dress would look like on them," explains Maloomian.

The Fashion Screen System is not just for stores. The inventor envisions them in freestanding kiosks in hotels, airports, and malls, where shoppers could "try on" clothes picked from catalogues and then actually make purchases using a credit card. Maloomian also sees the day when the system is installed in the average American home, allowing shoppers to "try on" clothes from any store in the world right in their living rooms.

But first things first. Maloomian sees his service being offered free to shoppers in stores. "The advantages so outweigh the costs that it's insane for the stores to pass on the cost to the consumer."

BRAILLE HANDRAILS

Little things mean a lot when you're trying to find your way in a sightless world. So a few small Braille letters etched into handrails on stairs could help vision-impaired people mount or descend steps with greater confidence and ease.

ODDS: 25%
ETA: 1995
PRICE: NA

This "little" idea, called Handi-Rail, comes from Katherine Ann Szudy, an eighth-grader from Parma, Ohio. "At the very bottom of the steps, the handrail has a letter *B* in Braille, for bottom," Katherine explained. "Then each step is numbered in Braille. At the top, there is a letter *T* on the handrail to let people know they have reached the top."

As you can imagine, these Braille letters can become extremely important in a fire or other emergency.

Katherine, who has come up with a lot of bright ideas to help the handicapped, came by her concern simply from watching the world around her. "My family goes to downtown Cleveland sometimes, and I see handicapped people," she explains.

Katherine plans to become either a biomedical engineer or a lawyer so she can help people.

STOLEN VEHICLE LOCATION SERVICE

•••••

ODDS: 100%

ETA: 1992

PRICE: $500–$700

•••••

We all know the sound and we all hate it. At 3 A.M., an annoying alarm is wailing away because some couple leaned against a parked car for a smooch. Thank goodness the car alarm is about to join the Edsel.

What will take its place is a fantastic high-tech system offered by International Teletrac Systems, an Inglewood, California, company. Called Stolen Vehicle Location Service, it should put the fear of God into car thieves.

An alarm device mounted in your car works in conjunction with computer software supplied to the police. Working in real time, the police know the instant your car is stolen. They also have a complete physical description of the vehicle and know where it was parked, the direction in which it is headed, and its speed.

Stolen Vehicle Locator Units will be manufactured by companies such as Mitsubishi International, Kenwood, Samsung, and Matsushita Electronics Ltd. Subscriptions to the locating service will be available at electronics stores.

The actual unit in your car is about the size of a paperback book and very inconspicuous looking. It sends a signal to the police department computer if anyone steals the car. "Eighty percent of all cars stolen are hot-wired or started with something other than the owner's key," says Maurice Nieman, Teletrac's vice president of marketing. "This system also has an optional towing alert guard to protect luxury cars, which are often abducted onto flatbed trucks.

"The system works with no antennas, no stickers, nothing to let the thief know the car is protected," Nieman continues. "In our marketing research, we've found that consumers want to catch crooks and that cops working on a stolen car case would much rather catch people stealing than find burned-out, stripped automobiles and collect information for insurance companies."

The Teletrac system can do other things besides locate stolen vehicles. Its emergency alert service can provide a twenty-four-hour communications channel between the driver on the road and an operator who can provide help. "Some models will have a flat tire button, for instance," Nieman explains, "that will give operators your exact location so that assistance can be sent out to you immediately." Other applications include a signal that means the air bag has been detonated, so medical help will be alerted.

"The Mitsubishi model has a battery run-down function. Our operator would be alerted that your battery was running low and would be able to call you at home or at your office and tell you about it before you got into your car."

The Stolen Vehicle Location Service is already available in Los Angeles and is presently being put in place in Chicago, Detroit, and Dallas–Fort Worth. Next in the expansion plans are New York, San Francisco, San Diego, Washington, Baltimore, Philadelphia, Atlanta, Miami, Houston, Boston, and Pittsburgh.

VOICE CREDIT CARDS

ODDS: 85%
ETA: 2001
PRICE: NA

The way we identify ourselves is going to change in a major way with the introduction of the voice-activated credit cards. Signatures and secret number codes will be left behind in the twentieth century, replaced in the twenty-first century by your voice, a more accurate and reliable proof of who you are.

The voice card system is being developed by Bell Communications Center (Bellcore) in New Jersey. The same size and weight as a regular credit card, the voice card has a flat microchip embedded in the plastic. Technical papers written by Tim Feustel and co-workers at Bellcore describe this research. The writers point out that this card means protection because it demands three things of the owner before it will release information. First, of course, you must have the card in your possession. Second, you must know the password. Finally, your voice must match the voiceprint on the card.

It is believed that this three-tiered "gatekeeping" is the most advanced form of credit security available, says Feustel. It's expected that every kind of credit card, from charge to phone to bank, will employ voiceprint technology.

Surprisingly, a voice credit card will not be expensive—about $5 when bought by companies in bulk—so the only downside is that the consumer must visit the credit card company's offices so the card can be programmed and its owner trained. This visit should be as popular with consumers as renewing an expired driver's license!

Ninety-nine times out of a hundred, the voice card will instantly recognize its owner when he or she speaks the password. If you are suffering from a cold or the flu, that percentage might drop slightly.

The day may come when consumers will carry a single Voice Credit Card that will work for competing charge companies, banks, supermarkets, and department stores.

NEW PRODUCT STORES

ODDS: 50%
ETA: 1992
PRICE: NA

Maybe you don't have to invent a better mousetrap to have the world beat a path to your door. Maybe you just need to open a better mousetrap store.

Brian Gray, a twenty-five-year-old Canadian entrepreneur, has done just that. After trying unsuccessfully to market original concepts to large manufacturers, he came up with the notion of The New Product Store, Inc. The first shop opened in Toronto in 1989, the second is slated for Beverly Hills in California. Tokyo is a possibility, and so is your home town.

As you might expect, these stores are for people who already have everything else. Not that the merchandise is frivolous stuff, mind you. The products represent the varied creativity of scores of inventors, most of whom have been frustrated in their attempts to market their ideas.

Inventors pay a fee to show their products, as well as a commission to the store on every sale. In return, they get exposure, feedback, a support system, a receptive audience and, hopefully, some revenue. Products range from a hydraulically adjustable toilet seat for the handicapped to a breast enlarger that works like a blood pressure cuff.

Is there anything in the store that hasn't sold at all?

"No," says Gray. "There is *someone* for everything."

Okay, who bought the boob pump?

CHAPTER 12

learning

PARIS IN A BOX

ODDS: 100%

ETA: 1992

PRICE: ABOUT $175

Ah, the French. Mispronounce one word and they threaten to take back the Statue of Liberty. To improve international relations and make learning French more fun, researchers at the Massachusetts Institute of Technology have invented a remarkable interactive video program called "Direction Paris."

To use this program you need a video disc player, a television set, a Macintosh computer, and one of two interactive video discs, "A la Rencontre de Philippe" or "Dans le Quartier St. Gervais."

When the student comes in and turns on the program, Philippe, the hero, is about to be thrown out of his apartment by his girlfriend (don't you love modern education!). He needs help, either to save his romance or to find another place to live.

The student directs the action on the television screen by replying to a menu of Philippe's questions on the computer monitor. There are no right or wrong answers. Rather, there are occasions where the student can intervene and make a difference in Philippe's life.

The student is capable of going through Philippe's apartment, listening to the messages on his answering machine, and using the phone to dial other characters in the story.

The student can also travel around Paris alone or with Philippe, looking at apartments for rent. And as he/she would during any apartment search in a foreign country, the student will learn a great deal about daily life in France.

All the while, the student can call up vocabulary words on the computer or study a map of Paris.

There are seven different ways the story can end, depending on the decisions the student has made.

"A la Rencontre de Philippe" is the invention of scientists and Francophiles at the Athena Language Learning Project in Cambridge, Massachusetts, under the direction of Dr. Janet H. Murray of MIT. Average episodes last about a half hour and map out a full month of language labs for the intermediate to advanced student.

Programs are designed to help students "understand language in a culturally authentic and task-centered situation," explained Murray. And to have fun doing it.

170 LITERATE COMPUTERS

ODDS: 70%

ETA: 1992

PRICE: NA

"What we have here is a failure to communicate." That memorable line from the Paul Newman movie *Cool Hand Luke* is well understood by anyone trying to get information out of a computer without knowing the correct program and/or the operating system language.

In the near future, it won't be necessary to be computer literate. The computer is learning to understand "natural language," everyday writing filled with imperfect grammar and idiomatic phrases. This computer "education" is being conducted at General Electric's Research and Development Center in Schenectady, New York, under the direction of Lisa Rau and her husband and fellow researcher, Paul S. Jacobs.

Rau and Jacobs have developed a software program known as SCISOR (System for Conceptual Information Summarization, Organization, and Retrieval). SCISOR has the ability to read a variety of printed material written in everyday language and then answer questions about the content.

One of the first tests SCISOR was subjected to involved "reading" 500 stories from a financial news service. It was asked to categorize the items according to the concepts with which they dealt, such as mergers and acquisitions. Finally, the user typed in questions, in plain English, about the content of stories.

For example:

USER: "What was offered for DTS?"

SCISOR: "Digital Communs agreed to acquire Digital Transmission Systems for $14 million in cash and Digital Communs common stock."

SCISOR has a 10,000-word lexicon and the ability to do a number of other tasks, such as summarizing stories and adding more facts to appropriate categories.

SCISOR was designed particularly for the casual, inexperienced, or phobic computer user. But it does so much so well and so easily that most likely it will be used by everyone. Right, SCISOR?

CUSTOMIZED TEXTBOOKS

ODDS: 75%

ETA: 1992

PRICE: VARIABLE

Visit the college campus in today's fast-changing world and you might (or you might not) be surprised to find textbooks woefully out-of-date. In a political science lecture, the professor could be discussing the 1990 reunification of Germany while the course textbook still describes two hostile nations.

Customized textbooks that can be updated in days are the wave of the future, not only at colleges, where they're already appearing, but in high schools and elementary schools as well. Using computers with large data bases of information, publishers can let teachers design tailor-made texts by ordering chapters from a wide array of sources.

"The result is a book that contains the order and the exact information that the teacher wants," says Robert Lynch, editor and director of custom publishing of the College Division of McGraw-Hill, Inc.

How quickly can changes be made? "On the fly," according to Lynch, because customized texts are produced on electronic desktop systems. McGraw-Hill can get a sample text into the hands of the professor forty-eight hours after the order has been placed. Students' copies hit the campus bookstore three to four weeks later.

What does all this mean to students? Instead of reading several chapters from a lot of books, the student will purchase one custom-made volume that contains a compilation of material from books, magazine articles, essays, experiments, reports, etc.—all handpicked by their instructor.

The book won't be of the same quality as a text produced by traditional offset methods, but it will have a table of contents, index, and seamless pagination. The syllabus will be bound in and the cover will include the name of the professor and the course and other information.

"It has the potential of reducing the out-of-pocket expense of the student," says Lynch. The theory being that even though customized books cost more, the student will be buying fewer books altogether.

More important, stresses Lynch, is that "teachers will no longer have to rely on the same things; they can be much more dynamic and responsive to their class needs."

However, there are limits to this dynamism, which need attention. Right now a publisher can only offer material that it owns or receives permission to include. Copyright owners will have to agree to grant reprint rights for the system to truly be successful.

INTERACTIVE BOOKS

ODDS: 40%

ETA: 1994

PRICE: $20

One afternoon, a man named Peter sits in his office staring out of the window, thinking. Suddenly he finds himself reflecting on the scene of a car wreck he passed on his way to work that day. As he explores the image in his mind, he realizes that the car he saw mangled on the side of the road belongs to his ex-wife.

"Do you want to hear about it?" he asks.

If you're not interested in Peter's thoughts at that moment, you can ignore the question and continue with the story. Or you can answer him by typing "yes" or "no" on your computer keyboard. If you tell him "no," he responds, "I know why you would not want to know." If you tell him "yes," he proceeds to tell you the terrible truth: "I may have seen my son die this morning."

Welcome to interactive fiction, a new form of computer-based literature. Also known as Hypertext, or multiple fiction, the genre does not move linearly from episode to episode as do conventional novels. Instead, it enables the individual reader to explore the story in a more personal way. You may choose to see events from another perspective, or learn more about the background of a particular character, or move into the mind of the protagonist.

The passage at the beginning of this write-up is from *Afternoon*, a multiple fiction novel by Michael Joyce, published by Eastgate Press and designed for an Apple Macintosh computer.

Although the form may seem very "now," Mark Bernstein, publisher of Eastgate, reminds us that multiple fiction really draws on the ancient tradition of storytelling. "In olden times, stories were a performed art," says Bernstein. "If the performer was sensitive to the audience, he or she would modify the performance for each audience. That's what we're trying to get back to here—to restore the sense of participation and dialogue with the audience."

Reading *Afternoon*, you make decisions as you move through the novel's 540 screens. You can press the RETURN key to continue on a given path, or you may decide to explore one of the many intertwining plots by selecting any word in the text that you find compelling. As you make selections, you will be led to interlinked segments of the narrative, all prepared by Joyce, who has anticipated a mind-boggling number of potential reader responses. "And the choices you make really matter," says the author.

"You begin to form the feeling that you're in conversation with the text," he explains. Each twist and turn the reader chooses adds up to a unique experience. "No two readers experience the same story."

So far, Eastgate has published one other Hypertext novel and two Hypertext political history books. In addition to text, all use special effects, such as graphics and dialogue from inanimate objects, to grab the reader's attention.

Afternoon has received critical acclaim and is being taught at Cornell and Yale Universities.

CHAPTER 13

hobbies

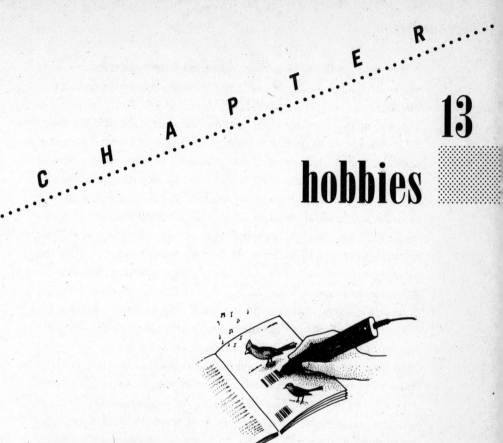

THE SONGWAND

What bird-watchers love to do most, next to actually seeing birds, is to listen to them. And not just for the pure joy of hearing the songs, but because sound helps to identify birds in the field. A new product called the SongWand should help all birders enjoy their avocation.

• • • • •

ODDS: 90%

ETA: 1992

PRICE: $289

• • • • •

The SongWand is a small, hand-held scanner that comes with peel-off labels called BirdCodes. The scanner, via a cord, plugs into a portable compact-disc player. Each BirdCode label has a bar code identified by the name of a particular bird. The labels are intended to be adhered into the margins of a bird-watching field guide. When the birder runs the tip of the SongWand over a BirdCode label, the song of that specific bird bursts forth from the CD.

So if you think that's a Black-Throated Green Warbler you hear singing in a tree, listen carefully to the song. Open your field guide and run the scanner over the Black-Throated Green Warbler bar code. You will hear the prerecorded sound of its song. Compare the two.

"It extends the printed material into the realm of sound," says Dan Kimball, SongWand's creator and president of Interactive Audio in Santa Barbara, California. Kimball came up with the idea after he saw, in a museum bookstore, an old bird guide he'd had a copy of when he was a child. Nostalgic, curious, Kimball bought the book. Inside he found pictures and descriptions of birds along with "sonagrams," little graphs that chart the frequency and melody of birdcalls. "I thought, 'Wouldn't it be nice if you could pass a wand over the sonogram and hear the song?' "

Which is exactly what Kimball, a software engineer, has accomplished. He understood that with optical disc technologies, "you could just put a code in a book and provide a device to read it."

He also knew enough to head for the Cornell Laboratory of Ornithology's library, which has probably the largest repository of recorded birdcalls in the world. The result will be the complete collection of birdcalls, titled *Eastern and Western Bird Songs of North America* on three compact discs.

The main purpose of the SongWand is to help birders brush up on their calls before going into the field. A memory function lets you input the series of calls you wish to study, and a quiz function plays random mystery songs to test your recognition.

However, birders realize that they can attract birds by actually playing the recorded calls in the field. This can upset birds if they feel their territory is being invaded. It may also take them away from the important task of feeding their young.

SongWand will come with instructions on how to use it "responsibly." As bird-watchers are normally staunch environmentalists, Kimball feels they will abide.

"The SongWand is basically an educational tool," says Kimball, who can see many additional uses for the technology. For example, foreign language instruction books and guides will come with bar codes and a wand. When a bar code is scanned, the student will hear a phrase spoken by a native.

"The technology provides interaction that is different from a cassette player," says Kimball. "It provides instant access to the sound."

HYPERCUBE PUZZLE

Students, you can bag the homework. Insomniacs, you'll beg for sleep. Obsessive-compulsives, enjoy! Hypercube could easily be the most addictive, challenging, and confounding puzzle-game since Rubik's Cube.

ODDS: 90%
ETA: 1992
PRICE: ABOUT $12

Madhukar Thakur, a doctoral candidate at the University of California, and Ravi Kuchimanchi, a doctoral candidate at the University of Maryland, have taken the infamous Rubik's Cube and given it a couple of diabolical twists.

Well, not totally diabolical. One intriguing feature of this new cube game is that it has an adjustable difficulty factor. You can add or remove colored bands, arrows, and numbers to change the complexity and challenge of the puzzle.

The result is a toy that will torture the whole family.

Its co-inventors describe Hypercube as a hybrid of a Rubik-type cube and the classic 15 Puzzle introduced in 1880, which you probably played as a kid. That's the one with a 4-by-4 grid holding fifteen numbered sliding squares and one empty space. You must get the scrambled numbers into order by sliding the squares horizontally or vertically into the empty space left by the previous move.

Hypercube has a similar sliding-square arrangement on each of its six surfaces. So each of the nine segments, or "facelets," on each side can rotate, à la Rubik, and slide. The facelets are colored and numbered. And there are removable colored bands on the outside edges.

Just how difficult is this game? Rubik's Cube had a measly 43

quintillion configurations—43 followed by 18 zeros. Hypercube's possible permutations total 10 to the one-hundredth power. That's 1 followed by 100 zeros. That's a very big number. It's more than the estimated number of atoms in the universe.

IMPROVED BALLET SLIPPER

ODDS: 25%

ETA: 1995

PRICE: $50 PER PAIR

Ballet dancers may look as graceful as swans, gazelles, and sugarplum fairies, but their bodies are taking a pounding.

Dancing in the pointe position (on the toes) puts tremendous stress on legs, feet, and ankles as dancers leap and pirouette, sustaining impact in the most unnatural positions. Over long periods, the strain can lead to chronic pain, injury, and even permanent debility.

Which brings us to the ballet shoe—the slight, soft, satiny slipper that has remained practically unchanged for the past 100 years. A shoe so delicate that in spite of the harder toe box, a professional's pair may be unusable after a single performance. (Even a casual student will use six or seven pairs a year, at $40 per.) Yet this tender bit of canvas, burlap, glue, and satin is all that protects the dancer.

Dr. Alan Tuckman, a former professional dancer turned orthopedic surgeon, intends to do for the ballet performer what some unsung hero did for the running enthusiast—use modern technological design to protect our skeletal structures.

The fit of the shoe is the most critical factor in avoiding injury, explains Dr. Tuckman from his office at the Albert Einstein Medical Center in Philadelphia. Using sophisticated techniques for biomechanical analysis, including pressure-sensitive films and video digitizing equipment, he has been studying the way standing on pointe puts stress on the ballerina. With a more complete understanding of how the foot reacts to movement on pointe, space-age materials, such as the thermoplastics, can be used to create a shoe that is molded exactly to the individual's foot, enhancing support and shock absorbancy, he says.

For all of that, Dr. Tuckman doesn't expect his finished product to be embraced by the leading ballet dancers of the late 1990s. Because of tradition, habit, and even superstition, experienced dancers, Dr. Tuckman suspects, will stick with the old-style slipper. But he believes that younger and nonprofessional dancers will love them—which is good since those dancers have relatively less muscle development and are therefore more injury prone.

With the specialization and improvement in the past decade of almost every form of athletic footwear from roller skates to bicycle shoes, an improvement in the ballet slipper should be welcomed by a generation very "into" what it puts on its feet.

ORNITHOPTER

• • • • •

ODDS: 10%

ETA: 1995

PRICE: $250 FOR MODEL KIT

• • • • •

Birds do it. Bats do it. The mythical Icarus got punished for doing it. And James DeLaurier of Toronto, Canada, and Jeremy Harris of Columbus, Ohio, spent fifteen years trying to do it.

And they finally did it. They actually built an engine-powered aircraft that flies by flapping its wings.

Now, this may not sound all that impressive to those of you who aren't aviators or ornithologists. But the fact is, flapping-wing flight is an incredibly complex and challenging problem. DeLaurier, an aeronautical engineer, and Harris, a mechanical engineer, happen to like incredibly complex and challenging problems, so in the late seventies, they decided to tackle the ornithopter.

"Actually, we would have saved ourselves a lot of work if we'd waited ten years," admits DeLaurier. "Back then, we were working with balsa wood and slide rules. Now we've got computers, carbon, and Kevlar." Computer modeling makes it easier to predict which configurations work and which ones don't. Carbon and Kevlar are space-age materials that are strong, lightweight, and flexible.

Anyway, why is it so difficult to fly the way birds do?

"Birds use muscles," explains DeLaurier. "Man has yet to produce anything equivalent to an artificial muscle. Instead, we have to use pulleys, belts, cranks . . . and an engine has to power them. Then the engine needs fuel, which adds weight. Then you must deal with very subtle aerodynamic adjustments. A bird's musculoskeletal system can perform infinite refinements almost instantly. A mechanical system can't."

Although computer projections indicate that a passenger-carrying ornithopter is feasible, to date, DeLaurier and Harris have built only scale models.

"Right now, we've got a radio-controlled, engine-powered, 8.6-pound version with a 9-foot wingspan. We're building a larger, more sophisticated model for Seville's Expo '92."

DeLaurier foresees a kit becoming available for model airplane enthusiasts within four or five years. But that's not what really intrigues him. He and his partner believe that man *can* fly like a bird, and they intend to prove it.

TEAM CHESS

ODDS: 90%

ETA: 1993

PRICE: $25 AND UP

The game of chess has remained virtually unchanged since its invention fifteen centuries ago in the Far East. Simple enough for children to play, yet so complex that it can challenge the most brilliant mind, chess stands as one of man's most ingenious and enduring accomplishments.

So it's probably about time that someone messed with the rules.

The man who has done that—and in a major way—is Richard A. Carlson of Cincinnati, Ohio, an illustrator for the Occupational Safety and Health Department of that city. Mr. Carlson has made a bigger board, almost doubled the pieces, created a completely new one, and added some radical new twists.

The result is that now four people, instead of two, can play the game.

"When the family would play chess, my young daughter was constantly asking to challenge the winner," Carlson explained. "I figured there must be a better way to do this."

It took two days to develop his concept for team chess.

Here's how it's played. The board has fifteen squares across by twelve squares from end to end. Lined up on the back row of those fifteen squares are 4 knights, 4 bishops, 4 rooks, 2 queens, and the king. In the front row there are 14 pawns and a new piece, called the warder, in front of the king.

As in regular chess, one team is black and one team is white. However, in team chess, pieces are further subdivided by the introduction of red and blue bands. Each member of a team plays half the pieces, either red or blue. The king and the warder are the only pieces that can be moved by either team member.

Now, the warder's special job is to protect the king while remaining in a nine-square area called the castle. The king can move anywhere, but as long as he stays in the castle, he gets the extra protection of the warder, who can move anywhere in the special zone in a single move.

"The warder is more or less unprotected by himself," Carlson explained. "On the other hand, he can't go outside of the castle. He's confined to that area. That's why I call him the warder. It's an old English term for jail keeper."

Purists from the parks of Greenwich Village to the chess clubs of Leningrad may resent what this family man from Cincinnati has done to their venerable game. Others will think that maybe chess was due for a change.

Carlson has a patent for Team Chess. Now he has to find a game manufacturer willing to break with 1,500 years of tradition.

SELF-WATERING PLANTS

If plants could talk, we'd have healthier plants. Your dieffenbachia would tell you when it's thirsty and when it's had enough. Communication would take the guesswork out of watering.

ODDS: 100%

ETA: 1992

PRICE: $3,000

There would be other advantages, too, especially if you had a lot of plants. You would conserve water and save money, and you would eliminate the runoff of nutrients and fertilizer.

Well, plants can't talk, but they can communicate their appetite for water in a very precise way. A research team at the Davis campus of the University of California has developed a greenhouse irrigation system that "listens" to plants.

Here's how it works, according to associate professors David W. Burger and J. Heinrich Lieth at the university's Department of Environmental Horticulture. One plant in the greenhouse is picked to be the "signal" plant. A tensiometer is placed in the flowerpot to monitor the tension created by drying soil. The reading is converted into electrical impulses, which are transmitted by connectors to a personal computer.

When the signals reach a certain level, the computer turns on the greenhouse irrigation system. When the tension decreases to a particular level, indicating that the plant has had enough to drink, the water gets turned off.

The University of California team estimates that water consumption can be reduced by an amazing 25 to 80 percent using this system.

According to Professor Burger, flowers grown using this "flower-signaling system" are slightly shorter, which is more aesthetic for pot chrysanthemums and other plants.

CHAPTER 14

sports stuff

LEVEL-ENHANCED GOLF PUTTER

ODDS: 85%
ETA: 1994
PRICE: NA

Putting can be a poky business, especially at the professional level, where every putt seems to take an eternity. Anyone who has ever watched a tournament on TV has probably seen Nicklaus or Palmer squatting on the green to examine the position of the ball and holding out his club for a reading of the green and the best angle for his putt. The whispering announcer, all the while, is trying to create dramatic tension out of this elaborate pantomime. Boring, with a capital *B*.

To the aid of golfers and the relief of spectators, a retiree from Sarasota, Florida, has actually designed a club that could do away with all this excessive squatting and looking. Albert A. Ronnick has patented a putter that has a built-in level indicator, just like the one that carpenters use to insure that shelves and other surfaces are level to the ground. The bubble inside a clear tube is located near the top of the club. It will give golfers an easier, more accurate read of the green and the position of the ball.

According to Ronnick, there are two additional advantages that his putter has over other clubs. First, the player cannot inadvertently hold it askew. Second, there is no risk that an asymmetrical weight distribution in the club will cause it to hang off center from the player's hand.

Ronnick doesn't actually play the game himself, but, an inveterate inventor, he had kicked the putter idea around for about ten years. Finally, he put club and level together and got a patent. Arnie, Jack, and the gallery will someday be grateful he did.

ONE-HANDED GOLF PUTTER

ODDS: 65%
ETA: 1993
PRICE: $90

There's no question that this odd-looking, one-handed golf putter will put you in the spotlight at your local golf course. There's also a good possibility that it will shave three to five strokes off your score. What isn't known is whether the U.S. Golf Association will ever put its stamp of approval on this unique club.

"It's definitely legal according to the rules of golf," says the club's inventor, John H. Scalf, of Allen, Kentucky. "But the USGA is a little unpredictable." In the meantime, Scalf is manufacturing and selling the clubs himself.

The putter is approximately the same size and weight as standard putters, but that's the end of similarities. The shaft curves slightly outward at the base, like a hockey stick, and bisects the wedge-shaped head. The head of the putter itself is a triple-grooved composite of aluminum and fiberglass. It rests on the surface of the green behind the ball when you're ready to putt. The player stands to one side of the ball and pushes it with a shuffleboard-type stroke, using either hand.

There are two main advantages to the one-handed stroke, says Scalf. Because the golfer is behind the ball, he can keep constant alignment while striking it; and because the head rests on the surface, it eliminates the tendency to push the ball off line to the right or to fan the putter and pull the ball off line to the left (for right-handed golfers).

An independent test by a longtime Sunday golfer confirmed that the shuffleboard stroke results in a truer, cleaner putt. However, this tester found it difficult to get a grip on the distance; most of his putts went farther than expected.

Scalf agrees that the average golfer will require an adjustment period of at least a dozen rounds to get a feel for the club. But he says the club has done wonders for him, reducing his handicap from 8 to 4.3 in just one season.

That, incidentally, was why he invented the club: His putting was killing his game and causing immense frustration. "For me, it is true that necessity was the mother of invention," Scalf says. "My putting had gotten so atrocious, I had to do something!"

Right now, Scalf is playing it cool as far as promoting his putter or looking for a national manufacturer are concerned. "One fellow on the pro circuit called wanting one, but I refused to sell to him. If he or some other pro were to win a tournament using the putter, the USGA would probably start hollering and make up some rule against it."

GOLF TRAINING HARNESS

If your golf game is causing you more pain and frustration than pleasure and elation, then this $40 shoulder harness may change your life.

ODDS: 80%
ETA: 1992
PRICE: $40

The brainchild of Gerald Kubo, a retired engineering professor from River Edge, New Jersey, it works on the premise that "muscles have memory"; that if you repeat a motion often enough, it becomes as automatic as walking.

The trick is to get the movement right.

Kubo, a golf addict for thirty-five years, thinks he has the solution. He calls it the G-SLOT Guide, a plastic, shoulder-mounted support that straps to the body and guides the golfer's swing.

Retired, determined, and with a ton of time to play, Kubo was frustrated to find his game getting worse, not better. The big problem was the inconsistency of his swing.

"I decided I was going to beat this game," he says. "But even though I practiced and took lessons, my game got worse."

So, applying his engineering skills to golf, Kubo came up with his harness. The support serves as a launching platform. As the golfer winds up to the top of his backswing, he rests the club in a groove on the shoulder mount and sets the course for the downswing.

The harness allows the golfer to aim his swing in the desired direction and, properly adjusted, it disallows swinging over the ball, hitting it too far on the left or right, or missing it entirely. In effect, the user can forget about the backswing and concentrate on the downswing.

With enough practice, says Kubo, muscles will memorize the correct motion and the harness can be eliminated.

The G-SLOT Guide won't turn hackers into Palmers, but if an erratic stroke is your problem, Kubo is convinced his invention will help.

The product can be ordered from G-SLOT Guide, P.O. Box 9205, Paramus, New Jersey, 07653.

SWING-STRENGTHENING BASEBALL BAT

• • • • •

ODDS: 75%

ETA: 1993

PRICE: NA

• • • • •

For all those players who dream about home runs but seldom hit any, a professional golfer and an aerospace engineer have teamed up to create a baseball training bat that can turn singles hitters into sluggers.

Larry Nelson is the golfer, and Richard Passamaneck is the engineer. Passamaneck is also a professor at the University of Colorado and a former catcher on a semipro team in the Braves' organization. He "knows a thing or two about hitting."

One thing Passamaneck knows is that in a power swing, bat velocity should be the greatest at the time of contact. With his training in aerodynamics, Passamaneck was able to devise a bat that would help strengthen those muscles needed to achieve maximum velocity at that critical instant in time.

The key to the training bat is a small fanlike device at the hitting end. When you swing, the fan is activated by the air pushed through it. Naturally, increased air resistance (which you can adjust the bat for) makes it much harder to move the bat forward.

According to Passamaneck, strengthening through air resistance is far better for a hitter than simply practicing with a weighted bat. The "fan" bat builds up only those muscles used in the swing and makes the player aware of which muscles are involved. Also, he says, their bat simulates a truer swing since a weighted bat will pull the batter in a direction perpendicular to the bat motion.

Nelson and Passamaneck, who also have a patent on a similar swing-strengthening golf club, plan to produce and market both devices themselves.

GRAPHITE BASEBALL BAT

ODDS: 100%
ETA: 1992
PRICE: $100

Wood to aluminum to graphite. Not as catchy as Tinkers to Evers to Chance, but nonetheless this may be the ultimate evolution of the baseball bat. Worth Inc., a sporting goods manufacturer in Tullahoma, Tennessee, has created a graphite bat that, they say, is superior to aluminum, sounds like wood, and has a real chance of making it to the major leagues.

If you are a baseball purist, this notion is revolting. However, if you are also an environmentalist, the Worth logic may soften you up a bit. According to Nelson Eddy (not *the* Nelson Eddy), a Worth spokesman, here are some reasons why they expect graphite bats in the "bigs" by 2001:

- It takes examination of 100 pieces of wood to find one of the proper grade to make a major-league bat.
- With Little Leaguers, high schoolers and college players using aluminum bats, there's not much of a market for the ninety-nine discarded bats.
- On average, a pro goes through six to nine dozen bats per season.
- There are about 500 batters in the big leagues. And each of the twenty-six major-league teams has several minor-league affiliates.

Eddy's message is that a lot of trees are dying in the name of the Great American Pastime.

But why graphite instead of aluminum? According to Eddy, the lighter graphite outperforms and outlasts aluminum. And what's more (and this is really important), graphite can be "tuned to sound like wood." The bat will "crack" on contact with the ball, a key concern for fans, who love the sound, and for fielders, who react to it.

Putting the "crack" in the bat is possible because graphite fibers have no distinctive sound of their own (unlike aluminum, with its ghostly metallic ping), and the polyurethane foam that fills the bat shell can be adjusted to produce a variety of sounds.

The Worth bat has been sampled by several major leaguers, including Wade Boggs, Chili Davis, and even Hank Aaron, who took a few cuts at an old-timers' game. The response, admits Eddy, was about fifty-fifty. "However, most of these guys are incredibly superstitious about their bats and don't even like the idea that something might be better than wood."

Better or not, like it or not, Worth is already making them—at the rate of twenty a day. And all the major bat companies are working on their own versions. Worth, the first with one-piece aluminum, also has the first U.S.-made graphite bat.

Wood to aluminum to graphite could be headed for a display case in Cooperstown.

SOFTER HARDBALL

ODDS: 100%

ETA: 1992

PRICE: SAME AS REGULAR BALL

Does it make any sense that nine-year-old Johnny playing Little League in the schoolyard is using the exact same baseballs as Jose Canseco and Doc Gooden?

If your answer is, "Yes, sure, what's the harm, they've got to learn the game," consider this fact: Baseball causes more serious injuries to children

than any other sport. According to the U.S. Product Safety Commission, in ten years, over fifty kids were killed by baseballs. That's right. Killed!

Worth Inc., a sporting goods company in Tullahoma, Tennessee, has developed a softer hardball that, they claim, will reduce injuries by 70 percent without affecting the way the game is played. The Reduced Injury Factor (RIF) ball "looks, feels, and plays like the real thing," says Worth spokesman Nelson Eddy. It has the same white cowhide cover with red stitching on the seams, the same diameter, the same weight, and the same aerodynamics. What it hasn't got is the same core.

The traditional ball's center is rubber and yarn. The RIF ball is filled with polyurethane foam, an aerospace material that Worth first used in the production of softballs. The foam, Eddy explained, has the capacity to compress over a greater area and for a longer period of time. The result is a softening of the blow when a ball hits a player in the head, chest, or other vital area.

"Instead of putting padding on players, like they do in football and hockey, we found a way to pad the ball without altering the way it plays," says Eddy.

The National Operating Committee on Standards for Athletic Equipment, whose stamp is on all official Little League helmets, tested the RIF ball on kids fourteen and under. It was determined that when a standard baseball thrown 60 miles per hour hits a kid in the head, there is a 90 to 99 percent chance of serious injury. With the RIF ball, that frightening percentage drops way down to 2 to 5 percent.

Despite the compelling safety advantage, Eddy acknowledges that the RIF ball has a long way to go before it gains widespread acceptance. While parents love the ball, coaches hate it. This is mostly a matter of machismo, Eddy believes. Coaches are quick to say the ball that "died on the warning track" would have been a home run with a "real" baseball, or that the bad hop wouldn't have happened with a "regulation" ball.

In the long run, Eddy expects the parents to win and the RIF ball to be officially sanctioned by the Little League. "It's like seat belts," Eddy says. "When they were first introduced, the engineers and car companies all knew how many lives they could save. But the public was slow to take to them because of a cowboy kind of attitude about driving. Now, wearing seat belts is the law in most states."

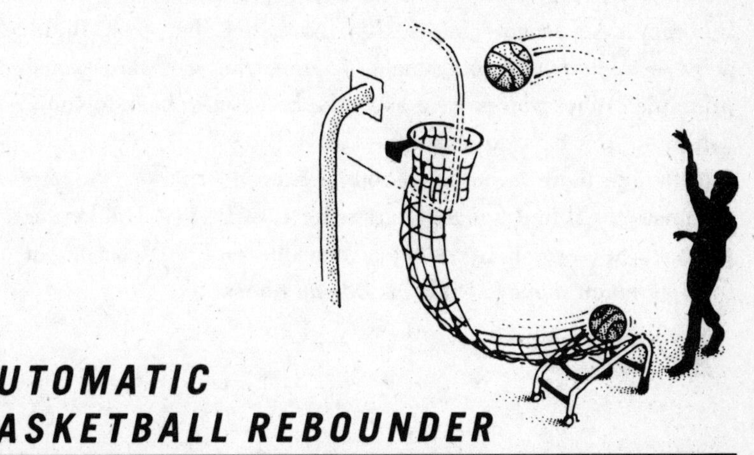

AUTOMATIC BASKETBALL REBOUNDER

ODDS: 85%

ETA: 1993

PRICE: $500

With this device," says modest inventor Bob Ackerman, "everybody will be shooting like Larry Bird by the year 2001."

Well . . . probably not.

But Ackerman's automatic basketball rebounder does make practicing easier, and it does provide players with an extra incentive to score.

Ackerman, the women's basketball coach at Spoon River Junior College in Canton, Illinois, calls his invention "Best Buddy" because "it takes a good friend to run around chasing rebounds for you."

The Best Buddy rebounder consists of a net chute that extends from the bottom of the regular net around the basketball hoop to a 24-inch-by-24-inch backboard on wheels. The player shoots from anywhere around this backboard. When he or she makes a basket, the ball runs down the net chute to the backboard and is deflected up into the player's hands.

Ackerman's patented prototype will work from a distance of 3 to 20 feet. The table has wheels so the shooter can easily move it around the court. It also has built-in steps to accommodate hooking the net chute to the hoop.

Tests at Spoon River College and at a summer program at North Carolina State resulted in a 20 percent improvement in shooting accuracy, Ackerman claims. It's his belief that Best Buddy can achieve such results because it operates on a reward-punishment principle. When you make a shot, the ball comes back to you. When you miss, you have to chase the ball.

Although there are other rebounders on the market, Ackerman is optimistic he'll find a manufacturer for Best Buddy. Unlike the competition, he says, his product is movable and will cost about one-third as much money. Under $500, he hopes.

THREE-PIECE ROWING SHELL

ODDS: 100%
ETA: 1992
PRICE: $2,500

Connecticut boat designer Robert Champlain was faced with an interesting problem. "Someone came to me one day and wanted to buy a rowing boat. The problem was he lived in Boston and space was at a premium. He couldn't find a place to store the boat so he never bought one.

"I thought to myself, 'How can I capitalize on this problem?' Then, driving home from work one day, it came to me like a bang! Make a boat that nests, like Tupperware."

After many months and many prototypes, Champlain created the boat he had envisioned: a three-piece rowing shell that could be easily carried and stored. The pieces are close to the same size but not exactly, so they can fit one inside the other, just like Tupperware. The boat weighs 43 pounds, an average weight for a recreational rowing shell of its size. Assembled, it's 20 feet long, 23 inches wide, and 15 inches deep.

That customer from Boston could easily have kept the pieces in an apartment closet, taken them down to the Charles River, assembled the boat, and gone for a row.

"This boat is really functional, and you don't have to be a rocket scientist to put it together," says Champlain. Ten minutes is all it takes to assemble the pieces. The longest section is 7 feet long, so it can stand up in a closet.

Called the Zipper, it's made of fiberglass and aluminum like most shells. It comes with two "decks" made of nylon that conveniently "zip" into place over the front and back sections to prevent water getting into the boat. The Zipper carries one passenger and is designed for the recreational oarsperson. It comes with sliding rowing seat and riggers, but does not include oars.

Champlain is selling the Zipper now from his company, Golden Era Boats, in Noank, Connecticut. He hopes to market the boat nationwide under the name Piece Boat.

HIGH-ALTITUDE SAFETY BAG

ODDS: 98%

ETA: 1992

PRICE: $2,500

Until recently, one golden rule has guided mountain climbers: Proceed slowly. If you are heading high above your home altitude, you ascend only about 2,000 feet per day. Altitude sickness brought on by a lack of oxygen results in dizziness, nausea, and disorientation. At very high altitudes, moving too high too fast can cost you your life. Estimates put high-altitude climbers' deaths at one in thirty from altitude sickness, technically known as cerebral and pulmonary edema. In this condition, the climber feels as though he or she is drowning. A gurgling noise wells up with each breath. The lungs and brain fill with body fluids. He or she loses balance and the ability to think. The climber's only chance is to get to a lower altitude.

Above 17,000 feet, almost every hiker will feel ill as the body stops digesting protein. At 20,000 feet, the life threat becomes severe. (Mount Everest is 29,028 feet.)

R. Igor Gamow is a professor of chemical engineering at the University of Colorado at Boulder. His interest in mountain climbing and saving lives has resulted in the Gamow Bag, a 14-pound, portable, inflatable, airtight "intensive care unit" for climbers.

A dizzy hiker is zippered into the 7-foot-long bag. His fellow climbers pump air into the bag until the air density is 2 pounds per square inch while a small pressure-relief valve lets out CO_2. The bag can make a climber at 23,000 feet feel like he or she is at a far more comfortable altitude of 16,000 feet.

Professor Gamow researched and tested the bag's use in the mountains of Nepal, Alaska, and South America. It has already been used by several American teams at Mount Everest. In one rescue in Tibet, an unconscious climber was placed in the Gamow Bag, which his colleagues pumped for eleven hours. The sick climber was then able to resume the ascent.

Already in limited production, the Gamow Bag has been purchased by the armies of India and Pakistan. Professor Gamow believes that every serious high-altitude hiker's backpack should include this life-saving device. Especially male hikers'. "Men are more aggressive climbers, they're more macho and go higher faster," he says. "Women have more sense."

SIX-SIDED TENNIS RACQUET

ODDS: 90%

ETA: 1992

PRICE: SAME AS REGULAR RACQUETS

And all this time you thought there was something wrong with your swing. Now hear this: There's something wrong with your tennis racquet.

It may be hard to believe that since day one, the tennis racquet has been misdesigned. That's the theory of a Cleveland inventor who claims the grip should have six sides, not eight. There is now considerable evidence that Andrew Brown, an actuary by profession, is right.

Brown claims his new grip will revolutionize the game, make eight-sided racquets obsolete, and change the tennis learning curve from four years to four weeks. His six-sided racquet may also prevent painful tennis elbow.

Brown took up tennis when he was in his forties. Frustrated by bad hits, he began to wonder if the fault might be the racquet's, not his. So he remade the handle—over and over again—until he "hit on the point where the ball went just where it should."

According to Brown, when you "shake hands," or grip a standard racquet to make a forehand shot, the face is turned 7 degrees upward. University studies have shown that a mere 1-degree difference means even a well-aimed ball travels 6 feet farther than intended. A 7-degree difference means the ball can go an extra 40 feet!

The backhand shot is similarly off kilter in a downward direction—as any hacker who drives the ball into the ground can attest.

The eight-sided grip has been around since the 1880s (before that, the handle was round). No one knows who invented the eight-sider, and, according to Brown, no one ever questioned its scientific merit. Until now.

His six-sided grip, on the other hand, is getting a lot of attention from scientists at a number of universities, most notably at the University of Massachusetts's Department of Exercise Sciences. Using a high-speed camera and a computer to measure wrist and racquet angles at impact, researchers there found a 14 percent improvement in the forehand and a 9 percent improvement in the backhand of subjects using the six-sided grip. And this after players had used the new racquet for only fifteen minutes.

As for tennis elbow and tennis wrist, "there's no question that the new grip should eliminate these problems," says Brown, since the player does not have to twist his arm to compensate for the off-line racquet face. "The six-sided grip simply allows the body to do what it does naturally."

STRAIGHT-LINE POOL CUE

Kim Davenport, the number 2 ranked pro in the world, calls it "a first-class idea." The number 6 player, Grady Matthews, says it "has to be the most innovative teaching aid in the history of the game." And trick-shot master Mike Massey calls it "a tool that can help every player."

ODDS: 85%

ETA: 1992

PRICE: 20% HIGHER THAN REGULAR CUE

The "it" is a new pool cue designed by Colorado Springs schoolteacher Marion J. Ross Jr. His twist on the conventional cue is a simple "aiming reference line" on the shaft that helps the player keep his or her stroke straight.

"Most people when they miss a shot have either a wobble or a twist in their stroke," explained Ross, an avid amateur player. "With a conventional clear shaft they can't see what they're doing wrong or how their stroke is off. This invention should help them keep their stroke straight."

The aiming reference line is a sixteenth-of-an-inch-thick strip of colored maple—the same wood used in most quality cues—that runs 18 inches up the shaft from the tip of the cue.

Ross, who is now president of Straight Line Shafts, Inc., says there are a number of ways to produce the new cues but the most commercially viable is to cut the shaft on a milling machine, insert the maple veneer, and then sand it down.

The idea of an aiming line, says Ross, is hardly new in sports. "Some bowling balls have a line on them to show the rotation of the ball while it moves down the lane. And in golf, there is a small line at the bottom of most putters to draw an imaginary line to the hole. With our cue, we have just taken this imaginary line and placed it on the shaft."

DIRTBOARD

Kids are going to read this and weep.

•••••

ODDS: 95%

ETA: 1992

PRICE: $195

•••••

The All Terrain Dirtboard is here, different, and most of all it's absolutely insane. The Dirtboard is a revolutionary skateboard that allows you to ride on just about any terrain, dirt hills, grass and mud just as if you were riding your regular skateboard on smooth concrete. The Dirtboard opens up a whole new world for you.
—First paragraph of the Dirtboard promotion brochure

If it does everything its creator, Mort Heilig, says it will, Dirtboard could be the hula hoop of the nineties. What makes this "board" special are the wheels. They're air-filled tires that measure 8 inches in diameter. Compare that with the 3-inch, solid wheels on regular skateboards. The larger size and the buoyancy make all the difference, says Heilig. "You can now ride on dirt and grass and gravel. And on concrete, the ride will be smoother, quieter, and faster than a conventional skateboard."

Bigger wheels are also safer. Thousands of skateboard accidents occur when hard wheels hit even a small twig and the rider goes flying, says Heilig.

This isn't the first unusual vehicle that Heilig has come up with since founding Supercruiser Inc. six years ago in Monterey Park,

California. But it could be the most successful. Why does he invent this stuff? "I like to fill a need that everyone else has overlooked. At first it looks like a crazy idea," he says.

But there's nothing crazy or "insane" about Dirtboard. It's a well-thought-out, sensible piece of design. Unlike a skateboard's tires, the Dirtboard's tires are set in so they can rise up above the platform. This way, despite the size of the tires, the board is still close enough to the ground so the rider can use his free foot to propel it forward. The back wheels are covered by fenders so that the rider can't step on a rotating wheel, causing an accident.

Dirtboard is 41 inches long and 12 inches wide, and it weighs 21 pounds. Early models are all red with blue and black trim.

City kids will love Dirtboard, but country kids, without a lot of sidewalk and pavement around, should love it even more.

Beyond awesome.

CHAPTER 15

bike stuff

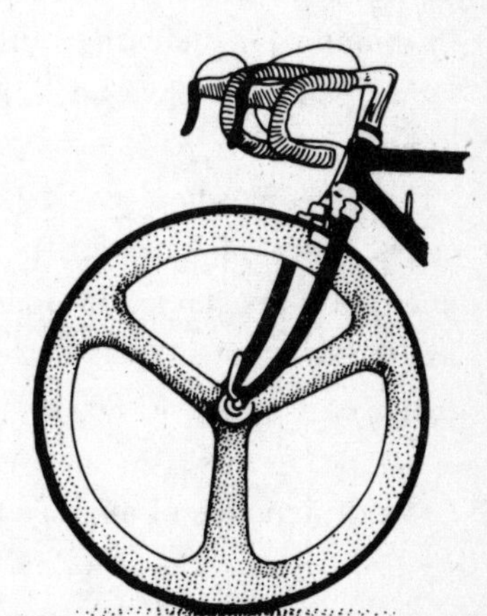

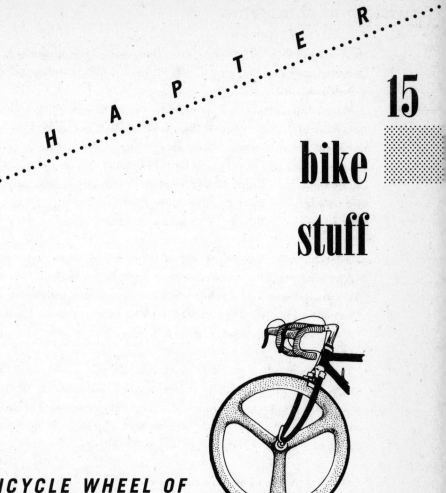

BICYCLE WHEEL OF THE FUTURE

ODDS: 100%

ETA: 1993

PRICE: $750 PER WHEEL

For bicycle enthusiasts, this is the future. A new wheel that's so revolutionary it advances the sport as much as turning the handlebars under or the introduction of gears did years ago.

Engineers at Dupont's Delaware headquarters came up with a design they call The Wheel of the Future, a three-bladed job (like a big peace sign) that will forever change the way bikes look and work.

"It definitely looks different on the road," says senior research engineer Mark W. Hopkins, who, along with his colleague Frank Principe, invented this new wheel. "It casts a different shadow. And it feels neat, too."

More to the point, the Dupont wheel produces a ride that is faster, smoother, and more efficient than anything that has come before it, including the disc wheel currently used by many racers. In its advertising brochure, Specialized Bicycle Components, of Morgan Hill, California, which supplied Dupont with design guidelines, calls the three-blader "the most aerodynamic wheel ever made." Their tests have shown that the wheel can save over ten minutes in a 100-mile race.

Selected racers have already used the wheel in actual competition and come away with a few victories, including a major upset in a Chicago triathlon. "Seasoned riders are saying that they've shaved two minutes off their times in 40-kilometer races," reports Hopkins. "Their responses have been uniformly favorable, and that's very exciting for us."

The Dupont wheel consists of an aluminum rim and three thick spokes made of carbon, epoxy resin, glass, and Kevlar fibers (a penetration-resistant substance used in bulletproof vests). The spokes form three airfoil shapes that, Hopkins says, slip through the air with greater ease because they create far less drag than conventional wire spokes do.

The design also eliminates the control problems that have plagued the disc wheel, says Hopkins. "Because the disc is solid, it has low drag, which is good, but it also tends to stall in crosswinds and it can be difficult to handle. With our wheel, the elements aren't a problem."

The Wheel of the Future is also a durable wheel. "We wanted the performance of a Formula 1 car, but with the reliability of a car you'd drive to the grocery store every day," asserted Hopkins. That decision added about a half-pound to each wheel compared to standard wheels. Not a problem, insists its co-inventor. "What slows down a bike is aerodynamics, not weight."

The only downside to the wheel right now is the price: an uphill $750. As you can imagine, that ticket and the limited availability have meant that only serious racers own Dupont wheels.

That won't always be the case though, hopes Hopkins. He expects that by the mid-'90s, all leisure riders, including children, will be able to buy The Wheel of the Future.

THE CLIP-ON BICYCLE MOTOR

ODDS: 90%

ETA: 1992

PRICE: $350

While others have done their part to preserve the environment by abandoning aerosol cans, riding public transportation, going to rock concerts for rain forests, and sorting their recyclable trash, Brits Douglas Barber and Paul Priestman have created a clip-on bicycle motor that will not only preserve leg power but will reduce the congestion and exhaust fumes on city streets.

And best of all for bike riders, their Power Ball means you don't have to pedal uphill!

When you are ready to start riding, attach the Power Ball, a soccerball–sized 30-cubic-centimeter gas engine, to the front of your bicycle just above the wheel and extend its accelerator cable until it clips on to the handlebars. Now pedal to the nearest gas station.

The Power Ball takes unleaded fuel, which is fed into the motor's gas tank through a filler spout just like those on motorbikes and lawnmowers. To start your motorized bike, simply depress the accelerator button on the handlebar and the Power Ball drops its roller directly onto the wheel. In seconds, the spinning roller takes over the job of powering your bike.

The Power Ball is made of plastic and ceramic. It comes with its own front light set into the ball and an output socket for a rear light. At the end of a trip, the Ball and its attachments can be easily removed and stored in its own canvas bag.

"The Power Ball is not a new idea," admit Priestman and Barber, "but it's one we felt was long overdue for reappraisal." In the late 1940s, a French manufacturer produced a removable bike motor similar to the Power Ball. "It's particularly pertinent today considering traffic congestion in the world's cities, rising fuel costs, environmental issues, and the ever-increasing emphasis on leisure activities."

NEON BIKE LIGHTS

This is one of those classic New York stories that could come right out of a 1930s movie. In fact, we've even cast it for you.

ODDS: 70%

ETA: 1994

PRICE: $200

Young Jimmy Cagney is "The Kid." Knocked over by a hit-and-run driver, he loses his ability to read and write. Down on his luck, he ends up living on the streets where he's befriended by a Pat O'Brien–type character who takes him into his home. The Kid comes up with a fabulous invention, makes a million bucks, and becomes the toast of Manhattan.

Well, in real life the story is not over yet. But up to the part about the "million bucks," it's all true. Raymond Cordero (The Kid), twenty-two, was a printer until he suffered head injuries in a hit-and-run accident. Hospitalized for months without any financial support, he loses everything, including his home. And when he gets out, without the facility to read or write, he also loses his job. He lives on the street and becomes a bicycle messenger.

Enter Richard Flores, a neon glass bender, who befriends Cordero and takes him into his home. "It's a very rare thing in New York City to have someone take you in that way," Cordero says. While with Flores, Cordero comes up with the idea for neon bike lights—long tubes of dazzling, colored lights that are attached to the frame of the bike, making it almost impossible for a driver not to see a cyclist.

"As a messenger, I've had so many close calls with cars, I decided I wanted to build a better light," Cordero explained. At first Flores was reluctant to get involved with his young protégé's idea. "But I kept pushing it," explained Cordero. "I got on his nerves until finally he said he'd help me just to get me off his back."

They built a prototype that was greeted enthusiastically by New York bicyclists. And they applied for a patent.

The lighting system involves three lengths of neon tubes attached with nylon straps to the bike's frame. The neon tubes are each fitted into an outer acrylic tube for protection. "You can ride over potholes or fall with the bike and they won't break," assures Flores.

The tubes are powered by a rechargeable battery pack (3½ inches by 3 inches) that clips on under the seat. The tubes range from 14 to 21 inches in length and the whole system weighs about 1 pound. The tubes are fluorescent coated in glowing colors.

Flores and Cordero are presently custom designing their neon-lighting systems for individual customers and talking to big companies about mass-producing the lights.

Hopefully, this story will have a happy ending—just like all those "Kid" Cagney movies of the thirties.

FLATLESS BICYCLE TIRES

ODDS: 60%

ETA: 1993

PRICE: $16 PER TIRE

In 1979, a California company began manufacturing a flatless polyurethane tire for wheelchairs. The market for such a product was obvious; the last thing a disabled person needed was a flat tire. Since their introduction, over 2 million of the wheelchair tires have been sold.

Now that company, Urethane Technology International, Inc., of Irvine, is making a limited number of flatless tires that can be used on wheelchairs and on certain bicycles. It's their plan to create a complete line of bike tires that won't ever go flat and that will have a service life far beyond that of conventional air-filled tires.

"They're for anyone who likes to ride a bike when he or she wants to, not when the tires let them," boasts UTI founder Vincent Panaroni. "Take bicycle messengers—they don't want to stop to pump their tires in the middle of a four-lane road.

"And you can bet their tires go bald fast. They won't with our product."

According to Panaroni, regular tires have a service life of about 1,500 miles compared with a UTI tire, which lasts at least 5,000 miles.

The tires are one solid unit of molded polyurethane foam. They are surprisingly light (they weigh less than pneumatic tires), and the ride is reportedly comfortable.

Another advantage of the flatless tire is that they won't deteriorate while in winter storage. According to Panaroni, the rubber on regular tires flattens when not in use and is then prone to cracking when filled with air in the spring. "UTI tires will not weather-crack because they are 100 percent reactive polymer," he says. "There are no plasticizers involved which catch and hold water—the cause of cracking."

ELECTRONIC BIKE DERAILLEUR

ODDS: 60%

ETA: 1993

PRICE: $80

If you are a bicycle rider, you know that horrible grinding sound you sometimes hear when you try to switch gears. You lose pedaling power and the chain jumps from sprocket to sprocket. Your heart jumps, too, as you wait for the worst to happen—for the chain to come right off.

The trouble here is the derailleur. For those of you who can't take your bikes apart, the derailleur is defined as the "gearshifting mechanism on a bicycle for controlling its speed by shifting the sprocket chain from one to another of a set of different-sized sprocket wheels," according to Mr. Webster. When the chain shifts to another sprocket wheel, it sometimes misses, causing the problem.

Now comes a new type of derailleur in which the chain never moves and therefore can never slip. Instead of the chain moving from sprocket wheel to sprocket wheel, the wheels move to the chain.

Got it? When you shift gears, the chain remains in a single, smoothly running plane. The sprocket wheels move to meet the chain.

This ingenious derailleur was invented by bike enthusiast John T. Siegart as his senior project in engineering at the University of Alabama. He has U.S. and foreign patents on his device, plus the support of Research Corporation Technologies, a technology transfer service company for nonprofit organizations.

Siegart named his invention the Sectorized Sprocket Transmission. The key to its design is the fusing of the sprockets (those concentric metal plates with the sawtooth edges) into clusters. Each cluster is then divided into four sectors. While the chain moves along a sprocket in one sector, the opposite sector is shifted electronically to the desired speed and rises to catch the chain.

The shifting apparatus is cam-powered by a 9-volt battery. The cyclist shifts gears by touching a button mounted on the handlebars.

The entire SST assembly weighs less than 3 ounces and can be installed on any multispeed bike.

DOUBLE-LOOPED PRETZEL BICYCLE LOCK

Robert Denison thinks like a petty thief. As owner of a chain of bicycle stores in New York City—a town where stealing bikes is almost a sport—he has to! For Denison's fondest desire is to foil bike thieves and protect bicycles everywhere.

ODDS: 90%

ETA: 1993

PRICE: $50

Denison thinks he's done it with his patented double-looped pretzel bicycle lock. "It's a primitive design," he explained, "but it's also a fun lock because of its strange shape."

The "strange shape" is key to the logic behind this lock. According to Denison, thieves currently crack the popular U-shaped lock in seconds with just a bit of pipe and a little leverage. You look out the window of the pizzeria and the $2,000 Trek mountain bike you locked to the stop-sign post is history.

A few years ago, with an increase in bike thefts, the manufacturers of the U-shaped locks were forced to cease guaranteeing their product in New York City. And that's when Denison, president of the Metro Bicycle Stores, started thinking like a thief.

Denison claims the second loop on his lock eliminates any place to gain the leverge to break the lock. The only way to crack the lock is by cracking the bike as well—which makes the whole theft pointless.

The double-looped pretzel bicycle lock is made of steel, weighs about 20 percent more than the standard U-shaped lock, and will be covered in rubber or vinyl when it reaches the marketplace. Denison plans to have his "fun-looking" pretzel locks available in all the colors of the rainbow.

CHAPTER 16

health & safety

NEW MIGRAINE MEDICINE

A new medicine that can shut down a migraine attack in just thirty minutes has proven successful in 80 percent of patients tested.

• • • • •

ODDS: 95%

ETA: 1993

PRICE: NA

• • • • •

The drug, called Sumatriptan, offers the best hope yet for migraine sufferers—and those who suffer with them. Debilitating migraine headaches—a complex and incurable disorder often accompanied by nausea and vomiting—affect at least 5 percent of the population.

Sumatriptan has been developed by the English pharmaceutical company Glaxo Holdings PLC, the maker of the antiulcer drug Zantac, the world's largest-selling medicine (according to the *Wall Street Journal*).

"Sumatriptan is the first drug in a long, long time developed specifically to treat migraines," says Jennifer McMillan, director of public affairs for Glaxo in the United States. The medication aborts the headache by dilating the constricted cranial blood vessels, which are thought to cause the pain of a migraine.

In classic migraines, there is interference with vision just prior to the onset of an attack. The medicine can be taken then or at any time during an attack. The company is seeking FDA approval for an injectable form of the drug. Clinical trials are underway on a tablet form as well.

In clinical trials with the injectable form, 80 percent of more than 5,000 patients tested reported a quick halt to their attacks. The side effects experienced by test subjects—warmth, dizziness, vertigo, and fatigue—were considered mild and dissipated within minutes.

If all goes well and the FDA approves Sumatriptan, migraine sufferers might have it here in the next three to four years. It will be available in the United Kingdom even sooner.

PAINLESS PERIODONTAL TREATMENT

ODDS: 95%

ETA: 1992

PRICE: PROBABLY LESS THAN SURGERY

If you've ever suffered from periodontal disease, a bacterial infection that affects the soft tissues and bones supporting the teeth, then you know about oral surgery. Ouch!

J. Max Goodson, D.D.S., head of the department of pharmacology at Forsyth Dental Center in Boston, is about to change the way periodontal disease is treated. He's removing the ouch.

For fourteen years, Dr. Goodson has worked to perfect a local drug delivery system called Actisite. With Actisite, the dentist takes an extremely narrow, threadlike fiber made of very soft plastic and gently places it in infected periodontal pockets. The fiber, manufactured by the ALZA Corporation of Palo Alto, California, is filled with tetracycline, a broad-spectrum antibiotic. To ensure that the "thread" stays in place, a "dressing" made of clear, gluelike material is applied over it.

For ten days the antibiotic is slowly and continuously released into the pocket. When the medicine is used up, the dressing is removed, and in most cases, the infection has healed.

"You can't say that one local drug delivery treatment lasts forever," says Dr. Goodson. "But a single treatment is often effective for years."

Actisite may not eliminate the need for surgery in every case, but it certainly is an improved method of first resort, and in most cases it will do the trick without anesthesia or sharp-edged instruments.

CONVENIENT HOME BLOOD TEST

• • • • •

ODDS: 85%

ETA: 1992

PRICE: LESS THAN $2 PER UNIT FOR GLUCOSE TESTER

• • • • •

Although the accuracy and range of chemical tests for such serum components as glucose, cholesterol, and various disease markers is ever increasing, these tests still have one unpleasant aspect—they must be performed on blood. And that usually means a trip to a laboratory, clinic, or doctor's office, where long needles, rubber tourniquets, and other medieval apparatus await. Not to mention the cost in terms of time and money.

For diabetics and others who require daily monitoring of blood chemistry, there are lancets. Little steel daggers to prick your finger. They hurt. They take real willpower. So blood tests, no matter how necessary and beneficial, become something to fear and avoid.

The TouchTester system solves this problem. Based on a research prototype called the PINSET (Painless Invisible Needle Serum Extract Tester), the TouchTester is a small, painless, inexpensive, convenient, disposable unit that takes just a tiny amount of blood practically before you've even noticed. Its developers, Safety Diagnostics, Inc., of Evanston, Illinois, expect that it will vastly expand the home diagnostics market.

To use it, you just set the little plastic device (about the size of two stacked LifeSaver candies) on a flat surface, press down on it enough to slightly prick your finger, and read the results. Easy. Discreet. And safe.

Due to a very sensitive chemistry system inside the device, less blood is required. Also, the sample is never exposed, so there's no chance of contaminating it or of exposing others to disease. The TouchTester is used just once and then discarded.

Self-testing is, of course, no substitute for a physician's care. But there are many instances in which it can either augment such care or indicate the need for it. Either way, the patient benefits.

HIP-GUARD

ODDS: 100%
ETA: 1992
PRICE: $80

"Aunt So-and-so fell and broke her hip." Not her arm, or her leg or ankle or wrist—her hip.

Elderly people break hips. It's one of those truths.

Well, a study conducted at Harvard University and reported in *Physician's Weekly* concluded that "generous padding may be more important in preventing older people's hip fractures than good bone density." The research team further suggested that such fractures could be prevented if thin seniors with fragile hips were to wear special protective padding.

Bob Ferber, a management consultant from Jackson Heights, New York, had come to the same conclusion some years earlier. When his mother fell and broke her arm, she told him, "If I hadn't been wearing a thick coat with a heavy lining, I would have broken my hip, too."

This conversation started the wheels turning. "It's a dreadful thing when someone breaks a hip and loses their independence," thought Ferber. Independently, he came to the same conclusion that the Harvard team would reach: A protective padding would help prevent broken hips.

Ferber is now president and technical director of Prevent-Wise, Inc., a start-up company that is manufacturing Hip-Guard, a girdle-like device that contains shock-absorbent material. It weighs less than half a pound, wraps around the buttocks and hips, and closes in the front with Velcro fasteners.

For the 2 to 3 hundred thousand elderly people who break their hips each year in this country, Hip-Guard could be an "independence saver."

HEALTHIER SALMON

ODDS: 90%

ETA: 1995

PRICE: SAME AS REGULAR SALMON

If Scandinavians generally seem a bit healthier than other nationalities, it may be because they eat a lot of the best salmon in the world. And scientists have discovered that eating salmon can prevent heart attacks and reduce the risk of arthritis.

It seems that salmon contains generous amounts of Omega-3 fatty acids, a polyunsaturated fat effective in combating cardiovascular and chronic inflammatory diseases. Humans get Omega-3 only from fish, who get it from green algae and smaller animals in the food chain.

The Norwegians intend to breed supersalmon that contain even larger quantities of Omega-3. A joint project of the Norwegian Fish Farmers Association, the Marketing Council for Norwegian Salmon, and some top independent scientists, the project was begun in 1989.

The director, Harald Skjervold, a retired professor of animal genetics and breeding from the Agricultural University of Norway, explained that, in fact, they are developing two new types of Norwegian salmon: a "light, slim" salmon that will be rich in Omega-3 despite a moderate fat content; and a Superior Salmon that will have even more Omega-3 than the light, but whose fat content will be equal to the salmon we already know.

"This Superior Salmon will have normal fatness but with an extremely high content of Omega-3," Skjervold explained.

"Genetic improvement is rather time-consuming, but we expect these new and improved fish to find a large market in Western countries," he added.

Skjervold is almost certainly right. New medical studies suggest that if the intake of Omega-3 fatty acid is increased from .5 to 1 gram a day, the risk of cardiovascular death in a middle-aged American male will be reduced by 40 percent. And new data also indicates that Omega-3 is effective in decreasing cancer mortality.

EYEBALL SCULPTING

ODDS: 80%

ETA: 1995

PRICE: $1,000–$2,000 PER EYE

Say good-bye to eyeglasses and so long to contact lenses! A simple operation performed under local anesthesia may do away with both of them forever.

The operation involves the use of a special laser scalpel called an excimer laser, or, more precisely, an argon fluoride 193 laser. The technique involved is known as photorefractive keratectomy, or PRK.

But enough of the big words. Unlike conventional lasers, the excimer does not cut tissue by generating heat. Instead, this laser produces a photochemical reaction. As the laser light makes contact with the cornea, it vaporizes microscopic layers of tissue to reshape the cornea. The whole procedure can take as little as thirty seconds!

Summit Technology, Inc., a medical device company in Waltham, Massachusetts, has already successfully tested the excimer laser on an initial group of partially blind patients and is now conducting tests on nearsighted volunteers. European trials have already indicated that the laser has the potential to restore sharp vision to people with this common vision problem.

Market estimates show that 140 million Americans could benefit if the procedure proves successful and is permitted in the U.S. General approval from the Food and Drug Administration is expected by 1994.

Western ophthalmologists see the excimer laser as a tremendous advance on radial keratotomy, a surgical procedure developed in the Soviet Union that can correct even extreme nearsightedness, but with unpredictable results.

It's been estimated that between 3 to 5 million operations will be performed each year on nearsighted individuals around the world within five years after FDA approval of excimer corneal sculpting.

SCRATCH-FREE EYEGLASSES

Long a source of mystery, diamonds are the hardest substance known to man. So man, naturally, has worked long and hard to find ways of artificially manufacturing diamonds. The newest process will use common gases to create diamonds suitable for a variety of applications.

ODDS: 90%
ETA: 1993
PRICE: 10% HIGHER THAN REGULAR GLASSES

One of those applications will be scratchproof eyeglasses. Coated with an ion-beam diamond made from "gas," the glasses will remain scratch-free many times longer than glasses presently on the market. "They're exactly the same, except that they don't scratch," says David

Hoover, vice president of technology at Diamonex, a leader in the development of the diamond-making technique called *ion-beam deposition*.

According to Hoover, ion-beam deposition is a process that creates diamond coatings by combining natural gases, including methane, with high voltage electrical power in a vacuum chamber called an *ion source*.

The ion source looks like a 2-pound coffee can with a series of screens on one end. When the gases and the electricity combine in the can, they create an "energy plasma," says Hoover. The ion source extracts carbon ions out of the plasma and sprays them across the vacuum chamber. As they hit the surface of the eyeglass lenses a diamond coating builds up.

The scratch-free eyeglasses should be here by 1993. "Further in the future," says Hoover, "maybe by the year 2000, we may have diamonds in windshields and the windows in airplanes."

NEW CONTACT LENS CLEANER

ODDS: 90%
ETA: 1992
PRICE: $70

The curse of contact lenses is cleaning them. So anyone who comes up with a better way should do okay.

New Jersey ophthalmologist Neville A. Baron has spent ten years working on the problems. Current methods use either heat or chemicals. Lenses treated with heat must cool off for several hours before use. Chemical cleaners frequently produce allergic reactions and are relatively expensive.

Dr. Baron's solution is to use a tiny ultraviolet lightbulb to sterilize the lenses. The light is carefully calibrated so as not to damage the delicate polymers of the lens. A tiny ultrasound generator cleans them. Lenses cleaned with Dr. Baron's process can be worn in less than an hour.

The whole apparatus is packaged in a carrying case the size of a cigarette box. It's made of lightweight, high-impact plastic, and it's completely portable as it relies on a recharging stand for power. The device even cleans and sterilizes the removable lens case at the same time it works on the lenses.

According to Dr. Baron, who also invented liquid sunglasses (see page 155), his cleaner will cost about half what a year's supply of chemicals would cost. He also believes that the ease of using his cleaner will result in better care of lenses, prolonging their life by up to four times.

CONTROLLED-RELEASE BIRTH CONTROL PILLS

ODDS: 80%

ETA: 1996

PRICE: ABOUT SAME AS REGULAR BIRTH CONTROL PILLS

Social historians already point to the advent of the birth control pill in the '60s as the single most important development in the sexual and political freedom of womankind. Today, 32 percent of all American women between the ages of fifteen and forty-four still use this method of birth control. And a new development that may alleviate some of the pill's side effects could increase that number.

The breakthrough has nothing to do with the content of the pill. Rather, the potential for increased safety is a result of a new delivery system that sends the hormones into the body at a slow, steady rate. (The conventional pill releases hormones from the gastrointestinal tract into the bloodstream all at once.)

The peak levels of drugs in your body are what are often associated with side effects, says a spokesperson for the ALZA Corporation of Palo Alto, California, which has developed the new technology. "For any drug, you can reduce side effects with a steady, controlled release that avoids what are called the 'peaks and valleys' of traditional drug delivery."

This new delivery system may sound similar to time-release capsules that have been around for years. Not so. Time-release capsules only work with water-soluble drugs, and the hormones in oral contraceptives are highly insoluble by water.

The new pill, based on what ALZA calls the Oros "push-pull" technology, will be a two-layer tablet surrounded by a semipermeable membrane. The tablet will also contain a tiny, laser-drilled hole through which the hormones are released.

Once the pill is swallowed, normal fluids in the gastrointestinal tract are pulled through the first layer of the pill. This fluid causes a swelling between the two layers. The swelling pushes the drug from the inner layer out through the laser-drilled orifice at a rate of about one to two drops per hour.

The rate is controlled by the outer, semipermeable membrane, designed to allow water in at a certain rate, thereby releasing the hormones out of the tablet at a certain rate.

The most common side effects of today's birth control pill are nausea, headaches, and breakthrough bleeding. On rare occasions, with higher dosage pills, more serious repercussions have been blood clots and even death. The ALZA Corporation will not yet get specific about which of today's pill's side effects will be alleviated by the new delivery system.

While the selling price of the new pills will be set by whoever markets them, the controlled-release technology is not necessarily expensive, according to ALZA. So the price of the pill may stay about the same.

DIAPHRAGM WITH SPERMICIDE SPONGE

If you're still using a diaphragm for contraception, then you must like its simplistic appeal. Few women, however, like dealing with those gooey jellies and creams. They're hard to wash off your hands, much less the diaphragm. And the "second application"—well, that's about as pleasant as PMS.

ODDS: 45%

ETA: 1995

PRICE: SAME AS CONTRACEPTIVE SPONGE

Dennis Treu, the president of Xtramedics in Deerfield, Illinois, is going to make a lot of women feel sexier about using a diaphragm. His company is developing a sponge of spermicide that adheres to the inside of a diaphragm. It will provide protection for at least twenty-four hours, and once it's in place, it won't come off until you remove it.

No more guessing about how much spermicide to use. No more mopping up the overflow. And should you make love a second time without a second application, no more worrying.

Called the Diaphragm Disk, the device is about the size of a fifty-cent piece. On one side is a mound of spermicide that's dry until moistened with water. On the other side is a state-of-the-art adhesive, similar to the stuff on a Post-It pad.

The disk is peeled off its packaging and moistened slightly before it's adhered to the inside of the diaphragm. The diaphragm is then inserted as usual, and you're safe for twenty-four hours. The same active ingredient as in all other spermicides will be released in proper amounts whenever "pressure" is applied.

Treu hopes that eventually the diaphragm sponge could provide protection for thirty-six or even forty-eight hours. Right now, the only thing holding back further development of the Diaphragm Disk is money. "It'll be very, very expensive to develop and test it on humans," says Treu. He's hoping that the success of his other invention, the feminine hygiene padette (see page 61), will provide funding for the revolutionary diaphragm disk.

CHOLESTEROL REDUCER

There's no question that cholesterol has put a crimp in the eating habits of Americans. Meat, cheese, and egg lovers have changed their diets to keep blood cholesterol levels down and reduce the risk of heart disease.

ODDS: 50%

ETA: 1996

PRICE: NA

While dietary change is certainly one way of reducing cholesterol intake, researchers at Iowa State University are convinced that there are other, less restrictive, ways. For example, if cholesterol could be reduced at the source—in the meat, egg, and dairy products themselves—then you could eat more of these foods without the health risk.

Donald C. Beitz, Ph.D., professor of animal science and biochemistry, is the leader of the Iowa State team. One method they are examining is the transformation of cholesterol into coprostanol, a naturally occuring compound that passes harmlessly out of the body. An enzyme called cholesterol reductase is the substance that changes cholesterol to coprostanol.

Until recently this enzyme had been found only in certain bacteria. Dr. Beitz and his team have discovered it in the leaves of green, leafy plants, notably alfalfa, cucumbers, and peas. Now the task is to concentrate the enzyme and apply it to foods high in cholesterol. "Depending on the food, you could reduce the cholesterol by 25 percent or more," says Dr. Beitz.

The enzyme could be applied by injection directly into the animal shortly before slaughter, during the processing of egg and dairy products, or even at the cooking stage in powder form.

So far, early tests on rats have been successful and tests on sheep are scheduled next. Still, there're years of work to be done before this cholesterol-reducing preparation reaches the marketplace, says Dr. Beitz. "It takes a lot of alfalfa leaves to get enough enzyme to be effective in treating significant quantities of foods. Our long-range plans are to transfer the gene from the alfalfa leaf into an easy-to-grow bacteria or yeast. We need to do this to have a commercial product."

Meat lovers everywhere, no doubt, wish Dr. Beitz speedy success.

AQUABAND BANDAGE

ODDS: 95%
ETA: 1992
PRICE: $3.75 A BOX

The newest thing in wound care since the 1920s," is the way Joel Martz, president of Laivan Corporation, describes his Aquaband bandage. And if it lives up to its promise, Aquaband may in fact revolutionize the bandage business.

It was in the 1920s that the Band-Aid as we know it was developed. So maybe it's time for something new and better. Martz's bandage totally seals a wound from outside water, dirt, and bacteria, he claims. It's also stretchable, good-looking, and has a high water-vapor transmission rate, which permits moisture to pass away from the wound to the surrounding air.

But the big thing is that the user can swim, bathe, and shower with the Aquaband in place. It is also thinner and more flexible than standard bandages, so "it feels as if nothing is there," says Martz.

Two existing technologies have been combined to create this patented bandage. An adhesive-coated, semipermeable (water-resistant) membrane is laminated to a nonwoven fabric, protective wound cover—creating the bandage.

Laivan Aquabands will be packaged for kids in the shape of cartoon characters, as well as in standard bandage shapes for adults.

FAT PREVENTION DRINK

If the battle of the scales is a battle you routinely lose, there's help on the way in the form of a drink that will reduce the amount of fat your body makes from what you eat.

•••••

ODDS: 50%

ETA: 2000

PRICE: $6 PER DAY FOREVER

•••••

A chemical compound, consisting of dihydroxyacetate and pyruvate, that occurs naturally in the human body appears to slow down the rate at which we accumulate fat. In one clinical study, when high concentrations of the compound were given to patients, their weight gain was 15 to 20 percent less than that of a control group given the same food intake but not the chemical compound.

Doctors at Montefiore Hospital in Pittsburgh who are developing the compound for patient use aren't certain what form—liquid, pill or capsule—the chemical will take, but liquid seems most viable. At present, they are conducting studies required by the FDA.

Montefiore's Dr. Ronald Stanko, an assistant professor of medicine in the department of clinical nutrition, has been working with dihydroxyacetate for seventeen years and feels it's a chemical with huge potential for helping mankind. "We have been finding that this substance has benefits for many people, including those with obesity, diabetes, and hyperlipidemia [high blood cholesterol]," says Dr. Stanko. "In addition, because it enhances endurance, it may be helpful to those with such chronic diseases as emphysema and congestive lung failure."

For people with ordinary weight problems, the idea of a drug that can reduce fat by up to 20 percent sounds very appealing. The hitch is that it won't come cheap. Six dollars a day, forever, adds up.

CIGARETTE CASE FOR QUITTERS

ODDS: 90%

ETA: 1994

PRICE: UNDER $35

If there are any smokers left in 1994, they may want to give this gizmo a chance. It's a cigarette case that's designed to humiliate the smoker.

Richard Drouin, an employee of the New York City Parks and Recreation Department, patented this plastic case with the built-in programmable electronic clock and other stuff. The clock is set to beep at regular intervals, indicating that it's okay for the addict to open the case and light up. Every day, the smoker resets the clock to increase the amount of time between cigarettes.

On the outside of the case are controls and a digital screen, which displays the total number of cigarettes smoked as the day progresses.

"It really makes you aware of how much time has elapsed between cigarettes," says Drouin. "I got the idea when someone said to me as I was lighting up, 'Hey, you just put one out a minute ago.' "

If the smoker tries to sneak a cigarette before the beeper goes off, the case makes an irritating buzzing sound. "There's definitely a humiliation factor," says Drouin, "because everyone within close range can hear that you didn't make it. It's a challenge."

The case can also be designed to play a jingle or flash a red light in place of making the irritating sound. Whichever the smoker likes least. As a last resort, the case can be constructed so that it won't open at all, "no matter what," says Drouin.

NONSURGICAL INCONTINENCE CURE

More people than you might think are eagerly awaiting a nonsurgical, relatively inexpensive cure for incontinence.

ODDS: 95%

ETA: 1992

PRICE: $2,000

According to the National Institute of Health, incontinence is the number one reason for nursing home admissions. In this country, $10 billion a year is spent managing the affliction, $1 billion on adult diapers alone.

The easy cure for many people with this embarrassing problem is a Teflon-based paste called Urethrin, which is now awaiting approval from the Food and Drug Administration. It is manufactured by the Mentor Corporation of Santa Barbara, California.

"Urethrin is injected around the sphincter muscle, which controls the flow of urine," Peter Shepard, Mentor's vice president of marketing and urology sales, explains. "The material helps support a sphincter that has been weakened, almost like a packing material. Urethrin provides bulk to the urethral tissue and increases resistance to urine flow."

The sphincter muscle has usually been weakened by age, childbirth, or prostate surgery.

At present, the only surgical methods for treating urinary incontinence are the placement of an artificial sphincter in males or a bladder suspension procedure in females. The most common procedure involves bolstering the sphincter with a type of sling. A hospital stay is required after the surgery, with a tab of $7,000 to $10,000. Urethrin treatment will cost about one-quarter that amount.

"One of the most encouraging aspects of Urethrin is that it is not an open surgical procedure but simply an injection that can be administered on an outpatient basis or in a physician's office," says Shepard.

The procedure was developed by Dr. Victor Politano, chairman of the department of urology at the University of Miami. Familiar with a procedure for using the Teflon paste to repair vocal chords, he believed a similar application would work to bolster weakened sphincter muscles.

Patients would naturally need to undergo urological tests prior to receiving the treatment to ensure that this method is right for them.

AMPLIFIED STETHOSCOPE

ODDS: 80%

ETA: 1993

PRICE: $500

Taiwanese medical student Stephen Shue was having trouble using a stethoscope. The breath and heartbeats of his patients seemed to come in muffled, soft tones.

Not every student would take it upon himself to start redesigning a medical instrument that had been around for centuries. But Shue is also a mechanical wizard. As a child he would take apart radios, TVs—anything he could get his hands on.

To improve the clarity of the stethoscope, Shue took a radio transmitter, an amplifier, and a microphone and inserted them into the instrument. This not only amplified the vital sounds, but it made it possible to transmit the sounds over the telephone or even an FM frequency.

At $500, the cost is a lot more than the usual $180 for a traditional stethoscope. But the advantages are as clear as the sound the instrument transmits. Patients who are unfamiliar with regular stethoscopes will have no trouble using this one at home to monitor their heartbeats. And a patient can transmit the sound to his doctor's office over the phone.

How did his advisors at Taiwan's Kaohsiung Medical College react to Shue's revolutionary stethoscope? "The president told me it was a very, very good idea," he said.

Shue is now an M.D., and, with the help of his brother, he's manufacturing his stethoscope in Taiwan.

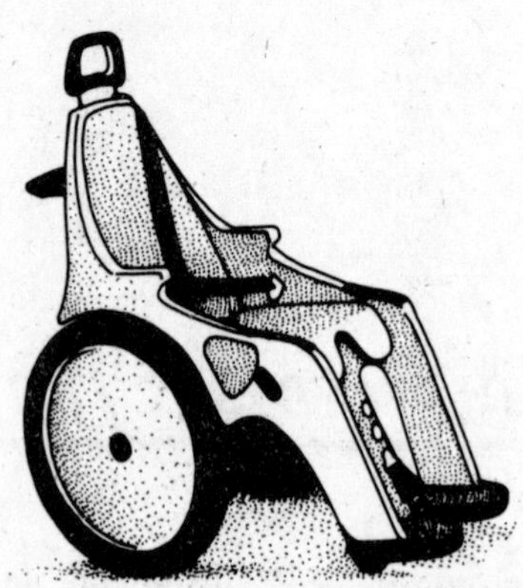

THE FRIENDLY WHEELCHAIR

The wheelchair is a vehicle like any other vehicle in that it has both major and minor malfunctions that can debilitate it or put it out of action—just like a car. If you've never used one, though, you probably never think of it this way.

ODDS: 90%
ETA: 1992
PRICE: $3,500

Benno Danecker, president of Kunstoff Service Danecker of Halfing, Germany, realized how troublesome a vehicle it can be because his wheelchair-confined employees were spending a lot of time in the company shop getting flats fixed, rust removed, brakes adjusted, and so on. Since Danecker's company is in the business of producing precision products for the transportation industry (they've done work for NASA), it made sense that KSD's engineers would come up with a modern wheelchair that's easier to use and maintain. "I wanted to help handicapped people have more dignity," says Danecker.

The result is KSD 1, referred to as Your Friend. Dieter Golumbek, a polio victim confined to a wheelchair and a mechanical engineer on staff at KSD, helped in the design of this revolutionary vehicle.

Your Friend sports two 100 percent polyurethane wheels that never go flat. In tests the tires hadn't thinned after 50,000 miles, says Danecker. The wheelchair weighs 10 pounds less than others on the market and is constructed of easy-to-clean plastic with no nooks and crannies that can impede overall disinfecting.

Your Friend comes with thick foam bumpers so it can't scratch furniture, an adjustable seat cushion that snaps out for easy washing, mudguards for the wheels, a headrest, even a built-in toilet. And the seat is ergonomically constructed for optimum comfort.

But Golumbek wouldn't let his boss stop there in the quest for the perfect wheelchair. The best feature is a hydraulic system that allows the user to raise and lower himself as required. Users will tell you that wheelchairs are almost always too high to fit under tables and desks.

Golumbek, by the way, is a Special Olympics medalist, so you can bet Your Friend is built for speed and balance, as well as comfort.

It looks good, too. Your Friend is available in twenty colors, from pink to glitter black.

"EXERCISE" WHEELCHAIR

ODDS: 95%
ETA: 1993
PRICE: $2,500 PLUS PRICE OF WHEELCHAIR

One man's desire to help one little girl has resulted in an invention that should benefit thousands of people.

Frank Mendel, an associate professor of anatomy at the State University of New York in Buffalo, wanted to help his accountant's six-year-old daughter, Sarah, who was confined to a wheelchair after being struck by a crippling virus. With hopes that she might someday walk again, her parents were determined to maintain the integrity of the girl's leg muscles.

Sarah was anxious to ride a "Big Wheel" tricycle along with her

little friends. So Mendel, with a team of therapists and designers, modified a Big Wheel to provide electrical stimulation to Sarah's paralyzed legs. The handle bars were replaced by hand cranks connected to the trike's pedals by chains and cams.

The trike was propelled by a combination of Sarah moving the hand cranks and the motion of her feet, held in stirrups, pushing on the pedals, as a result of electrical stimulation of two sets of muscles in the thigh of each leg.

Now Mendel and his team have used the same principles to develop a device that will turn some standard wheelchairs into "healthy wheelchairs." The device allows paraplegics to incorporate exercise of both their normal and paralyzed muscles into their daily activities. For many users this could improve their overall health and reduce the number of time-consuming and expensive physical therapy sessions.

The wheelchair works like this: Computer-controlled, muscle-stimulating electrodes are placed on the user's legs. When the rider works the hand cranks to power the chair, the computer triggers the leg muscles to drive reciprocating foot plates that augment propulsion of the wheelchair. The amount of leg-muscle stimulation is programmed into the device's computer by a physical therapist or physican to ensure that each rider gets exactly the right amount of exercise.

The benefits of this stimulation are many. Users may reduce swelling in the lower legs because of improved blood circulation, lower the risk of pressure sores, enhance cardiovascular health, and improve their appearance, which enhances self-image. Some riders may even develop enough leg strength to stand on their own, using electrical stimulation to trigger their muscles.

Mendel's design team includes Dale Fish, a physical therapist; William Tanski, a senior equipment designer at SUNY; and Robert Kell, a retired electrical engineer.

SMOOTH AMBULANCE RIDE

When you watch a shrieking ambulance zigzag through packed rush-hour streets, you can't help feeling sorry for the poor soul inside—fighting for life yet getting tossed about like old newspapers.

ODDS: 80%
ETA: 1992
PRICE: NA

Recognizing how uncomfortable and dangerous this can be, the German government asked a company called Technology Development to invent a way to make the actual ride, as well as getting in and out of the ambulance, smoother for the patient.

It was the German government that approached the Technology Development Corporation with the problem. The scientists there came up with two rather obvious solutions. The first was to mount the stretcher on a pedestal in the center of the vehicle rather than over the back wheels where the ride is bumpier. The second solution was to install a hydraulic system connected to the compressor of the car so that patients on stretchers could be kept level and steady during the ride and as they were placed in or removed from the ambulance.

"It smooths everything out for the patient," says Harald Wiesner, vice president and director of European Operations for Technology Development in Bonn. "The mechanics and the hydraulics of this system have all been used for years. None of this is tricky." Wiesner also pointed out that the system, called Ambulance Perfect, is easy to install and not expensive. As a result, he expects hospitals to pick up on the invention soon.

ELECTRONIC ECHO PATHFINDER

Several years ago, Adam Jorgensen witnessed his elderly father gradually lose his sight. Watching his father stumble or become disoriented in unfamiliar places was a frustrating, futile experience. Yet the younger Jorgensen could find no adequate navigational aide to help.

ODDS: 90%

ETA: 1992

PRICE: $550

An electrical engineer, he thought about the problem and all the people like his father, then decided to find his own solution. "Bats, owls, even submarine navigators use echoes to create precise guidance systems. I figured, 'Why not humans?' "

Jorgensen's Echo Location Device works like radar. The visually impaired individual wears tiny receptors behind the ears and carries a flashlight-like instrument. The instrument emits ultrasonic pulses that bounce off any object in its path. If the object is far away, it takes longer for the echo response to reach the ear receptors. If the object is close, the echo response is received quickly.

A built-in artificial delay helps to fine-tune the process, since the human ear has difficulty distinguishing the small differences in time. The delay of the echo-return times allows the user to make a better judgment.

The device also filters out extraneous noises that could confuse the listener. According to Jorgensen, this is the main problem with similar instruments.

"What I've done is helped create an acoustic image of an area," he says. That concept is good enough to have attracted the National Eye Institute, which hopes to produce and market his invention.

Specially trained people will have to work with the visually impaired until they become comfortable with the device. But Jorgensen is confident that the blind will learn to "hear distances" as well as they read Braille.

ROBOT GUIDE DOG

ODDS: 50%
ETA: 1995
PRICE: $10,000

The Seeing Eye dog, like the old nag that used to pull milk wagons, is about to be replaced by automation. A robot guide that can better serve the blind is in the early stages of development.

And while it may be a little sad to witness one more instance of machine replacing animal, for those who cannot see, the robot guide dog will be a technological blessing.

A team of five researchers at North Carolina State University, under the direction of electrical engineer Ren C. Luo, have already built a small prototype of the robot using a toy four-wheel truck. It's armed with a computer and an arsenal of ultrasonic, electromagnetic, photoelectric, and laser sensors that allow the contraption to figure out where it's going, what hazards lie ahead, and the best path to pursue.

"Our goal is to build more than a household type of robot to help the handicapped," expained Luo. "Because blind people go out in the street and need help, the robot needs to see and hear for an outside environment."

To that end, Luo has equipped the robot with what he calls an "outdoor data base"—so the computer is capable of recognizing and responding to everything from traffic noises to elevator buttons.

The full-size prototype, which Luo and his crew expect to have completed in 1992, will be about the size of a filing cabinet and weigh about the same as a well-fed German shepherd. In appearance, it will resemble a dog, with at least one operating paw capable of picking things up.

A synthetic voice box that talks, instead of barking, will issue warnings about potholes, red lights, and bus stops. "Our robot will be easier to train than a real guide dog," predicts Luo.

Several high-tech companies have already expressed interest in manufacturing the robot guide dog. "The price will depend on what kind of profit they want to make, but it's worth at least $10,000," says Luo.

SMOKE PROTECTION PILLOW

It's every traveler's nightmare. You're asleep in a high-rise hotel when suddenly you're awakened by screams and sirens. You open your eyes and see the room filling with smoke . . .

ODDS: 70%
ETA: 1993
PRICE: $12

Two-thirds of fire-related deaths are caused by smoke inhalation. Yet an aid that could save lives is right at hand. The pillow.

Any pillow can keep you alive and help you escape from a fire. But an inventor in Topeka, Kansas, has improved on the basic pillow to improve your chances of surviving.

Thomas Dolsky came up with the idea for the fire-protection pillow in the aftermath of the MGM Grand Hotel fire in 1985. He remembered something from his youth that he believed could have permitted people to escape from that tragedy.

"As a boy I worked on a farm," Dolsky explained, "and every year when we were clearing timber, some of us would be overcome by thick smoke produced by burning undergrowth. We discovered that we could hold our old, down-filled pillows in front of our faces and breathe through them to avoid the ill effects of the smoke. If only the people at the MGM Grand had known that their hotel room pillows could filter the smoke—I started thinking I could improve on the idea."

Dolsky's pillow has a transparent polymer hood attached to the end of the pillow inside the zippered casing. The pillow is made of Dacron 808 Holofil batting, found in many regular pillows and also in disposable respirators.

In the event of fire, the user unzips the bag and pulls out the transparent hood. The hood's free end fits over the entire head, while the other end remains attached to the pillow, which is held against the chest. In this way the user can breathe air filtered through the batting and still see through the hood.

The problem that Dolsky had to solve was finding the right polymer for the hood. "We tried many combinations of plastics. Mylar has the strength, and it can withstand temperatures up to 400 degrees Fahrenheit, which is far higher than most people can withstand," Dolsky explained. "But Mylar crinkles noisily, and that's not what people want when they're trying to sleep."

The solution was a quietening mix of one thousandth of an inch Mylar and two thousandth of an inch vinyl.

Dolsky's patented pillow has been tested in dense smoke for up to forty-five minutes, more time than is usually needed to escape or be rescued from a fire.

"This product needs to be on the market," says the inventor. "It can save lives."

GUARDIAN ANGEL SMOKE ALARM/ FIRE EXTINGUISHER

ODDS: 60%
ETA: 1994
PRICE: NA

Liz Cecelia, a ten-year-old fifth-grader from Baldwin Borough, Pennsylvania, was shocked by the number of fires around Christmastime that she saw reported on the TV news. "I love our Christmas tree and I thought it could catch on fire if it got too hot," she explained.

So what Liz did was imagine a Christmas ornament—an angel, in fact—that would not only decorate the tree but protect it too. Hidden beneath the angel's skirt would be a smoke/heat detector and a fire extinguisher (Liz learned about this stuff in school). She called her idea the Guardian Angel.

Coming up soon was the Invent America contest, the largest national invention competition for schoolchildren. To find out if her idea could actually be made, Liz spoke to her mom's cousin, who is an engineer, and to an industrial arts teacher who teaches at the same school as her dad. They both said that the Guardian Angel could work.

The doll's body, which is between 12 and 18 inches long, sits on top of the Christmas tree. It holds a dry chemical powder that can be released through three fire extinguisher jets at the bottom of the angel's dress. The powder is released at the same instant that the detector senses fire and sets off the alarm.

At first, Guardian Angel was to be just a fire detector. But Liz added the extinguisher in case no one was at home to hear the alarm.

Liz and her Guardian Angel were fifth-grade national winners in the Invent America contest.

LIFE DETECTOR

ODDS: 85%

ETA: 1996

PRICE: $20,000

The worst moment for a rescue team is when the decision is made to give up the search for buried victims of an earthquake, avalanche, or other disaster. There is always the possibility that some poor soul is still alive and waiting to be rescued.

Now the same technology that heats TV dinners is going to help save lives. Microwaves have the ability to detect life through walls and piles of rubble better than any other technique being used.

"The microwave uses an invisible electromagnetic beam that, when shone on the surface of a body, will cause a modulation that will register signs of movement on the microwave beam," explained Prof. Kun-Mu Chen of Michigan State University, the man who has developed the technology.

Using the sign of movement as the indicator that someone is buried alive is considered a surer method than other techniques using acoustic devices. "Right now the microwave technology can penetrate walls that are 2 and 3 feet in thickness," reports Chen.

Thermal techniques that detect warm bodies also have limitations, according to Chen. "These systems are just not good enough. A body without a heartbeat may be warm for some time."

The U.S. Defense Department asked Professor Chen to come up with a better rescue device for the navy. The Life Detector, which represents four years of Chen's life, is the result.

"The navy needed me to devise a better system than what they had," he related. "In conditions where it is dangerous to send out a helicopter, they needed a system that would let them know if the soldier out there was alive or not."

The microwave Life Detector could also prove invaluable should soldiers be felled by chemical weapons. Explained Chen: "Given the protective clothing, the physiological status of a soldier can be detected by a microwave life detector through the clothing."

Chen believes his work in microwave systems is just the beginning and that less expensive detectors able to penetrate deeper will be developed for local emergency teams in the years to come.

CHAPTER 17

sleep-easy stuff

SINGING PILLOW

If you can't stop replaying the day, or if you think too much about tomorrow, or if street noises and plumbing sounds keep you awake, consider this clever, though pricey, pillow from Japan. It can make all kinds of soothing sounds capable of lullabying even the crankiest adult into dreamland.

• • • • •

ODDS: 60%

ETA: 1995

PRICE: $500

• • • • •

In Japan they call it the Makura no Sōshi, which, translated, means "notes of the pillow," or *The Pillow Book*, a book about beautiful feelings written over 1,000 years ago by the court consort Sei Shōnagon. When the pillow comes to America, it will probably be called something like the Singing Pillow.

Developed by Victor Sound Equipment and the Biox Corporation, both of Tokyo, the pillow contains a small player mechanism operated by integrated-circuit memory cards. The cards come in a variety of "restful" programs including "Rattling of the Railroad Track," "Chirping of Frogs," and "Dripping Sounds of Water." A timer can be set to play the sounds for ten to eighty minutes.

The pillow can also provide insomniacs with the sounds of the radio, TV, or stereo.

Makura no Sōshi has been available to consumers in Japan since April of 1990. It has also been introduced in Sakura Hospital in Chiba-Ken, Japan.

One would think Americans need as much help sleeping as the Japanese. So for those who have everything they want—except enough sleep—look for singing pillows in department stores by 1995.

AFTERGLOW LIGHT BULB

ODDS: 40%

ETA: 1993

PRICE: NA

The afterglow light bulb is one of those wonderful gadgets that only a five-year-old could invent.

Hey, when you're a kid going to sleep is a big deal, and it's scary to go from bright light to total darkness. You need some in-between time.

Kacy White of Louisville, Kentucky, is the five-year-old who came up with the idea for the afterglow light bulb. Fortunately, her father, Tom, is a high-tech director in a middle school for gifted children, so he knows his way around an invention. He was able to conceive what Kacy could only imagine.

"When my light burned out, I was afraid," Kacy said, explaining where the inspiration began. Also, she feels that older people need time to get safely under the covers before the light goes out completely. "My grandpa tripped," she said.

Kacy was already hunting for an invention idea when the bulb in her room burned out. Her brother, Jamey, eight, is an avid inventor who enters the annual Invent America contests, and Kacy wanted to join him.

On that fateful night, Kacy asked her father why light bulbs go off so fast. "With me being a teacher, of course, I wouldn't tell her the answer," says Tom. "I asked *her* a lot of questions."

By citing objects already in Kacy's world, like glow-in-the-dark toys, Tom helped her discover that she could paint the light bulbs so they would glow in the dark all the time. But that's not what she wanted.

Kacy also knew about solar-powered stuff, like little airplanes and windmills that sit on windowsills and run all day. She understood that you could store energy and use it later. With her dad's help, she was able to suggest that a light bulb could also glow by using solar energy.

"As the light is on, glowing, it is storing energy," Tom explained. "When it is turned off, the energy is released and the bulb continues to burn for another minute."

Or as Kacy explains it: "When you turn the light off, it doesn't go off. It glows in the dark."

Tom hopes that Kacy, who won a regional award in the Invent America contest as well as the National Kindergarten Award, will earn enough from her idea to pay for her college education.

CAFFEINE-FREE COFFEE BEANS

If you're a coffee lover and a health nut, you know the dilemma. Caffeine just makes you so-o-o-o jittery, yet coffee tastes just so-o-o-o good. Water process decaf is a step in the right direction, but it's an expensive process that gets rid of flavor as well as caffeine.

ODDS: 85%

ETA: 2001

PRICE: A LITTLE MORE THAN REGULAR

So what's a desperate, coffee-loving, sleep-loving fanatic to do? Send positive-energy vibes to a research team developing a naturally caffeine-free coffee bean.

Richard Laster, president of DNA Plant Technology in Mount Kisco, New York, is spearheading the project. According to Laster, one of two possibilities should net a healthy coffee beverage by the turn of the century.

One direction involves recombinant DNA, which could alter the genetic structure of the coffee bean and block the caffeine gene from manufacturing caffeine in the plant.

The other possibility involves a bunch of coffee trees, currently growing in Brazil, that began life in petri dishes in New Jersey! These trees were developed through a process called somaclonal variation in which cells are taken from the body of a plant and cultured in a lab. Technicians can develop different varieties that might normally take the plant generations to grow. In this case, the variety being sought is a caffeine-free coffee bean.

"We won't know until they're fully grown whether we have the variety of coffee trees we're trying to develop," says Laster. "A coffee plant takes between five and seven years to grow to maturity and give its first harvest."

Laster's Brazilian crop is close to revealing results. The trees are five years old and have had their first miniharvest. "But we need to evaluate them over years to see if they have the qualities we're trying to develop," he says.

By one method or the other, Laster is confident that coffee drinkers in the next millennium—a few short years away—will enjoy their favorite drink, guilt- and caffeine-free.

HANGOVER-FREE WINE

If you love drinking wine but pay for it the next day with a hangover the size of France, or if you can't drink wine at all because of allergies, then you might want to raise a glass to a couple of researchers at Cornell University. Because the days of wine and wooziness are almost over.

ODDS: 90%

ETA: 2000

PRICE: SAME AS REGULAR WINES

The hangover problem is not caused entirely by the wine; the sulfites added to keep the beverage from oxidizing and turning brown make a contribution. Sulfites can cause headaches, or worse, allergic reactions. On rare occasions, severe allergic reactions have caused death.

The solution is honey. It can act as a natural antioxidant without harmful side effects and without affecting the taste of the wine. A scientist at Cornell's Department of Food Science and Technology in Geneva, New York, made this discovery by "weird luck."

Robert W. Kime, a researcher, had added honey to cider in preparation for turning it into apple wine. At that point he found he was out of yeast and left the mixture sitting overnight. The next day when the yeast was to be added, Kime found that the honey had totally clarified the cider.

The cider was much lighter in color as well. Kime realized that honey is not only a clarifying agent but also an antioxidant, which means it could replace the sulfites currently used in wine. Dr. Chang Y. Lee, professor of food science, did experiments to prove that honey's natural protein is responsible for these reactions.

The honey itself is transformed into alcohol during the fermentation process so the flavor of the wine is not affected. Taste tests have already been successfully conducted, with most panelists actually preferring the honey-preserved wine.

Lee and Kime have patented their honey clarifying and preserving processes and enquiries are pouring in from wine-producing countries, including France, Italy, Spain, and Portugal.

GAS-FREE BEANS

•••••

ODDS: 25%

ETA: 1999

PRICE: SAME AS REGULAR BEANS

•••••

Although beans are a versatile, inexpensive source of low-fat, high-quality protein, many people avoid eating them because of flatulence. So-called gas is both physically uncomfortable and socially unpopular.

While this may not seem like a problem of earth-shaking proportions, it is important enough that researchers at the University of California at Berkeley are working on a way to isolate and eliminate the flatulence factor.

New genetic engineering techniques are making it possible to reprogram a bean's genes so that they are no longer able to make a particular enzyme that is responsible for producing a class of carbohydrates called raffinose oligosaccharides. We cannot completely digest raffinose oligosaccharides. Instead this stuff ferments in our lower digestive tracts, producing gas. So eliminating the enzyme may eliminate gas. However, food scientists don't all agree that raffinose oligosaccharides are the only cause of flatulence.

Now the reason the humble bean merits so much attention, according to Ben de Lumen, leader of the University of California research team, is that beans contain significant quantities of fiber, vitamins, minerals, and essential amino acids. And, as lowlifes on the food chain, beans are extremely efficient to grow in terms of acre-for-acre food production compared with silage (fodder) crops that take a large amount of land to produce enough fodder to feed livestock.

In other words, beans are ecologically righteous. Nutritionists figure that if the flatulence factor can be removed, more people will eat beans and more farmers will plant them, freeing up valuable farmland currently used to grow feed for livestock.

EXIT TRAVELER

For Batman and Bruce Willis, swinging down the side of a burning building in the dead of night is just another day at the office. For the rest of us, however, it's a pretty terrifying thought.

ODDS: 100%

ETA: 1992

PRICE: $398

On the other hand, the alternative, being trapped high up in a blazing apartment or hotel room, is even worse.

A plan for escaping from a hotel fire is not something many of us think about in preparing for a vacation or a business trip. Then a tragedy like the fire at the MGM Grand Hotel in Las Vegas happens, and for a while every traveler gets super safety conscious.

This product, the Exit Traveler, is expensive. But for people who take trips often, it's probably worth it. At least you know you're prepared and that, no matter what, you have a good chance to save your own life.

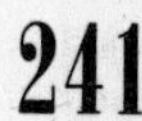

Similar to a mountaineer's harness, the Exit Traveler is small enough (10 inches by 16 inches) to fit in a suitcase, yet strong enough and long enough when extended to lower you to the ground from a twelfth-story window. In an emergency, you simply loop the braided, stainless-steel cord around a closed door hinge or a structural beam in the hotel room. You slip into the adjustable harness at the other end and head for the window.

This is the bravery part—climbing out the window and lowering yourself down the side of the building. The Exit Traveler makes it easier and safer than you think. No Batman or Bruce acrobatics needed. The fireproof cable lowers you to the ground slowly, at the controlled rate of 18 inches per second. There is even an emergency light stick, in case of a power failure.

Although there are no regulatory standards for such devices in the United States, there are in the Netherlands and West Germany, where the Exit Traveler passed tests with flying colors, according to Rick Denzien, president of R.A.W. Rescue Products in Ambler, Pennsylvania.

CHAPTER 18 for parents

STATIONARY INFANT WALKER

• • • • •

ODDS: 90%

ETA: 1993

PRICE: $60–$80

• • • • •

If you are the parent of an infant, get him or her out of that baby walker. Those innocent-looking child-minders are hell on wheels.

Every year in the U.S., there are 24,000 accidents attributed to infant walkers. According to *Consumer Reports*, many of those tragedies occur with an adult in the room. In 1989, Canadian legislators proposed a ban on the sale of infant walkers because they are so dangerous. Unfortunately, there is no movement afoot to do the same here.

Which brings us to Doctors Daniel and Lois Fermaglich, husband and wife pediatricians from Mountain Lakes, New Jersey. They have invented a baby walker that's safe, sensible, and, most important of all, stationary.

Their walker is called the Infant Exerciser. It uses a treadmill so that infants, suspended from the harness-type seat, can practice walking all they want, without moving around a room, bumping into stuff, or tumbling downstairs.

The Infant Exerciser functions as a play and feeding station. The suspended seat is hexagonal in shape, allowing the child to rotate completely around. Each of the six sides is a traylike module where the infant can play with toys or eat while moving his little feet on the treadmill below.

The Doctors Fermaglich were moved to invent the Infant Exerciser after twenty years of treating infants injured in conventional walkers. The frustrating thing, says Lois Fermaglich, is that many people just don't know about the danger of walkers.

And what's even more frustrating, she says, is that "even if they were banned, people would buy used ones. They're used as babysitters, and there is a high percentage of babies that are back in walkers within two months of sustaining a serious injury.

"The answer is an alternative to the mobile walker," she says, "and there may be others, but we designed ours to be safe."

The Fermagliches have been given the runaround by the leading manufacturers of juvenile products. Big companies like the idea, but not the price tag—which would be a few dollars more than traditional, unsafe walkers.

"They don't want to be innovative," says a determined Lois Fermaglich, "so we're taking the Infant Exerciser straight to investors."

BETTER BABY SEAT

It may be that conventional baby seats are designed all wrong. That instead of the infant sitting upright, he should be supported on his stomach at a slight angle.

ODDS: 90%

ETA: 1993

PRICE: $40

This is the theory of husband and wife pediatricians Daniel and Lois Fermaglich. And there's a lot of logic and research to back it up.

In medical school, Daniel remembers, professors advised that the best way to stop a child from crying was to hold him face down on your arm with his behind in the palm of your hand held slightly higher than his head. The baby's chest is then supported by the forearm. The grip is similar to the way a football player carries the ball, one handed. For years, the Fermagliches gave the same advice to parents in their hometown of Mountain Lakes, New Jersey. And it worked—hundreds of times.

There is medical evidence that babies under six months are not strong enough to support their heads while sitting upright. There's also research indicating that pressure on the abdomen will decrease colic, crying, and spitting up.

Armed with this knowledge and their own practical experience, the Fermagliches designed the Better Baby Seat based on the "football hold." The cushioned seat, which is saddlelike, is mounted at an incline on a plastic stand. The baby is tilted forward on its stomach and is strapped in, with legs dangling. The seat curves slightly away from the child at the top, so he can raise his head.

"The nice thing about the Better Baby Seat," explains Lois Fermaglich, "is it allows the baby to be in a position to interact with his environment."

WOMB-SIMULATING CRIB

Dr. Avrum H. Blitzer suggests that if the CIA can't break a foreign spy, a colicky child might do the trick.

ODDS: 70%
ETA: 1993
PRICE: $125

Dr. Blitzer, a gastroenterologist, and his wife, Edlyn, parented a colic child. The experience was so difficult and the baby's discomfort so distressing that it motivated the Connecticut physician to develop a crib to simulate the movements of the womb. It's Dr. Blitzer's theory that if the infant's neural systems are not optimally activated at birth, then the transition from womb to "hard outside world" can result in colic, or even dysfunctions, such as dyslexia.

"What the crib does," Dr. Blitzer explained, "is try to recapitulate a touchstone—a previously soothing experience—by creating a wave form analogous to water." This artificial return to the womb stops the child from crying.

The utilization of a series of cams (wheels on a rotating shaft) allows "waves" to be created by slats that move up and down under the 24-inch-by-36-inch mattress. The gentle motion is similar to ripples on an otherwise-calm pond. The crib is battery powered, has protective sides and bumpers, and looks a lot like a typical portable crib.

Does it really quiet down a child? A small study done in conjunction with Hartford Hospital indicates it does, reports the doctor.

The Blitzers now have their own company, called Doctors' Own Inc., to market the patented crib. They should do all right. Colic occurs in 15 percent of all infants, which works out to about 3.5 million babies in this country.

KNEE PADS FOR TODDLERS

ODDS: 90%

ETA: 1994

PRICE: $6 PER PAIR

Any toddler would tell you (if they knew the words) that skinned knees are the number-one occupational hazard of crawling around on the ground all day. And even adults know how much a skinned knee can hurt.

Daphne Bailie, a pediatric nurse in Toronto, Canada, became acutely aware of the problem when her firstborn child, Claire, started to crawl. Claire skinned her knees constantly as she made her way around the Bailie's hardwood floors and the cement deck by the pool. "The scabs barely healed before she was skinning her knees again," remembers Bailie. "It was becoming a real problem."

Bailie went to Toys "Я" Us to see their infant knee pads, assuming that such a product existed. Wrong. All she got from the sales staff were blank stares.

Undaunted, Bailie went home and took to her sewing machine. After several attempts, she produced a viable set of infant knee pads.

Soon her daughter was sporting color-coordinated, "completely functional, and very cute" knee pads. Little Claire became the rage around her neighborhood in suburban Scarborough.

"Wherever I went," says Bailie, "mothers stopped me. They wanted to know where I bought them."

A hundred or so enquiries later, Bailie decided that maybe Claire shouldn't wear her knee pads outside for a while. In the meantime, mother headed for a patent lawyer.

Two years of development later, Knifty Knees, a one-size-fits-all, oval-shaped knee pad, made of molded foam (about a half-inch thick) and covered in fabric, are a reality. "They actually form to the child's individual knee," says Daphne. The 3-by-4-inch pad cups the child's kneecap and is held in place by thick, soft, white elastic.

Knifty Knees, in a variety of colors, are already available in Canada.

CHILD'S HANDRAIL

ODDS: 75%

ETA: 1996

PRICE: $50

Just thinking about a small child trying to go up a flight of stairs makes you realize that bannisters weren't made with kids in mind. Toddlers have to hang onto an adult or crawl or stagger on their own, risking a fall. It suddenly seems so obvious that kids need their own little bannisters.

John Gatzemeyer, a design student at Syracuse University, has come up with something that makes even more sense: a special child's handrail that hooks onto the adult rail. It's low enough for kids one and a half to five and the right circumference (1 inch) for their little hands.

The plastic (polyvinyl chloride), modular rail has clamps that hook onto the adult handrail. The rail comes in 42-inch sections, so it can be made to fit the length of any stairway. There is one clamp per section.

The rail can be adjusted to suit the height of the child. And when the child is old enough to use the regular rail, the "child bannister" can be removed and stored. Since the clamps leave no marks and there are no screws or nails involved, the adult rail is left undamaged.

In 1989 Gatzemeyer won first prize for most innovative product in a Juvenile Products Manufacturers Association Contest, a yearly contest held at Syracuse University. His patented child's handrail was seen by the panel of judges as not only a useful safety device for kids, but one that instills a good habit early—always use the handrail.

BED-WETTER CLOCK

A vibrating alarm clock, invented to aid the hard of hearing, is proving to be an effective tool in the treatment of that frustrating and embarrassing childhood problem, nocturnal enuresis (bed-wetting).

ODDS: 100%

ETA: 1992

PRICE: $80

According to urologist John C. Stockman, M.D., enuresis can be caused by a number of different factors, which is why sufferers should always be evaluated medically. In children, the condition is usually related to physical and neurological maturation. Quite simply, some children take longer than others to develop sufficient bladder capacity and control. So while parents may feel confident that their child will grow out of the problem, they still have to deal with wet bedding, plastic sheets, nightly disturbances, and the effects on the child's emotional health and self-esteem.

A new treatment system—the QUIETWAKE Enuresis Management Program—doesn't cure the ailment, but it does solve many of the problems related to bed-wetting. Dr. Stockman, who helped develop the program, explained that QUIETWAKE offers a sense of control to the child.

The program is based around New Jersey inventor Jack Meister's vibrating alarm clock, designed for the hard of hearing and for those who want to wake up without waking their mates. It works for sufferers of enuresis because bed-wetting usually occurs at the same time each night.

The silent alarm is set so that the child can use the bathroom before an accident occurs. No one else hears the alarm, so no one else is awakened. And most important for the child: if he's at summer camp, has a playmate sleeping over, or teasing siblings—there is no embarrassment.

The QUIETWAKE clock is battery operated, lightweight, and portable. It attaches easily to an ordinary pillow or it can be used with a special pillow that amplifies the vibrations for heavy sleepers.

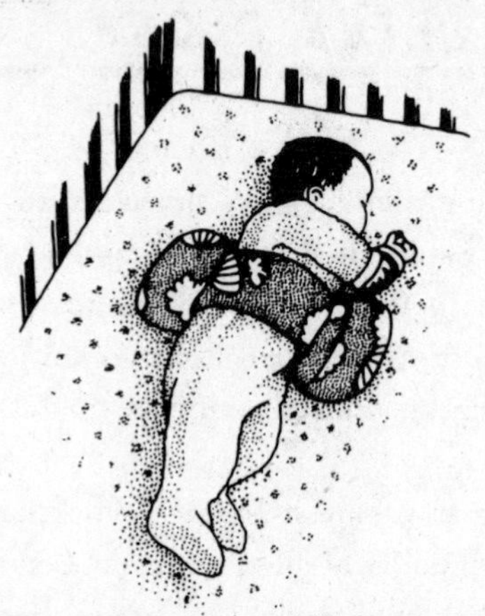

BABY SAFE

ODDS: 90%

ETA: 1992

PRICE: $25

The debate has gone on for generations. Which way should a baby lie in a crib? On its stomach or on its side, or does it matter? Well, now most doctors say the best way is on its side—less chance of choking, suffocating, or jawbone damage.

But how are you going to keep the child from rolling around?

A Canadian who worked in Indonesia as an underwater welder and construction supervisor returned to the West with a solution. Strange the way the world works.

Cuyler Cotton learned to value babies greatly from his Indonesian hosts. His product, Baby Safe, is based on an ancient Asian practice of keeping infants wrapped and warm as though they were still in the womb.

But Cotton's product does more than warm and cuddle. It keeps the baby secure in whatever position is most beneficial.

Picture two 4-inch-wide pouches, one on either end of an 18-inch-long band of nontoxic, washable flannelette quilting. Inside each pouch is a removable 3-pound bag of rice. The band is placed over the baby's waist to keep its inner organs warm and to help it feel secure. One weighted end is snuggled next to the baby's tummy, the other next to its back. The bags of rice (in waterproof casings) hold the baby on its side. The rice absorbs some heat from the baby, which also helps to keep the baby warm.

Already in use in some Canadian hospitals and private homes, Baby Safe, Cotton expects, should be available in the U.S. soon.

Nurses in maternity wards have found that Baby Safe keeps a child comforted for a long period of time—a fact that should be appreciated by mothers.

And when baby gets too old for Baby Safe, it works wonders as leg weights for Mama's exercises.

Cotton and the two women who helped him develop his idea—Dr. Beverly Brodie, an obstetrician, and Debbie Cutler, a nurse—have agreed to give a portion of the profits from Baby Safe to the Queen Elizabeth Hospital in Charlottetown, Prince Edward Island, where they all live.

MAGNETIC CHILDPROOF PLUG PROTECTOR

ODDS: 80%

ETA: 1994

PRICE: $10 FOR 4 COVER PLATES AND 1 MAGNET

Mark Menninga is an inventor with a long memory. When he was seven, he draped a necklace over a night-light and nearly set the room on fire.

"Flames shot 10 inches up the wall. I went screaming for Mom!" he recalled. The problem was an exposed prong that was shorted by the necklace. "It was an experience I never forgot."

Menninga, twenty-nine, of Des Moines, Iowa, has a patented product that will protect children from the same kind of near-tragedy he experienced. Now you might be thinking that there are all kinds of products that "babyproof" electrical outlets. True, but Menninga's is different and better.

Many parents insert plastic plugs into outlets so kids can't put stuff in holes. But these don't protect the child from touching the metal prongs of a live plug when the outlet is in use. Also, there are boxes that completely surround a plug. But they can all be opened manually.

Menninga's box solves both problems. It permits two plugs to be inserted while completely covering the outlet, and it can be removed only by using a strong magnet. To ensure safety, parents just have to keep the "key" out of the reach of kids.

BABY-FEEDING NIPPLE

Some new inventions make such simple sense you have to wonder why they haven't been around for years. The feeding nipple is one of those devices.

If babies are fed liquid through rubber nipples, why can't they also be fed strained foods? All that's needed is a specially designed opening.

ODDS: 80%

ETA: 1992

PRICE: ABOUT THE SAME AS REGULAR NIPPLES

Lois Smith, a painter, writer, and mother of four from Tucson, Arizona, is the inventor of the feeding nipple. She was inspired, she says, "by my own personal need."

And that "need" was inspired by her infant son, who was having a difficult time making the transition from bottle to spoon. Feeding time became nightmare time—long, trying, and not very successful.

As a result, her little boy was not receiving enough nourishment and was not sleeping properly. It was an unhealthy cycle for this child and mother, as it undoubtedly is for thousands more with the same problem.

So Smith, creative in her professional life, got creative in motherhood. She designed a nipple with a hole in the center and four more around the sides, all slightly larger than the openings in regular nipples. Her son was able to suck the strained foods without difficulty.

The innovative nipple is the same size, texture, and shape as a conventional one and can be used with either traditionally shaped or collapsible bottles. And it works well, Smith reports, with babies who have been bottle- or breast-fed.

Smith has a patent on the feeding nipple and a major company has already conducted market research.

TOTAL INFANT ORGANIZER

ODDS: 50%

ETA: 1993

PRICE: $75

"Don't get offended," says Pascal Mahvi, a California father of three, "but a baby bag is like a lady's purse. Everything gets lost in it! When dads try to find something in there, they can't."

Pascal, an organized kind of guy, got to really thinking about this dilemma one day when his wife, Caryl, complained about things "disappearing" from the bag. A civilian pilot, he is used to operating in tight quarters and storing stuff in small compartments.

Utilizing this knowledge, he devised a multicompartment baby bag that doubles as a kid's booster seat for restaurant dining.

The bag, called Bare Necessities, sports its own cooler, large enough for six bottles. The cooler keeps the milk cold, while its hard shell serves as the base for the booster seat. Above the cooler is a detachable accessory bag for toys, clothes, and other necessities. In the back is the diaper organizer compartment where the diapers, powder, wipes, and changing pad are all kept in executive order.

Outer pockets are designed for pacifiers, keys, magazines, and airline tickets. There's even a slim pocket that can hold an umbrella—closed for traveling or open for shade. The canvas bag can be worn over the shoulder, as a handbag, or as a backpack.

"When the kids get to be about three or four, you can use the bag for yourself," says Mahvi. "Put a camera in the accessory bag; cold soda and sandwiches in the cooler."

The seat, though small, can hold the weight of an adult. Mahvi, a 180 pounder, has tried it.

CHAPTER 19 food stuff

NOISE-DRIED ORANGE JUICE

ODDS: 50%

ETA: 1995

PRICE: 10% INCREASE

The earsplitting sound of jet engines has penetrated food science. Your morning orange juice may soon take the form of a powder produced by machinery based on World War II German rockets.

Purdue University researchers have developed a technique called acoustic drying to preserve foods that cannot be successfully or economically dehydrated by other means. Such foods include orange juice, apple juice, honey, soy sauce, and corn syrup. The use of sonic energy instead of thermal energy to dry these foods means that fewer nutrients are lost, while overall quality and flavor are preserved.

Dehydrated drink mixes and sweeteners have long been popular because they're convenient, lightweight, long lasting, and space saving. Also a plus is the fact that they don't require refrigeration and that they lend themselves to single servings, reducing waste. However, most of these products are only analogs—combinations of ingredients and flavorings that mimic the originals.

At Purdue, researchers are producing the real thing—powdered forms of the natural products. So the sonic-dried orange juice that you'll stir into a glass of water in the morning and the powdered honey for your oatmeal will be virtually identical in flavor and nutritional value to their fresh counterparts. These foods will be lighter and smaller, and they'll last longer too.

Good news for campers who have to carry foodstuffs up mountain trails. And good news for the rest of us, who just have to carry the groceries to the far end of the supermarket parking lot.

CRISPY CANNED VEGETABLES

Napoleon's troops ate canned vegetables during France's invasion of Russia. The chow turned out to be the best part of the campaign.

Nothing much has changed in the world of canned vegetables since those times. They were mushy then. They're mushy now.

•••••

ODDS: 85%

ETA: 1996

PRICE: 5 CENTS MORE THAN REGULAR CANNED VEGETABLES

•••••

Which is why research at Cornell University is sure to cause a stir with homemakers from Moscow to Paris to Toledo. Scientists have found a way to put the crunch back into carrots, green beans, cauliflower, and most other legumes à la can.

Malcolm Bourne, a professor of food science and technology at Cornell's New York State Agricultural Experiment Station in Geneva, New York, spent years experimenting with timing, temperature, and additives. His objective: to make tinned veggies just as crisp as frozen or fresh.

Bourne has done it. A patent application has been filed for a preserving process involving lower-than-normal cooking temperatures, a brief holding period to allow a naturally occurring enzyme to "fix" the firmness, and the addition of calcium and citric acid. Vegetables canned this way, he says, come out 25 percent crisper.

Canning requires two cooking periods, Bourne explained. A relatively short blanching in boiling water to drive out gases so more vegetables can be packed in the can is followed by a long period of heating to sterilize the food. It is a process, Bourne says, "that hasn't changed very much since 1810, when Frenchman Nicholas Appert invented it in response to a 12,000-franc prize offered by Napoleon. He was preparing for the Russian campaign and wanted a better means of preserving food for his troops."

In changing the process, Bourne knew that "we couldn't cut short the sterilization; nobody likes to die of botulism. But we suspected the vegetables were losing their firmness during the blanching stage and wondered if using less heat at that point would preserve the crispness."

Bourne and his colleagues prepared thousands of cans of vegetables at various temperatures and holding times. The holding time was key because an enzyme in the plant tissue called PME has the capacity to reverse the softening effect of cooking by "building salt bridges out of the spare calcium atoms in the vegetables." The researchers eventually found the ideal conditions under which PME could work to restore the vegetable's natural texture before the sterilization began.

They also found that they could further enhance the quality by adding calcium and citric acid, which acts to lower the pH and permit a gentler heat treatment during sterilization.

More good news: No amount of added cooking in soups or stews could make the vegetables mushy.

Bourne's new process has, as you can imagine, generated a great deal of interest from canners, whose profits have slipped with the increasing availability of fresh produce—not to mention the popularity of frozen vegetables.

Still, there are problems. Lowering the blanching temperatures in industrial-sized tanks, which are often operated twenty-four hours a day, may result in microorganisms that produce a sour taste. Also, the holding time and the need for new machinery has some companies worried about their profit margins.

All of this can be worked out, Bourne believes. So the question is: Will the public pay an extra nickel for a crunchier canned carrot? Or more precisely: Will industry give the public the chance to pay an extra nickel for a crunchier canned carrot?

FISH DOGS

ODDS: 80%

ETA: 1994

PRICE: SAME AS HOT DOGS

Americans, increasingly health-conscious, are eating more fish and less red meat. So it only stands to reason that the hot dog might someday contain menhaden (that's fish).

If a sausage made of fish doesn't sound as appealing (or as all-American) as the regulation dog, consider that we've already been hit with turkey dogs, chicken dogs, and even tofu dogs. Fish dogs are coming.

They are under development now. Menhaden and Atlantic mackerel, two not-very-popular fish, are being turned into dogs at the Marine Foods Laboratory of the University of Massachusetts in Gloucester. There are a number of advantages to fish, explained Professor Herb Hultin. For example, the gel-like texture needed for dogs can be achieved in fish—unlike meat or poultry—without salt. Also, fish contain Omega-3 fatty acids, which some researchers believe are good for your heart.

The challenge to producing a saleable sea sausage from fatty fish is to prevent development of off-odors. Professor Hultin is expecting success. "It's something like the soybean thirty years ago. Fish derivatives will be in a lot of future products, and people will never even realize they're there."

ORANGE CAULIFLOWER

Twenty years ago, a Canadian farmer in the Bradford Marsh area of Ontario noticed something strange in his cauliflower field. Sitting there amidst the thousands of white-headed cauliflowers was one orange one. He'd never seen anything like it.

ODDS: 95%

ETA: 1995

PRICE: SAME AS WHITE

The unusual cauliflower ended up under the microscope at the University of British Columbia, where it was determined that what made this vegetable unique was a beta carotene (vitamin A) level 100 times higher than that of a normal cauliflower. As you can imagine, this was hot news in the vegetable world. Scientists everywhere began trying to direct this genetic variation into a new strain of vegetable.

One of those scientists is Mike Dickson, a horticulture and vegetable breeding expert at Cornell University. Ten years ago he was given orange cauliflower seeds by a friend at the National Vegetable Research Station in England. Dickson's been hooked on producing orange cauliflower ever since.

Inbreeding and cross-pollinating orange cauliflower seeds with other orange cauliflower seeds hasn't worked. The results have been "yellow curds too small to do anyone any good," says Dickson. "The only way to produce an orange cauliflower is to produce a hybrid." By cross-pollinating white and orange cauliflowers with a pair of tweezers, Dickson has been able to make a small number of hybrids.

How do they taste? "If you were blindfolded, I don't think you'd know the difference if you tasted both," he says. In fact, Dickson sold his hybrids at a local roadside vegetable stand for a while and got a "very positive" response.

So what's the problem in getting this healthy new vegetable onto the nation's dinner plates? "It's all a question of genetics," says Dickson. "To get the right genes, you've got to find the special white cauliflower that will accept seed from the orange cauliflower."

It becomes a matter of trial and error and a lot of time. Dickson has been on the case for ten years now. "Most plant breeding is a game of numbers and chance."

Perfecting the plant will be well worth it, no matter how long it takes. Commercial producers are panting for the chance to grow orange cauliflowers. White cauliflowers are already renowned as a source of vitamin C and as an anticarcinogenic agent. Add a giant dose of beta carotene, also an anticarcinogenic, and you have a truly spectacular vegetable.

Not only that, notes Dickson. The orange color gives the cauliflower greater versatility. For example, one would never serve white cauliflower with fish and potatoes—far too pale a dish. Ahhh, but add a dash of orange. That's completely different!

CHOLESTEROL-LOWERING PEANUT OIL

By now we all know the benefits of cooking with olive oil—that it's high in monounsaturated fat, which helps lower serum blood cholesterol. In a few years, olive oil should be in for some healthy competition for a place in your kitchen cupboard.

ODDS: 90%

ETA: 1996

PRICE: SAME AS PEANUT OIL

The challenger to the oil of choice is derived from a peanut variety that is higher in monounsaturates—up to 80 percent, compared with 75 percent found in olive oil.

These are very special peanuts, however, as your standard variety has only about 50 to 55 percent monounsaturated fat. Agronomist David Knauft of the Institute of Food and Agricultural Sciences at the University of Florida, who is working with the new nuts, explained how they came to be. "A peanut variety planted here 30 years ago mutated sometime between 1977 and 1981, becoming much higher in oleic acid. This produces an oil higher in monounsaturates that may be more effective than polyunsaturates in lowering cholesterol."

The mutation will also mean a stronger shelf life for products like peanut butter and candy, according to Knauft. Because the fats are less unsaturated, they are more stable, which prevents rancidity.

In addition, the mutated peanut should reduce the amount of saturated fat in meat. Studies conducted at Texas A&M University show that when it was used in hog feed, monounsaturated oil lowered the proportion of saturated fat in the meat from 40 to 15 percent.

The one problem with the new nut is a split-pod characteristic that makes it commercially undesirable to plant. So Knauft and his team at the University of Florida are crossing the mutated peanut with other varieties. This time-consuming endeavor should delay the arrival of healthier peanut products until about 1996.

MAYHAW

ODDS: 100%
ETA: 1994
PRICE: $5 FOR JAR OF JELLY

Strictly speaking, there's nothing new about the mayhaw. A small, red fruit that grows wild in the swamps and bogs of southwest Georgia, mayhaws have been in America since before the *Mayflower*.

But unless you grew up in that corner of the country, chances are that the mayhaw is news to you. Good news.

Mayhaw jelly is a rare and old-fashioned delicacy whose time has come. Domestication of the mayhaw tree and an expanding cottage industry devoted to developing mayhaw products mean that this distinctively sweet, tart, tangy confection (too tart and tangy for most palates to be eaten raw) will soon be brightening breakfasts from coast to coast.

Like elderberries or fiddlehead ferns, mayhaws—cousins to the crab apple—have traditionally been picked by knowledgeable natives

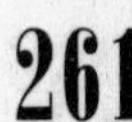

for their own use. During the brief three-week period in May when the fruit is ripe, locals descend upon area wetlands to brave the thorny, bushy trees (and bugs and snakes and . . .) to collect the bright red, half-inch "berries."

Now certain mayhaw varieties are being propagated and grown under orchard conditions. "This means greatly increased production and more efficient harvesting," explains Gerard Krewer, of the University of Georgia Extension Horticulture Department, who has been working with Jerry Payne of the USDA-ARS Southeastern Fruit and Tree Nut Laboratory on this project.

All in all, it will mean a lot more fruit. This is an especially exciting development for Joy Jinks, Pat Bush, Betty Jo Toole, and Dot Wainright in the farming community of Colquitt, Georgia. These ladies started The Mayhaw Tree, Inc., in 1980 to produce and distribute mayhaw jelly and other products. And, not incidentally, to produce jobs in a region hard hit by the farm crisis.

You can order their mayhaw products toll free. Dial 1-800-677-3227.

FLAVOR ENHANCER FOR LEFTOVERS

ODDS: 65%

ETA: 1993

PRICE: $1 FOR 6 OUNCES CONTAINING 1% OF ACTIVE INGREDIENT

If your mother fed you leftovers a lot and they didn't taste nearly as good as they'd tasted the day before (or the day before that), then you know that meat doesn't hold its flavor. Tuesday's succulent pot roast becomes Wednesday's rubber surprise.

Addressing the problem on behalf of families everywhere is the work of John Vercellotti and Allen Saint Angelo, scientists at the USDA's Agricultural Research Service in New Orleans. The solution, they feel, will soon be on your supermarket shelf.

Vercellotti and Saint Angelo have found a way to inhibit the natural processes that cause meat to deteriorate. The problem stems from iron in the meat binding with oxygen to form a chemical complex that reacts with polyunsaturated fats in the meat through oxygen free radicals. The breakdown products of these fats cause the meat to taste like cardboard, which means it's flaccid and bland by the time you warm it over.

The derivative is called N-carboxymethychitosan (quite a mouthful). It's also known as NCMC, and it will work on chicken and fish as well as red meat. The use of NCMC to prevent warmed-over flavor and for preservation of meat-containing materials has recently been patented by Saint Angelo and Vercellotti in U.S. Patent #4,871,556.

NCMC is a flavorless white powder that dissolves in water and blends invisibly with food. It's nontoxic and nonallergenic.

Vercellotti thinks that NCMC will do the most good in frozen meat entrees and microwavable prepared foods, both for the home and for restaurants and hospital commissaries. NCMC can be applied to the meat right in the slaughterhouse or during processing.

Homemakers will be able to buy NCMC in small seasoning cans and apply it before or after cooking or by adding it to gravy.

SAFER CHICKEN

ODDS: 50%

ETA: 1992

PRICE: 5 CENTS MORE PER CHICKEN

Two to four million Americans suffer some degree of salmonella poisoning every year, according to the Communicable Disease Center in Atlanta. That's a lot of suffering, caused by a lot of bad food. But now the Agricultural Research Service (ARS), a division of the USDA, has found a way to eliminate salmonella growth from at least one popular food item—chicken.

ARS researchers have found that lactose, a milk sugar, working in conjunction with bacteria in the intestinal tract of the chicken, inhibits salmonella growth. According to Dr. Donald Corrier, a research veterinary pathologist at ARS, "Lactose increases the acidity in the intestinal tract, which in turn enhances the bacteria static action of the volatile fatty acids, which fight the salmonella bacteria."

Whey, a byproduct of cheese production, contains primarily protein and lactose. The dairy industry isolates the protein for sale as animal feed, but the lactose has no market. So the industry is naturally interested in what's happening at the USDA, hoping that a large market will suddenly be created for this waste product.

The Agricultural Research Service is presently buying whey permeate for 12 cents a pound, which works out to about 12 to 15 cents a bird.

The lactose is added directly to the chicken's feed rations, constituting about 5 percent of the total diet. Researchers are continuing to experiment in the hope of bringing this percentage down and thereby cutting the cost to about 5 cents per chicken. Corrier believes that's the point where farmers would be willing to buy the bacteria-fighting food supplement.

By the way, if you've never been exposed to or seen anyone poisoned by salmonella, it is a gut-wrenching experience that can be fatal. To prevent it is certainly worth a nickel a chicken.

CHOLESTEROL-FREE MILK

ODDS: 75%

ETA: 1996

PRICE: SLIGHTLY MORE THAN REGULAR

Cholesterol counters will have one less food to worry about if dairy companies can find a way to remove the stuff from milk at a reasonable cost.

The process for making milk cholesterol free while leaving other tasty fats behind has already been developed at Cornell University and by some private companies. What's keeping the milk off the market is economics not technology, says Professor Syed Rizvi, head of Cornell's research team.

The decholesterolizing procedure is known as supercritical fluid extraction, the same technique as that used to decaffeinate coffee. In this process, carbon dioxide (CO_2) is forced through butterfat under extremely high pressure. As a result of the pressure, the CO_2 becomes what is called a *supercritical fluid:* It remains a gas but behaves like a liquid.

In this state, the carbon dioxide picks up cholesterol and other fats and flows into a second vat. Here, the pressure and temperature are manipulated so that the CO_2 releases the cholesterol only. Then, in a third vat maintained at normal atmospheric pressure, the CO_2 dissipates, releasing the other fats. These fats can be returned to the milk or used to make other dairy products, such as butter, cheese, and ice cream.

The process is long and complicated and, as a result, expensive. Too expensive to put cholesterol-free milk in supermarket dairy cases now.

But it should get there someday. And when it does, says Rizvi, who has worked on this project for four years, the consumer will not be able to detect any difference in flavor or consistency.

FLAVORED BARBECUE BLOCKS

For backyard barbecuers, tailgate partiers, and all-around gourmands, flavored barbecue blocks will probably be the next big rage in outdoor cooking. Just throw one of these lumps on the fire and whatever you're cooking turns out spicy as well as smoked.

ODDS: 80%
ETA: 1993
PRICE: $1 PER UNIT (1 MEAL FOR 4–6 PEOPLE)

The blocks, invented by Los Angeles chef/caterer Emerson B. Holmes, are made of sawdust, gelatin, and seasonings, such as garlic, pepper, turmeric, and tarragon. Right now, Holmes has four mixes—one each for seafood, fowl, red meat, and pork.

The flavored blocks are simply added to the charcoal fire when the flame is low. The result, says Holmes, is an incredibly moist and flavorful dish.

"The smoke does all the work," he explained. "You don't need to do anything else—no marinating, basting, or spicing." Or salting, which means this method of cooking and flavoring is good for people on low-sodium diets. It's also good for people on low-calorie diets because there is no need to add oil or grease to the grilled food.

SUPERSWEET SUGAR SUBSTITUTE

Imagine a substance that is 200,000 times as sweet as sugar. The NutraSweet Company has several such substances, and one of them is destined to be the new sugar substitute of the 1990s.

ODDS: 80%

ETA: 1996

PRICE: SLIGHTLY LESS THAN SUGAR

First of all, why do we need a new low-calorie sugar substitute? NutraSweet's own aspartame (200 times as sweet as sugar) is already everywhere, and judging from the phenomenal sales of "lite" products, it's doing quite nicely.

The answer is money. According to NutraSweet spokesperson Richard Nelson, "The new compound will be less expensive to produce because it is so intensely sweet; therefore you'll need less of it. Food companies would use less of it as well."

The new sweeteners were developed by NutraSweet in collaboration with two French scientists, Claud Nofre and Jean-Marie Tinti. Nofre and Tinti studied the sweetness receptors on the human tongue and how they reacted to various compounds.

NutraSweet hasn't yet decided which of the supersweet compounds it will develop for consumer use. Nor have they come up with a snappy name for the stuff. The scientific names for the sweeteners are aryl ureas and trisubstituted guanidines.

What will the new low-calorie sugar substitute taste like? "Similar to aspartame and sucrose," says Nelson. "What you look for is a sweetener that mimics as closely as possible the taste characteristics of sucrose."

After more testing, NutraSweet will submit its supersweet sugar substitute to the FDA for final approval.

MUSH-FREE TOMATOES

ODDS: 80%

ETA: 1994

PRICE: NA

Imagine going into your local supermarket and buying a tomato that tastes like a tomato.

Yes, Virginia, there is such a thing as a tasty tomato. But most of us who rely on the store-bought kind have no idea whatsoever what a ripe tomato tastes like. That's because ripe tomatoes are soft and fragile. They bruise easily, spoil quickly, and definitely don't travel well. And since most produce is grown a long way from where it's sold, ripe tomatoes would arrive bruised, old, and mushy.

To prevent this, tomato people ship 'em while they're still green. At that point, tomatoes have the consistency—and the flavor—of baseballs. And by the way, no matter how long you leave those suckers on the windowsill, they're never going to taste any better. Flavor is developed only when the tomato is ripened on the vine.

Enter the folks at Calgene, Inc., of Davis, California. They think they can create tomatoes, and other fragile fruits, that can ripen on the vine in their own sweet time and still be shippable for a week to ten days before turning mushy.

William Hiatt, the head of Calgene's tomato project, explained that the new tomato is the result of genetic engineering techniques. Instead of the slow and uncertain process of hybridization, genetic engineers can use so-called restriction enzymes and gene cloning. These techniques can be used to control specific regions of DNA to produce specific mutations. In this case, the gene for mushiness is being deactivated. The result will be a ripe, yet firm, tomato.

So, Virginia, if you believe in DNA, enzymes, and mutations, then there is such a thing as a tasty tomato.

MELON-SWEETNESS METER

ODDS: 80%

ETA: 1995

PRICE: NA

Okay, here's the scene: Captain Kirk of the starship *Enterprise* and his main man Spock from the planet Vulcan are shopping in the produce section of their local supermarket sometime in the twenty-second century. As they approach the melon counter, Spock pulls out a trusty scanner from his belt holster. Selecting a firm cantaloupe, he activates the meter.

"What's the reading?" a grim-faced Kirk asks.

Spock, expressionless as always, replies, "Eleven."

"Good. Let's take it," says Kirk.

"Anything else?" asks the emotionless Spock.

"No," Kirk responds. He pulls out his pocket transmitter. "Beam us up, Scottie."

Shopping for melon in 1995 will be "Star Trek"–like. However, instead of carrying a melon-sweetness meter on your belt, you'll be supplied with one by the supermarket. It'll be right there in the produce aisle.

Developed by the United States Department of Agriculture, the melon-sweetness meter uses near-infrared light to determine the soluble sugar content of individual fruits and vegetables, particularly melons. According to USDA researcher Gerald G. Dull, who developed the meter, a reading of 9 percent or more soluble solids is the industry-wide standard for melon ripeness.

The meter directs the light beam to the middle of the melon. Upon entering the fruit, the light scatters through the flesh. The meter then detects how much light is absorbed and uses this data to determine the melon's content of soluble solids. About 85 percent of these solids are sugar in most melons.

"Every person has his or her idea of what a ripe fruit is," says Dull. "We'll tell you what the sugar content is. Anything less than 9 percent probably won't satisfy anyone."

And in case you're wondering, melons and other fruits don't get sweeter with time. "The fruit may get softer, but if the sugar's not there, it'll never get sweeter," asserts Dull.

The first melon-sweetness meter is being developed for large-scale commercial use by food distributors and will cost about $5,000. By the mid-'90s, a smaller supermarket version should be ready for customer use. And a pocket "Star Trek" version could be on the way anytime after that. "It's not totally out of the question," says Dull.

STRAWBERRY-FLAVORED BANANAS

ODDS: 70%

ETA: 1994

PRICE: LESS THAN SLICED FRUIT IN CAFETERIAS

Everyone has been exposed to institutional cooking at one time or another. And the verdict is—and it's unanimous—that such meals really leave a lot to be desired.

Not only is the food usually overcooked and ranging in color from beige to gray; there are seldom any fresh fruits or vegetables. The reason for their absence is the high cost of labor to peel, clean, slice, and chop. And since you can't exactly serve a whole cucumber, pineapple, or even a carrot, forget it. Slicing machines might seem to be the answer, but

they're expensive and still require labor. The bottom line is that institutions don't serve much raw stuff.

When the U.S. Department of Agriculture became aware of this situation, a team of researchers set out to solve the problem.

The team, headed by Dr. Attila Pavlath in Albany, California, figured that preparing the fresh fruits and vegetables in a central location, like a manufacturing plant, and then shipping them to institutional kitchens would be the best idea.

However, we all know that a cut apple looks like a pile of rusty razor blades in mere hours. Not discouraged, the USDA set out to develop a thin, edible film that would adhere to a piece of cut fruit (vegetables will come later) to protect it against dehydration and color change.

"We only used natural ingredients because the FDA would take too long to approve anything that was artificial," says Pavlath. The film consists of minute amounts of three elements: simple proteins found in corn, soybeans, or milk that help the film adhere to the fruit's moist surface; carbohydrates that protect the surface from oxygen, which causes fruit to turn brown; and wax to protect the surface from drying.

So far, the formula they have come up with can protect a piece of cut fruit six to eight days. Not long enough, says Pavlath. His team is aiming for fourteen days, which would make the shipping of fresh-cut fruit a reality.

By the way, if you're wondering why this write-up is called "Strawberry-Flavored Bananas," it's because the scientists have tried using fruit pulp left over from making juices for the carbohydrates in the film coating. That means strawberry-coated bananas, orange-flavored peaches, and pineapples covered with raspberry.

How do these exotic fruits taste? Says Pavlath, "As far as I'm concerned, I like them, but I'm adventurous." First things first, however. Expect to see sliced fruits with a flavorless film in chow lines initially.

C H A P T E R 20

snacks

MINIMELONS

The best thing about melons is the taste. The bad part is that they're too big to put in your pocket or pack in a lunch box.

• • • • •

ODDS: 90%

ETA: 1996

PRICE: NA

• • • • •

Now if honeydews and cantaloupes came in convenient single-serving sizes, chances are we'd snack on them the way we do on apples, oranges, and plums.

Minimelons are what Perry E. Nugent, a research horticulturalist at the U.S. Vegetable Laboratory in Charleston, South Carolina, has been working to develop for the past four years.

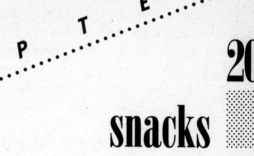

"I'd thought about it off and on for a long time," he explained. Then a few years ago at a meeting in California, he met a man in the vending machine business who suggested he develop a nutritious fruit snack the size of a soda can that could fit into the machines.

Ever since, Nugent has been working on his "miniloups." When his work is completed, we'll have seedless melons (or melons with edible seeds) that have a thin edible skin and a shelf life as long as that of apples or oranges. The vitamin content will be high and the color appealing.

So far, by cross-breeding small wild varieties with commercial ones, Nugent has produced fruit that is naturally resistant to some insects and diseases (so there's little or no spraying), in sizes as small as cherry tomatoes, and in shapes from round to oblong. He has melons whose edible skins are bright green, orange, and yellow, and some with stripes and speckles.

The hard part is making them seedless so that you can eat a minimelon anywhere without making a mess. Patience is required, says Nugent. "After all, they've spent fifty years or so trying to make seedless watermelons."

Getting that perfect melon is Nugent's aim. "It's like playing a big slot machine with about seventy wheels, and each wheel is a different characteristic," he says. "You crank the handle and the best melon will be the right combination of all seventy."

Real success, Nugent believes, will only come if the melon's flavor is right and if the vitamin and sugar content is high.

Nugent is now collaborating with Doyle Smittle, a professor of horticulture at the University of Georgia, who will soon begin taste testing and quality evaluations.

"Melons come in a tremendous range of flavors, from fruit punch to lemon to apple," says Nugent. "The perfect flavor and color combination may turn out to be a matter of good fortune and chance."

POPPED NUÑAS

Nuñas pop like popcorn, taste like roasted peanuts, come in an array of colors from purple to pure white, and have a history that dates to the Incas. Talk about *Back to the Future*. This bean could be the hot "new" snack food of 2001.

ODDS: 85%
ETA: 2001
PRICE: NA

The nuña (pronounced "noon-ya") is a most unusual bean that is grown, and known, only in the highland pockets of Peru, Ecuador, and Bolivia. Although a member of the kidney and pinto family, the nuña has properties unique to its high-altitude existence that make it a crop with enormous potential in developing and developed countries alike.

According to Stephen Spaeth, a U.S. Department of Agriculture plant physiologist based at Washington State University, the most notable of the nuña's special properties is the bean's ability to pop in a very short time when heated in oil, hot air, or a microwave (unlike popcorn, the beans do not change shape, but merely puff up and split in half). The rapid cooking time, Spaeth points out, is important at high elevations where it takes more time—and therefore more energy—to cook by boiling. In underdeveloped countries, where fuel is in short supply, the nuña could become a food staple.

In Peru, where remnants of the bean have been found at archeological sites dating back 11,000 years, nuñas are served as a side dish to the main meal. But in America, Spaeth believes, the future of the nuña is probably as a snack food.

Either way, the beans have a pleasingly crunchy texture, similar to that of peanuts, but without the oil. They're rich in protein, high in fiber, and low in fat. You could do worse than to snack on a bag of popped nuñas.

Commercial growers see the potential and want to produce nuña crops in the U.S. There are, however, a few kinks to be worked out. Plants grown at high latitudes—without the same light-to-dark ratios found in the native equatorial environment—fail to produce seed.

Scientists are working to create a seed suitable for cultivation in temperate climates. Spaeth feels confident they will succeed and that nuñas will be a hit circa 2001.

LONG-LASTING VEGETABLE SNACKS

Carrot and celery sticks, bite-size cucumbers, and small seedless peppers are about to become more versatile foods now that someone has invented a way to keep them fresh and good-tasting for nearly thirty days in the produce section.

• • • • •

ODDS: 95%

ETA: 1992

PRICE: COMPARABLE TO OTHER VEGETABLES

• • • • •

VegiSnax is what they're called, and if you live in Portland, Seattle, Santa Barbara, or Philadelphia, you might have already seen them being test-marketed at supermarkets and fast food restaurants.

The DNA Plant Technology Corporation of Cinnaminson, New Jersey, working with E.I. du Pont de Nemours & Company, has several patents on a process that extends the shelf life of these vegetables.

"Our aim is to use agricultural biotechnology to arrive at new foods," says DNA Plant Technology president Richard Laster. "We want to improve on aspects such as taste and vitamin level. We want to combine flavor, texture, and shelf life."

Using a method called somaclonal variation, the natural processes of plant evolution are accelerated. "We look for plants that might show the sorts of variations we want to encourage," Laster explained. "By taking a small sample to culture in the laboratory, we can induce varieties that would take years, if not centuries, to develop in nature."

Another method used by DNA Plant Technology is called gametalclonal variation. This involves using *protoplast fusion,* by which the walls of sex cells from two plants are fused to combine particular qualities of both. "The techniques are not so different from traditional plant breeding," says Laster, "just much faster."

The result is that Laster's company has been able to develop plants that produce high-quality, good-tasting vegetables with remarkable shelf lives.

RHUBARB-BASED FROZEN TREATS

ODDS: 95%

ETA: 1992

PRICE: $2.50 A PINT

In *Future Stuff* we told you about potato ice cream. The product was amusing enough and good enough to cause a stir wherever we promoted the book. Well, move over, potato ice cream, and make way for rhubarb-based frozen treats.

As you might expect, turning rhubarb into an ice-cream–like confection happened by accident. New York inventor John Harra explained, "I had nothing to do with the food business, other than being an overeater." Especially an overeater of ice cream. "One container of Häagen-Dazs while I watched Ted Koppel, another container for the late show."

Realizing that he had to do something about all those calories, Harra, who designs machine tools, figured he could also design a great-tasting, less-fattening dessert. So he bought an ice-cream machine. But after six months of experimenting, Harra was nowhere.

Then, late one night while baking a strawberry-rhubarb pie for his brother, Harra burned the crust. Disgusted, he poured the filling of strawberries, rhubarb, and sugar into the ice-cream maker. What came out a while later tasted great.

Excited, but worried that his invention was a fluke, Harra stayed up until 2:30 A.M. to duplicate his frozen treat. It tasted the same every time, he says.

Harra is now president of SuperNatural Foods, which is testing Fruit Treat, his patented frozen rhubarb dessert. Harra describes it as a high-carbohydrate, all-natural, nondairy, salt-free, low-calorie, high-calcium, fat-free, cholesterol-free, all-fruit treat. He also claims that it's twice as effective as oat bran in lowering LDL blood serum cholesterol levels.

The rhubarb base provides a large quantity of soluble fiber, giving his dessert the "mouth feel" of a high-fat, premium ice cream. But calorie-wise, there are only 19½ per ounce compared with 60 to 90 per ounce in most ice creams.

NASA has recently expressed interest in Harra's Fruit Treats. "Two things make it interesting to the space agency," Harra explained. First, there is no protein, so if it should spoil, it won't support harmful bacteria. Second, it doesn't drip when it melts. Instead, it stays together in a cohesive mass. "This is significant," says Harra, "because if they took it into space and it dripped, astronauts would be licking it off the walls."

Before this rhubarb-based dessert makes it to space, it should turn up in your supermarket, probably in 1992. Look for it in strawberry, banana, raspberry, and peach flavors.

FAST-FOOD PIROSHKI

ODDS: 90%

ETA: 1993

PRICE: $2–$3 DEPENDING ON FILLING

We gave Big Macs to the Russians. In return (hopefully, not in revenge), they are about to give us piroshki.

What's a piroshki? you might ask. Picture something like a knish, a burrito, a calzone, or a wonton. It's a big dumpling—a packet of dough stuffed with a choice of fillings then baked or fried and eaten hot.

The men who will bring piroshki to America are Sam Werbel of Virginia Beach, Virginia, and Mark Aynbinder, a Soviet immigrant from Kiev. They have formed a trading company called Chesapeake

International, which is in possession of an industrial-size piroshki maker manufactured in Kiev.

In the Soviet Union piroshki are usually filled with potatoes, cabbage, onions, and maybe mushrooms. Americans, with their proclivity for mishmashes, will likely stuff them with any combination that's remotely edible.

"We've been trying all sorts of things—broccoli soufflé, pepperoni and cheese, taco filling—with great success," says Werbel. "Russians are now eating Big Macs, and they love them. We think Americans will feel the same way about piroshki."

Werbel and Aynbinder are so high on piroshki, they are even considering "carrying coals to Newcastle."

"We may actually open a franchise in Moscow," says Werbel. "Although piroshki is a very common food there, marketing it as an American-style fast food is a brand-new idea. They find the whole concept very exciting."

What is even more exciting, however, is the idea of the U.S. and the USSR exchanging hamburgers and dumplings instead of barbs and bullets.

TOTALLY POPPED POPCORN

ODDS: 85%

ETA: 1995

PRICE: LESS THAN REGULAR MICROWAVE POPCORN

It sort of makes sense that a scientist who loves popcorn and who specializes in microencapsulating would develop a way of microwaving popcorn so that every last kernel gets popped.

Chel W. Lew and his colleague Darren E. Barlow of the Southwest Research Institute in San Antonio, Texas, spent two years searching for a way to get rid of those nasty, hard kernels at the bottom of every bag.

"If you open a bag of microwave popcorn, you'll find a plastic film

lining the bag," says Lew. "The bag is lined with this layer to contain the fats, flavoring, and a microwave energy absorbent. But it doesn't pop all of them.

"In our process," Lew continues, "each kernel is coated with a combination of low-melting-temperature fat and an edible polymer. This dual coating—which encapsulates the kernel like a chocolate-coated peanut—provides better storage stability for each and every kernel and should make them all pop."

There are two additional advantages, Lew notes. "Since this popcorn does not need to be popped in a specially coated bag—it can be popped in a plain paper bag—consumers can adjust the serving size to whatever suits their diet." And food companies can lower the price—since they won't need all that fancy, specialized packaging.

SELF-HEATING CAN

• • • • •

ODDS: 20%

ETA: 1994

PRICE: $3.50

• • • • •

A hot meal anywhere, anytime, is what Nissin Foods of Japan is promising with their new Super Boil Noodles. Packaged in an ingenious, self-heating can, the Oriental-style noodles can be cooked up piping hot in just five minutes.

It took Nissin three years of research to develop the product, which is now being tested in Japan. The technology can also be used to heat other kinds of food products besides noodles.

The self-cooking can looks different from a regular can in three ways. It is covered in an insulating cloth. It comes with a key. And there is a coasterlike apparatus attached to its bottom.

When it's time to eat, you open the can and add water to the noodles. You take the key and insert it into the "coaster" at the bottom of the container. This loosens the coaster and allows it to be turned. You rotate the coaster five times, activating an oxidation-reduction heating mechanism.

Basically, what happens is that two chemicals, separated until the coaster is turned, unite and create enough heat to boil the water and cook the noodles.

The special insulating cloth around the container prevents burns. Also, for safety's sake, the heating unit can't be activated unless water has first been added to the noodles.

The big question is whether or not Nissin will distribute their self-heating meals in the U.S. through their American division. The company has no plans to do so. However, an overwhelming success in the Japanese market would probably change their minds.

The product that Nissin is now testing comes in two flavors: Kaisen Ramen, a seafood concoction; and Kyofu Nabeyaki-Udon, traditional style.

TIME-RELEASE FLAVORED CHEWING GUM

• • • • •

ODDS: 75%

ETA: 1994

PRICE: SAME AS REGULAR GUM

• • • • •

Flavor that lasts and lasts is what any gum chewer worth his wad wants from his favorite brand. Yet we all know that no matter what advertisements might promise, the flavor's gone in a flash.

Look for a whole new ballgame as soon as one of the world's largest gum companies has teamed up with a high-tech California outfit to create a time-release gum that renews its flavor with every chew.

The trouble with chewing gum as we know it now is that every flavor—mint, cinnamon, grape, bubblegum, whatever—gets dissolved by our saliva in about five minutes.

Enter microsponge technology, pioneered by Advanced Polymer Systems of Redwood City, California. According to Dr. Sergio Nacht, the company's VP of R and D, inert-polymer microsponges (tiny, tiny sponges) in the gum are able to trap flavor in nooks and crannies then release it slowly every time they are squeezed (chewed).

Although certain details of the gum-microsponge merger cannot yet be revealed, Dr. Nacht was able to offer a general illustration of the sponge's incredible storage capacity.

"Each microsponge is approximately 1/1,000 of an inch, or about the same size as a speck of talcum powder. Yet each sponge holds about 10 feet of pores. With just 1 gram of microsponges, you'd have a tube that stretched from here to the moon!"

Microsponges are made of synthetic material, similar to the stuff used to make soft contact lenses. Because they are so tiny, however, the gum chewer will never be aware of their presence. They are non-biodegradable and not absorbed by the body, but passed through.

Microsponges were developed by Advanced Polymer as a time-release delivery system for drugs and cosmetics, including a self-moisturizing lipstick that was described in *Future Stuff*. The idea to apply the technology to gum was, says Dr. Nacht, the serendipitous result of a company brainstorming session. A large chewing-gum company took an option on the right to the technology and set up a joint research and development team.

CHAPTER 21

rodents & bugs

EDIBLE INSECTS

ODDS: 50%

ETA: 1995

PRICE: VARIES

It's time Westerners got wise. Most of the rest of the world knows how delicious and nutritious insects can be. In Africa, Asia, Latin America, and the Western Pacific insects are valuable and traditional food sources. So what gives with Europeans and North Americans?

From time to time, insects have made minuscule dents in the American diet. Chocolate-covered ants were a minor rage for a couple of seconds in the fifties. Though mostly people giggled at the idea rather than actually eat the delicacy.

But now, as the world's population continues to explode, entomologists, such as Dr. Gene DeFoliart at the University of Wisconsin, are trying hard to disabuse Westerners of the notion that insects make inelegant eating.

For starters, insects are nutritionally superior to most foods, he notes. Bugs are high in protein, unsaturated fatty acids, such vitamins as thiamine and riboflavin, and minerals like iron and zinc (important for vegetarians).

Ah, but what do they taste like? In Bangkok, the giant (3-inch) waterbug is considered as good as lobster (they are cracked open and eaten similarly). Emperor Hirohito's favorite dish was rice and wasps. In many countries, insects are used to give flavor to rice and cassava.

Insects are also very efficient in food conversion. With a small amount of plant feed, you can produce far more edible insect protein than you could if you were feeding cows, chickens, or most other animals. This efficiency would help to reduce soil erosion and other problems of crop overproduction. And insect harvesting itself would bolster rural economies.

Still, despite all the advantages, Westerners remain squeamish. Perhaps it's because we see insects all the time and know too much about them. Dr. DeFoliart claims that, contrary to what we might think, insects are as clean as can be. "After all, their food is primarily leaves. Crickets and waterbugs are much cleaner than shrimp, crabs, or lobsters. You wouldn't want to see what those scavengers eat."

Besides timid eaters, the biggest obstacle right now to commercialization is mass production. Most edible insects are harvested from nature. Should they become popular, a more efficient method would be required. Genetic engineering is one way of increasing production, suggests Dr. DeFoliart.

By the way, if you are interested in buying some wasps, a real delicacy, they sell for about $8 for 2½ ounces in Asian-American neighborhoods. Silkworms go for about $1.19 for 3½ ounces. Prepare them roasted or fried.

Bon appétit!

MOUSE REPELLENT

If you suffer mice infestation, you have basically two options: (1) kill them with baited traps or poison; (2) drive them away using an ultrasound device.

A third option, preferable to both the abovementioned, has a chance of being available at the start of the next millennium. It's a mouse repellent that uses the rodent's own scent as its primary ingredient.

• • • • •

ODDS: 10%

ETA: 2001

PRICE: $5 FOR 6 OUNCES

• • • • •

Mice are social rodents with a clearly defined hierarchy. Dominant male mice excrete chemicals called pheromones that inhibit other mice from moving into their territory. The idea, which originates with Dr. Milos Novotny of Indiana University's Department of Chemistry, is to use this and other pheromones to repel mice.

Dr. John Creange at Research Corporation Technologies of Tucson, Arizona, the company licensing the repellent, explained that the idea is to "harness the way mice work to man's own use." But that's not all. Other compounds in the repellent delay puberty and generally "muck up the breeding cycle."

The repellent is nontoxic, biodegradable, and fragrant to humans, says Creange. It could be used anywhere mice call home, including restaurants, stores, warehouses, food-processing plants, and your house.

The form would depend on the location. In grain warehouses, the repellent would be in solid chunks, scattered around like bait. At your house it would be in a spray container.

The problem in developing this repellent is the practicality of extracting the chemicals from the mice. Another source may have to be developed, Creange believes. And environmental groups might want to take a good look at the effect on the food chain.

HAMSTER FITNESS CENTER

You know what a rat race is, right?

No, no, no, we're not talking about nine-to-five-mortgage-payments-car-loans-keep-up-with-the-Joneses. We're talking about those metal exercise wheels used by hamsters, gerbils, and other rodent pets. These little creatures enjoy only three activities: eating, running, and reproducing. Alone in a cage, they have a lot of time for eating and running.

• • • • •

ODDS: 65%

ETA: 1992

PRICE: $16

• • • • •

Behind bars, their only way to work out is on an exercise wheel. Just like a human on a treadmill, no matter how fast or how long the gerbil runs, he never goes anywhere. That's the rat race.

Elliot Rais, a former computer engineer and now a real estate developer, became intrigued by these little dynamos while visiting friends whose son has a pet hamster.

"That wheel kept going the whole evening," Rais recalls. "The squeaking was driving me to distraction."

It also drove him to think that there must be a way to harness all this energy, which led him to think of his invention, the hamster fitness center. But Rais, a technical type, knew that before he could do anything with the energy, he had to measure it.

And how do you measure the energy output of a hamster? You build it a fitness center.

"Just like stationary bicycles in health spas, my hamster fitness center calculates and displays miles per hour, total mileage, and calories burned," Rais explains. And to further motivate the little guys, Rais's fitness center includes a tiny hamster exercise outfit.

"Using Lycra might be stretching it," says Rais, "but I'm confident our hamster aerobic wear will be both comfortable and flattering."

So if you've ever wondered how far or how fast that hamster really runs, Rais's fitness center with its LCD display screen is just the ticket.

The inventor is now hard at work on the second half of the equation—figuring out how to apply all that energy. "Light bulbs? Fans? Swizzle sticks?" he muses. "We could generate power for any number of things."

Hamsters of the world, it's time to unionize!

SAFE FLEA TRAP

ODDS: 85%

ETA: 1992

PRICE: $20

Flea killing has come a long way since 1909. Back then, some inventive dog owner used a light to lure the varmints and a bowl of soapy water to drown them.

In more modern times, chemical remedies have been popular—though some suspect that these mixtures may be harmful to pets.

Now a Canadian inventor has jazzed up the old attract-and-kill-them concept to make a flea exterminator that's safe and effective. Mario Visca, a pet product manufacturer, rejected the chemical solutions because they often contain a cancer-causing chemical. And

he didn't like the old light bulb–soapy water bit any better, because an electric bulb near water can cause hazardous shocks.

A couple of years ago, when his hometown of Hamilton, Ontario, was having a bad run of fleas, Mario conceived what he feels is the perfect solution. It's chemical free and safe.

The Mavco Flea and Bug Trap uses a specially colored light bulb to attract the insects, but instead of soapy water, there's a removable gummed surface, like fly paper, that kills the pests.

The sticky pad is semienclosed so kids and animals can't get at it, but insects can. It's easy to replace the pad—it slides in and out of its base—without ever touching the sticky part. There's a specially colored light instead of a yellow or white one—the better, apparently, to lure large numbers of fleas. The trap's 8-foot electrical cord plugs into normal household sockets.

The Mavco Flea and Bug Trap will also rid your home of other light-sensitive insects, like flies, moths, and mosquitoes.

ROACH REPELLENT INSULATION

ODDS: 80%
ETA: 1995
PRICE: NA

A world without roaches is the Utopia that Dr. Richard J. Brenner, government entomologist, dreams about. Second best is to get these disgusting nuisances out of America's homes. Brenner has a good shot at plan B.

According to Brenner, who works for the U.S. Department of Agriculture's Medical and Veterinary Entomology Research Laboratory in Gainesville, Florida, a new product being developed by a partnership of government and private industry promises to put a roach repellent right into a building's insulation. The idea is to "use technology more and pesticides less to insectproof homes," says Brenner.

To this end, the Agricultural Research Service (ARS) has signed a technology transfer agreement with Air Vent, a company that will work with ARS to impregnate home insulations with cockroach repellents developed and patented by ARS.

With a corporate and government lineup like this facing it, does the cockroach have a chance?

Although the cockroach is as resilient as anything alive, Brenner thinks repellent insulation is the answer. "These cockroaches will stay out under bright lights without food and water and starve to death before they'll go into a surface treated with these materials," he says.

The repellent will be tested in Florida homes with serious roach infestations.

STINKY GARBAGE BAGS

ODDS: 98%

ETA: 1992

PRICE: COMPETITIVE WITH OTHER BAGS

There's nothing like the smell of ripe garbage in the morning. Nothing can match the sight of ripped trash bags and garbage strewn across the lawn. For sheer displeasure, picking up trash before you head for the office is hard to beat.

No more will you have to face that chore. DuPont has developed a plastic bag that smells so bad even the hungriest rodent will leave your garbage alone.

Charles Atkinson, product marketing manager and self-described maverick at DuPont's Sabine River Works plant in Orange, Texas, is the man responsible for the odor-emitting bags. Called Petmaster, they're made of a chemically treated plastic with a smell that repels curbside scavengers. To humans, however, the scent is fine—like cedar or pine—and masks the smell of household garbage.

Coming up with stuff that smells bad to one species and good to another and then getting it into the plastic was tough, Atkinson admits. "I quickly developed a way to get just about any kind of chemical into plastic during manufacture, but it proved too complicated and expensive," he explained. "I don't know whether it's because I'm a simple-minded man or a brave one, but I couldn't let go of the idea. So I began to really look at things in nature and then I started to make rapid strides."

Atkinson won't reveal the secret process, but he did offer this analogy: "Say you get into an elevator with a man who is wearing too much cologne. Although the scent was designed to be attractive, when it is not used in the correct proportions, it becomes unattractive, even repellent."

Another hint from Atkinson: "Man's threshold of smell and the animals' are two different worlds. I just found a way to exploit those thresholds."

However he did it, Petmasters have already been successfully test-marketed in Houston, where street garbage cans are banned. A few more tests, then reports certifying Petmaster's performance, and Petmaster will be in your supermarket.

Bad news for scavengers. Good news for people who hate the smell of garbage in the morning.

CHAPTER 22

home office stuff

SUPERSCREEN COMPUTERS

Charles Haynes, technochief at PSI (Plasma Superscreen Inc.) is on a mission to change the personal computer as we know it. He plans to get rid of the CRT (the TV-style box display) and the keyboard and replace them with a large, flat panel like a drafting table. Haynes's computer will act both as a

ODDS: 100%
ETA: 1992
PRICE: $25,000

durable work surface and a display screen that shows thirty-five times more information than a CRT.

Does this sound fantastic and far in the future? Well, fantastic, yes. Far in the future, no. The Canadian and American armies are already using Plasma's Superscreens for battle planning.

When Superscreens become available to the public at affordable prices, "they will triple the size of the computer market," Haynes predicts. The reason, he believes, is that the current design of the PC presents too many obstacles for the average person. Any user has to be typewriter literate and understand the logic of operating systems.

Also, says Haynes, the CRT screen is far too small: about 9 inches by 6½ inches. Superscreen's work spaces range from 24 inches by 32 inches to 60 inches by 60 inches.

To operate Superscreen, the user works with a digitizing pen to press icons or pictures that appear on the display. The image or information is then produced directly on the Superscreen work surface, not on a separate screen.

"This computer will do what the Apple Computer company wanted to do—get a computer into every house. It is a work surface. It could be mounted on the inside of cupboards and used as a central processor for all appliances in the home," explained Haynes.

Superscreen is based on "panel display technology." Between two pieces of heavy glass, there are a series of fine wires and a substance known as plasma gas. A clear plastic sheet, called a digitizer overlay, is mounted on top of the glass. It makes the pictures and icons accessible for the user to touch with the digitizer pen.

The main advantage of Superscreen is its size. On one screen it can show the entire bottom-line status of a huge corporation or compare two manuscripts on one screen. It can run the gamut, from organizing households to directing armies. Haynes and his colleagues at Plasma Superscreen in North Vancouver, British Columbia, see an incredible future for this new computer.

And while some futurists worry that computers will someday dominate man, Haynes thinks the opposite. "In the future we will begin to deal with the computer as a slave, in a master-servant relationship," he predicts. "The way of man is to oppress. We can't oppress women anymore or employees. Computers will fill that gap."

Whew, women and employees (and especially women employees) everywhere can breathe a sigh of relief.

VOICE-FAX MACHINE

What do you get when you cross an answering machine with a fax machine? If you're a technophobe, you get flustered and confused. But if you're one of the MIT graduates who started Brook Trout Technologies in Needham, Massachusetts, you get Flash Fax.

ODDS: 95%

ETA: 1996

PRICE: $300

Here's some of what this amazing hybrid system can do:

- If you are talking on the phone or receiving another fax, Flash Fax won't interrupt. Instead it will wait for a more opportune time to forward an incoming fax.
- If you are away for an extended period, Flash Fax will record and hold any faxes sent to you. At your convenience, you can call in and have your faxes forwarded to any fax machine anywhere in the world.
- Flash Fax will soon come with voice/fax capability. When you send or receive printed material, an audible explanation can accompany it. So when those complicated papers arrive from your lawyer, his comforting voice will tell you where to sign!

According to Steve Ide, vice president of Brook Trout, all the equipment needed for Flash Fax hookup is a touch-tone phone and a monitor (a TV or computer CRT will do). The system makes use of digital signaling processing, which allows any data to be digitized and transmitted.

Flash Fax is already being test-marketed in a few large companies.

People like it, says Ide, because "they don't want to deal with personal computers and keyboards. The phone and the TV are idiotproof."

Ide is cagey about the price, only because he can't imagine why the phone company wouldn't just give Flash Fax away. "The sale of the unit is minuscule compared to the amount of money the phone companies will receive from the cost of connect time. Each time a fax is sent and resent, the phone company collects twice!"

Flash Fax should be ready for home use in three years; with voice capacity, in five.

COMPUTER THAT READS LIPS

• • • • •

ODDS: 80%

ETA: 1998

PRICE: NA

• • • • •

Voice activation is just around the corner. Soon we're going to have houses, robots, cars, typewriters, personal computers, and tools of every kind that we operate simply by talking.

The technology exists, but so far the machines are imprecise—which can be a problem if you plan to fly planes, drive cars, or operate spaceships all by the sound of a human voice.

Steve Smith, an engineer with Hamilton Standard in Windsor Locks, Connecticut, believes that one way to improve comprehension is to develop a computer that can also read lips. Which is exactly what he's doing.

Smith begins by focusing a video camera on the user's lips. He then has the computer analyze the video signal for lip movements that characterize a word. The results are combined with the results from the voice recognition system. This double-check method should be far more accurate, according to Smith.

"There are many problems at present with systems that rely on recognizing voice instructions, especially with similar-sounding words," Smith explained. "This should be a low-cost way of improving accuracy."

Smith, an assistant flight engineer, was quite naturally thinking about on-board computers when he developed his lipreading system. A particular problem in an airplane is the high noise levels, which complicate voice recognition. The computer's ability to read lips could solve that problem.

It should also enhance voice activation anywhere it is applied—from automated bank-teller machines to security systems to home appliances. "Just about anywhere that humans are required to interact with computers," says Smith.

There are still a few kinks to be ironed out before the electronic lip-readers are ready for the marketplace. In particular, the recognition process is too slow and the effect of different lighting on human lips can cause confusion. Smith is working on both problems.

WRITE-ON CALCULATOR

ODDS: 20%

ETA: 2001

PRICE: $500

Now that minicalculators are used everywhere, from IGA's aisles to MIT's halls, who really remembers how to do long division, square roots, and all that other stuff?

Not many of us. But for those who miss that cranking-brain sensation that only a good math problem can bring on, a calculator fit for figuring is on the way. Canon's IN-3000 will make you feel like a kid (at the blackboard) again.

Unlike standard calculators, which read keys as they are pressed, the IN-3000 reads what you write. It doesn't even *have* a keyboard. The handy (5½-inch-by-8½-inch) calculator has only a blank, pressure-sensitive screen. Using a stylus, you write out your calculations just as you would in a notebook. As fast as with a regular calculator, the correct answer appears alongside the problem—printed in standard, boring, boxlike numbers.

According to a Canon spokesman, the calculator does not really read your handwriting, so your numbers and letters can be sloppy or neat. What it does recognize are writing strokes—the motions we learned in elementary school.

In Japan, engineers managed to create software for all number and character strokes as well as for quick conversions of Japanese and Chinese ideograms. The IN-3000 is already on sale and a big hit with Japanese yuppies.

Creating an American model will prove far more difficult, according to Canon, because there's a system and orderliness to Japanese writing strokes that isn't found in the way Americans write English. In other words, the motions we learned in elementary school aren't uniform from place to place, and we don't necessarily continue to write the way we were taught. "American people are so free," says the Canon spokesperson.

It may take the Japanese a while, but we're convinced they'll solve the problem and come up with software suitable for free-writing Americans.

ERGONOMIC KEYBOARD

ODDS: 70%
ETA: 1994
PRICE: $125

Like many writers, Villy Diernisse of Westwood, New Jersey, would get frustrated with the standard typewriter keyboard. "For a long time I knew that there was a much better way to arrange a keyboard that would provide more accuracy, enable more speed, and require less work."

The main problem with the standard QWERTY keyboard, Diernisse feels, is that the layout strains the weaker fingers and leaves the stronger thumbs relatively idle.

Diernisse did more than just curse at his computer. He designed the Ergonomic Keyboard. What guided him, he said, was the desire to provide the same functions and capabilities as the traditional keyboard but to do it with fewer keys, arranged where the fingers naturally fall.

"In the standard QWERTY keyboard, eight fingers do all the functions and enter all the information. On the Ergonomic Keyboard, keys are arranged so that the strongest, fastest fingers do the most work."

There are two distinct areas on this new keyboard: one for thumbs and one for other fingers. The thumbs activate twenty function keys that control the computer's software and hardware. The forty information keys, including the numbers and letters, are worked by the other eight fingers.

All the vowels are on the left side of the Ergonomic Keyboard, while the most frequently used consonants are on the right side.

Because there are fewer keys (sixty as compared with about one hundred on a computer QWERTY), Diernisse claims the Ergonomic is easier to learn. After seventy hours of training, he says, his students are typing 100 words per minute, as opposed to QWERTY students, who hit 65 words per minute after 100 training hours.

Despite all of this good news, the patented Ergonomic Keyboard has a rough road ahead. Unlike Diernisse, a lot of writers and other typists would rather bitch about their keyboard than switch.

COMPUTER SAFETY GLASSES

Spend six, seven, eight hours a day staring at a computer video display screen and your eyes are going to suffer. If they get very bad, causing headaches and blurred vision, then you need to get help.

ODDS: 95%

ETA: 1992

PRICE: $50

But help has been in short supply. What computer users have

needed and are about to get are special glasses that make staring at a screen easier on the eyes.

Computer safety glasses are coming from the Technology Development Corporation of Bonn, Germany, and more specifically from Dr. Helmut Kellner, who is also the inventor of the special 3-D glasses (see page 28).

The natural position of the eyes at rest produces parallel sight lines that peer into infinity. When faced with a screen—or a book, for that matter—sight lines bend in toward the object. Look at the same object for a long time and your eyes become strained. What Kellner has done with his Switch Glasses is to trick your eyes (and brain) into thinking that they're looking at something 7 to 8 feet away. The muscles that normally pull your eyes in to see the object up close relax, causing less fatigue.

The Switch Glasses look exactly like normal eyeglasses. If you already wear glasses, the Switch technology can be incorporated into your regular prescription.

When Dr. Kellner's invention was reported in the computer trade publication *Design Fax*, Technology Development Corporation's office in Orlando, Florida, received nearly 2,000 inquiries—including letters from IBM and Ford.

COMPUTER TRACKER

ODDS: 90%

ETA: 1992

PRICE: $49

A thief breaks into your home and steals your personal computer (along with everything else). Months later, the police raid a warehouse where they find scores of stolen computers that look just like yours. How do the cops identify your PC and get it back to you?

As personal computer use and crime both increase, so does this dilemma. Scratch on an ID number and thieves just scratch over it. Almost anything you can do, a good thief can undo.

So here comes Identifax, a Setauket, New York, company with eighteen years in the ID business. Their solution is to give your PC its own special series of beeps that sound every time you turn on the machine.

The system works by loading a unique beep code onto the hard drive of your computer with a one-time-use disc. Your personal code is registered in a central computer at Identifax headquarters. When the police recover a stolen computer, they simply hold the phone receiver next to the computer and turn it on. The Identifax base system will trace the sound code and give the police your name.

"This system was developed with the idea that, generally, only the computer itself is found, not the keyboard or screen," says Warner Loeb, president of Identifax. "So, even though the code will show on the monitor, the attachments aren't necessary for identification. Also, police aren't always computer literate, so this makes it easier."

It's also practically impossible, Loeb points out, for thieves to erase the code because it's hidden in the hard-disc drive.

CHAPTER 23

car stuff

ROADWAY-POWERED CARS

The idea of electric automobiles on a powered roadway has always seemed to belong more in the realm of distant science fiction than in near reality. But as pollution and energy problems persist, roadway-powered electric vehicles are looking more and more like a practical solution.

• • • • •

ODDS: 35%

ETA: 2001

PRICE: NA

• • • • •

We are at the point of serious experimentation. In a Los Angeles project, 1,000 feet of roadway is being wired with buried electrical cables that will provide energy for specially fitted cars. The vehicles will pick up this energy by magnetic induction—transferred by a magnetic field—without any direct contact with the buried power lines. Non contact means there is no possibility of electrical hazard.

The experiment is a joint effort of the Southern California Edison Company and the City of Los Angeles, Department of Water & Power.

According to Howard R. Ross, who is managing the consortium designing the system for Edison, motorists of the future will drive their electric cars from home to the nearest powered roadway (probably no more than a few miles) using battery power. "Then, on the freeway, the road itself will provide energy for propulsion and recharging the vehicle's battery."

In the Los Angeles experiment, two specially fitted electric vans are the first test vehicles to operate on the powered roadway. Should it all work well, electrified highways, at a cost of $1.5 million per lane-mile, will begin to find their place on America's regular highways, particularly in urban areas.

Smog, pollution, and our dependence on foreign oil could all then be problems of a century just passed.

TALKING CAR NAVIGATOR

ODDS: 80%

ETA: 2000

PRICE: $500, PLUS $150 ANNUALLY

British transport engineers have long been concerned that so many of their countrymen have trouble getting from point A to point B in a timely and direct fashion. So they created a formula for efficiency. It goes like this: One intelligent car plus one intelligent road equals one quick trip.

And that's exactly what scientists at the British Department of Transport's Transport and Road Research Laboratory have designed. It's called Autoguide, and negotiations are currently in progress with GEC Autoguide, a unit of GEC, P.L.C., in the United Kingdom to install a pilot scheme in London.

The first part of the equation is the intelligent car. A computerized navigational system is installed in the instrument panel, and an electronic compass is placed in the trunk. Before departing, the driver activates the Autoguide by entering his destination into the in-car system. That information is transmitted to a central computer at GEC headquarters.

Once the driver is on the road, three controls work in unison to direct him. An LCD screen indicates with a pointer arrow which direction should be taken. A synthesized voice calls out instructions, like, "Right turn ahead," whenever it's necessary to change direction. Finally, a bar graph on the display area decreases in height (at 30-meter intervals) as the car approaches a junction at which the driver should turn.

The second part of the equation is the intelligent road. Along the route there are roadside beacons that transmit up to 8 kilobytes of digital data to a receiver hidden behind the car's rearview mirror. That's enough road and traffic information to get the car to the next beacon, where new information is supplied.

The information flow goes both ways. Autoguide already knows the car's destination and has set the car's route. The travel time of the car in the system is also fed to the central computer, which compares the time with a preprogrammed norm for the distance between each pair of beacons. If a particular trip is taking longer than average, the computer concludes there's a traffic delay and reroutes other cars heading in that direction.

Julian Slater, GEC Autoguide's business director, says the system "should enable people to cut travel time by 10 percent and reduce the number of miles traveled by 6 to 10 percent."

There's no question that this is an expensive system to set up. But the British believe that by diverting traffic away from overcrowded roads, municipalities will actually come out ahead by saving on upgrades and repairs.

A bonus benefit is that fuel consumption, and therefore pollution, will be significantly reduced.

The British are already well into testing the system, using five beacons and fifteen Autoguide-equipped cars, on a network of streets in the London area. It could be commercially available in England by 1994 and in the U.S. by the turn of the century.

LIGHT ENGINE

If you checked all around your car, you'd find approximately eighty different light sources, ranging from headlights to glove compartment light to directional signals to the lights on your dashboard. Naturally, each light requires its own special bulb.

ODDS: 25%

ETA: 1999

PRICE: NA

Actually, not so "naturally." For the car of the future will have just one bulb to light all of those eighty-odd places. General Electric calls it the Light Engine Central Lighting System. "All of the lights we now use in our cars can be replaced in the future by one central source," says John Davenport, manager of concept development at the Advanced Technology Department of GE Lighting.

Light from this centrally located source will be "piped" to the headlamps, taillights, dashboard, and every other location via fiber-optic rods.

The breakthrough that will make this possible is low-wattage, instant-on, metal halide technology coupled with an integrated optical system, which is designed like a star-shaped arc. The metal halide high-intensity discharge bulb uses no more electrical power than a pair of present-day headlamps.

This futuristic bulb will simplify automobile lighting systems and make the awkward job of replacing bulbs in a car a thing of the past.

But even more important, the Light Engine will change the shape of cars, enabling designers to make them more aerodynamic than ever. "The new concept allows a headlight to be less than an inch high. It really becomes nothing more than a line of light," says Ben Anderson-Ray, General Electric's manager of Automotive Discharge Lighting.

AUTOMATIC MOOD MUSIC FINDER

• • • • •

ODDS: 95%

ETA: 1993

PRICE: $20 ADDED TO THE COST OF A RADIO

• • • • •

You are getting twanged to death by country music as you roll down the highway through Tennessee. What you wouldn't give for a little Grateful Dead or some R and B. But you can't find anything on your car radio except pickers and preachers.

Have faith! An incredible new technology is on the way. Radio Data Systems (RDS) will automatically help you locate the nearest station carrying the kind of programming you like. Simply push a button on the radio—NEWS, COUNTRY AND WESTERN, RHYTHM AND BLUES, CLASSICAL, JAZZ . . . whatever your choice. The device in your car scans the wires for a little message from participating radio broadcasters as to the nature of their programming.

Sage Alerting Systems of Stamford, Connecticut, is the company spearheading RDS in this country. The technology, says Sage's Jerry LeBow, consists of a 1,200-byte-per-second digital data stream, or subcarrier, that is installed by an FM radio station at a cost of about $6,000. LeBow likens it to a "miniature radio station riding alongside a big radio station."

This subcarrier, which contains the program type code, was developed by a European consortium of broadcasters who made it royalty and patent free to encourage its proliferation. It delivers digital information about the station's programming to radios in cars and homes equipped to receive it.

In addition, RDS will display the station's call letters, as well as the frequency, on the radio dial.

The price of a car radio will go up about $20 if it's equipped with Radio Data Systems. Well worth the price if you get stuck in country music land and don't like it.

SIDE-IMPACT CAR AIR BAGS

• • • • •

ODDS: 65%

ETA: 1998

PRICE: $1,500

• • • • •

After years of hearing about the safety benefits of air bags, we finally got them in the late '80s, at least on the driver's side. It's only now that air bags are being fitted on the passenger side, where so many terrible injuries occur. The next giant step is to get air bags on the sides of car seats.

You've probably never given it much thought, but the so-called passive restraint devices—seat belts and air bags—only protect people in the event of a frontal crash. A collision from the side (the second most common accident type after head-on collisions) is potentially more harmful because there's less car to absorb the crash. On the sides, you have only doors; in front, you have the frame, engine, and dashboard.

Sweden's Volvo Car Corporation, long known for leading the way (and for touting that leadership) in occupant-protection technology, is working on a design for a smaller air bag specifically for side-impact situations. The air bag and its propellant device would be integrated in the car's door.

Says Volvo safety researcher Hugo Mellander, "The side air bag is an interesting alternative, providing good protection without encroaching on the space in the passenger compartment."

As was the case with air bags for frontal collisions, however, it will probably take years and a public clamor before these side air bags are installed in most cars.

REARVIEW MIRROR RADAR

•••••

ODDS: 85%

ETA: 1993

PRICE: $150

•••••

The rearview mirror is sort of the belly button of a car. Every vehicle has one, but no one really pays attention to the thing. It's just there. And while every other part of the car seems to be getting computerized, digitized, and generally gadgetized, nothing has happened to the rearview mirror.

Well, get ready, folks! Changes that will make your head spin are about to revolutionize the world of rearview mirrors.

First off comes the memory-activated positioning control. As soon as you start the engine with your personalized key, the mirror (along with the seat, pedals, and other parts of the car) will adjust to just the way you like it.

Next up is the self-darkening rearview mirror. It will automatically compensate for bright headlights behind you.

But the pièce de résistance is a rearview mirror that can detect a vehicle that you can't even see. The Gilardini subsidiary of Italy's Fiat Group is developing a rearview mirror based on the technology of radar. The radar recognizes a vehicle approaching from the rear before it's visible in the mirror. A warning light on the rearview mirror will blink when a car is on its way into view.

Gilardini acquired the world rights to the mirror from its Swedish inventor, Dr. Goeran Sjoehel. Its most important use will come on high-speed, open roads, like the Autobahn, where cars can suddenly appear from the rear at high speeds.

HEAT-STORING DEVICE

ODDS: 60%

ETA: 1995

PRICE: $475

Drivers in Minnesota, the Dakotas, and Canada will certainly be pleased to hear that German engineers are developing a car engine that starts warm even in the coldest weather.

Schatz Thermo Engineering, under contract with Volkswagen, is working on a "heat storing device" that can store the heat of a running engine and reclaim it at a later time. The result is that on even the coldest morning, engines would start instantly, the passenger space would be quickly warmed, and the windows defrosted in a minute.

The device is a thermoslike sealed canister containing barium hydroxide. The unit is plumbed into the engine's radiator hoses. While the engine is running, the hot water inside melts the chemicals, which absorb heat in the process. The heat can be stored for up to three days, even during freezing temperatures.

A cold-morning start will extract all of the heat from the device by cooling and solidifying the chemicals. However, with just a few minutes of driving, the battery recharges and will be ready to supply the car with another warm start.

Another advantage of the heat battery, according to Volkswagen, is that prewarmed starts result in fewer exhaust emissions, reducing pollution.

FOOLPROOF CAR SUSPENSION

•••••

ODDS: 20%

ETA: 1995

PRICE: $2,000

•••••

Even the best of drivers can't violate the laws of physics and get away with it. For example, when a fast-moving car turns a corner, the dynamic forces acting upon it will shift a portion of the car's weight to the pair of wheels on the outside of the curve. This is what causes a car's body to "lean" into a turn. Now, if 100 percent of the weight gets transferred to the outside pair of tires, a catastrophic event follows almost immediately: a rollover.

Good drivers can easily sense when this catastrophe is about to take place and can usually avoid it. Bad drivers can't always. But all drivers, even professional ones, can sometimes be forced into situations where there's no choice.

Engineers at Toyota Motor Company, using a complicated mathematical formula to calculate the point at which a vehicle will be likely to turn over, have devised a way to utilize active suspension technology to prevent rollovers.

In actual use, the Toyota active suspension system would employ, inside the car, a computer that would monitor the speed and steering angle as well as the degree of body lean. Active suspension controls body weight, roll, pitch, and dive, as well as ride comfort, according to road conditions. If all factors pointed to a rollover, the computer would automatically activate hydraulic pumps. The pumps would fill and extend telescoping chambers mounted at each corner of the car. These devices would raise the low side of the car, bringing it to a more level—and more stable—position. All this in a fraction of a second!

This amazing suspension would be particularly useful in high-riding, rollover-prone vehicles, such as four-wheel-drive trucks and off-road sports vehicles.

The high projected price—$2,000—is likely to keep this foolproof balancing act off the market until Toyota can get its costs down.

SMALLER HEADLIGHTS

It may not sound like much, but a new light bulb that is just an inch or two smaller than the kind currently used in your automobile headlamps is going to radically change the shape of cars to come.

ODDS: 50%
ETA: 1994
PRICE: $200 PER ASSEMBLY

How can one little light bulb make such a difference?

It's not just the size factor. John M. Davenport, a researcher at General Electric, who has spearheaded the development of this light bulb, explains that it uses a different technology—high intensity discharge, or HID—to produce light. Today's incandescent bulbs use heated filaments. The new bulb, known as an arc discharge lamp, uses an electronically controlled spark between two electrodes to heat gases to a glowing white light. On a tiny scale, it's like lightning in a tube.

So how will this affect the body of your car?

Arc discharge lamps are not only smaller than conventional bulbs, they're far more durable and efficient. There's no filament to burn out. And increased efficiency means that the bulbs not only produce more light per watt (by a factor of 4), but they give off less heat.

Since the bulb itself is cooler, the lenses that amplify and focus the light can be made of polycarbonate (plastic) instead of glass. With the use of plastic the whole assembly will be lighter, tougher, and smaller in both height and depth. This makes for a quantum leap in design flexibility.

The result is a more streamlined automobile with better aerodynamics and improved gas mileage.

And all from one little light bulb. Illuminating.

ULTRAVIOLET HEADLIGHTS

If you've ever seen the eerie glow of a white shirt under the "black light" of a disco dance floor, then you can understand how ultraviolet headlights will be able to light up the night for drivers.

ODDS: 50%

ETA: 1996

PRICE: $250

In fact, cars fitted with ultraviolet beams will more than double the driver's range of vision by making distant objects "glow" in the dark. These beams will also penetrate mist, fog, snow, and rain better than standard car lights.

But the really fascinating property of ultraviolet light is that the wavelength is too short to be seen by the human eye. Therefore these headlights will not blind the drivers of oncoming cars.

These new nondazzle lights have been developed by Swedish inventor Lars Bergqvist, in cooperation with Saab, Volvo, and the Swedish Transport Research Commission.

Although UV light is invisible to humans, many surfaces that it illuminates, particularly fluorescent colors, become highly visible. If such colors were used for road signs and markings, on bridge pillars and other vehicles, motorists would see everything far sooner without blinding one other. And since many ordinary items of clothing, such as white shirts and jeans, are clearly visible in UV light, drivers would spot pedestrians sooner as well.

So what's keeping ultraviolet light off the world's roads? Tests. "What matters," says Hans-Ove Nilson of Volvo, "is to evaluate the impact of UV light on our health and environment."

BUILT-IN CHILD'S CAR SEAT

When you take a child anywhere, it seems like a hundred pounds of equipment goes with you. Well, some relief is in sight. Volkswagen engineers have designed an integrated child's car seat that folds away when not in use.

ODDS: 90%
ETA: 1994
PRICE: NA

The seat is in a prototype vehicle of the future called the Futura (see "The Self-Parking Car," page 7). While not as flashy an innovation as automatic parking, the child's seat may ultimately prove to be more in demand with the American public.

The child's seat is built into the upholstery of the car's right-hand rear seat. The upholstered sides and the front barrier are easily folded upwards and form the basic frame for the safety seat. There are a number of different settings enabling the seat to be positioned correctly for the size of the child. The seat can accommodate an infant—or even a ten-year-old.

A regular seat belt can be applied for even more protection. The cross barrier is unlocked and automatically resets so the child can get in and out easily.

The whole apparatus can be folded away so that an adult can sit in the space when Junior's not around.

REMOVABLE STEERING WHEEL

For years bicyclists in big cities have been taking one wheel with them whenever they park their bicycles. It's an effective deterrent because thieves would rather ride than carry their bounty away. Virgil Johnson, an inventor-janitor whose car has been stolen five times, believes that a removable steering wheel would work just as well for automobiles.

ODDS: 25%

ETA: 1997

PRICE: $600

Johnson now has a patent pending on a wheel that you take with you or lock away in the trunk whenever you park. It can be disengaged and reconnected only with a special key. And while you're parked, a special steel "stopper," 3 inches in diameter, locks into place over the steering column so that an enterprising thief can't attach his own steering wheel. When the cover is not in use, it locks into a hub on the underside of the steering column.

It sounds like Johnson, of Southfield, Michigan, has thought of everything. Even so, he admits it wouldn't stop all car thieves. They can still tow cars away. "But I can stop 60 percent of all auto thefts in this country," he says. "It's like the old saying: 'If you don't let the horse out of the corral, you don't have to get him back in.' "

You might think that car manufacturers would be lining up to get their hands on Johnson's wheel. Not so. In fact, the big three American car companies have all turned it down. "They don't want it to work because when a car gets stolen, they make money," Johnson reasons.

In lieu of new cars coming equipped with his removable wheel, Johnson is working on an adapter that would convert the standard steering wheels on current cars and make them removable.

One way or the other, Johnson is determined to put a significant dent in the stolen-car market. "I'm a crime fighter," he says.

CHAPTER 24

why didn't i think of this?

SEE-THROUGH CONVERTIBLE TOASTER

In 1989, Black and Decker, the tool and appliance people, ran a contest called Toast to the Future. The idea was for ordinary folks to come up with improved designs for the everyday toaster.

Imagine the excitement. Toaster enthusiasts all over the world began tinkering away, trying to improve on what seemed

• • • • •

ODDS: 80%

ETA: 1995

PRICE: TWICE AS MUCH AS A REGULAR TOASTER

• • • • •

to be a perfectly okay little appliance. After all, how many ways can there be to darken bread?

Well, as it turns out, Black and Decker received 350 spectacular responses from eleven countries. And the very best one came from John Cupit, of Cleveland, Ohio, who walked off with the $10,000 first prize.

Cupit's toaster is see-through, so you know exactly how dark your bread is getting! The sides of the toaster are heat-resistant glass panels which house the heating elements. The glass is easily removed for cleaning. Now, add to this unique feature the ability to toast both horizontally and vertically, and you have one dynamic toaster.

When you want to heat something on your bread, like cheese or tuna fish, you push down a little handle, and the toaster rotates 90 degrees to a flat position. A tray (stored in the toaster base) is used to slide the bread and topping into the toaster slot.

"At present, the toaster exists only as an industrial design model," says Gary Van Deursen, director of Black and Decker's New Product Concepts and Industrial Design Department, "but with new technology, it could be on the market by 1995.

"It will be more expensive than a regular toaster," Van Deursen continued, "but we think people will be willing to pay for the convenience and innovative design."

PERMANENT BUTTONS

ODDS: 50%

ETA: 1999

PRICE: LESS THAN REGULAR BUTTONS

If you ever happen to visit Scandinavia, take a close look at the buttons on some men's shirts and women's blouses. What you might see is rather revolutionary: buttons bonded to garments ultrasonically, so they *never* come off!

The technology, invented in Sweden by Bengt Petersson, was further developed and marketed by Combitex, a company in Norway. The button is made of plastic and has a stem. The stem is melted through the fabric of the shirt and bonded ultrasonically forever. The "bonding" machine can do the customary seven buttons on the front of a shirt and the two on the cuffs in twenty to thirty seconds. Permanent buttons can be bonded to any type of fabric—cotton, synthetic, or blends—at the same price it costs for regular buttons to be sewn on.

No more thread, or more needles; no more lost buttons? Charles Murray of Murray Associates, Inc., a U.S. technology marketing firm, has been trying to interest American shirt manufacturers in the technology. To date, it's a no go. "Appearance-wise, it's not as good as a pearl button," Murray admits. "But it's a question of economics, too. So far, permanent buttons don't save enough on labor costs to convince shirt manufacturers to change over. And the machine only works now for shirts."

Yes, but how about the poor consumer who's tired of the button game? You know how it goes: Lose a button, find a button (but not the same button), find the right color thread, get a needle, oops! dropped the needle, there it is, where's the thimble?

Permanent buttons are too good not to make it to our shores. Murray figures that when plastic buttons that look like pearl buttons are developed, companies with enough volume will find it worth their while to invest in the button-bonding machines.

Oh, heck! Now where did I put that button?

NO-MISTAKE STEAK COOKER

•••••

ODDS: 80%

ETA: 1993

PRICE: $10

•••••

It was a nightmare," admitted Cathy Denomme. Here she was, a former counselor for the mentally and physically handicapped, suddenly transformed into a cook for dozens of hungry men, and she couldn't barbecue a steak properly. *Aggggghhhhhh!*

But there was no waking from this nightmare, because it was real. Denomme, a Canadian mother of two, found herself in High Falls, Ontario, where her husband took a new job with the Great Lakes Power Company. Eager to work too, she found employment in an old farmhouse cooking for crews of linemen and electricians. So far, so good.

However, every Thursday night was T-bone steak night. "It was a nightmare because I never could get the steaks right," she recalled. "You can't cut them up when you're supposed to be a professional cook, which, of course, I wasn't."

Denomme started researching the subject. *"Rien."* Nothing. Professional chefs told her that in a mere three to five years, she'd be able to detect doneness just by pressing on the steak. "But I didn't have three to five years to develop the touch test," she said.

Instead, she developed her own implement to determine exactly when a steak or hamburger is ready. Her homemade invention was made out of wood and stainless steel (mass-produced models are made of plastic) with a spring inside that protrudes out the bottom. When the device is placed on top of the meat, the protruding spring measures how firm the steak is. An indicator on top will register R, or M or W.

Denomme's "No-Misteak" worked so well and people liked it so much that she patented her little invention. Hotline, a North Dakota distributor and marketer, will be selling No-Misteak in this country.

IMPROVED STAPLE REMOVER

ODDS: 75%

ETA: 1993

PRICE: $5

Anything that gets rid of any of life's annoyances for five bucks is okay in our book. So an improved staple remover is certainly worth a few lines.

You know the micro-madness that occurs when the staple remover doesn't pull out both sides of the staple you're trying to remove. The damn thing gets stuck half in and half out. One nasty little point stares up at you, threatening a wound that won't heal for a week. And the staple remover is now useless; the only thing to do is remove the errant metal with your fingers (or teeth).

Larry Strickland, a mechanical engineer in Morgantown, West Virginia, has a better (and safer) way. One day it just hit him: "Why not put a mini pliers on the back of the staple remover?"

It works perfectly, says Strickland. The mini pliers are activated by the original handles and operate like a big tweezer.

Strickland hasn't landed a manufacturer yet, but he's determined to get his product to market. "I've spoken to many, many, many people and they all say they want one."

"I NEED MORE" STICKERS

ODDS: 25%

ETA: 1994

PRICE: NA

"Mom," called fourth-grader Jonathan Merickel from the upstairs bathroom, "we're out of toothpaste!"

Jonathan is a responsible kind of guy. You ask him to take out the trash, he takes out the trash. You ask him to brush his teeth before bedtime, he brushes his teeth. You ask him to tell you when he's out of toothpaste, he tells you.

But if you're Jonathan's mother and you're thinking about laundry and school lunches and the new house you're building, you may forget to write "toothpaste" on your shopping list.

And if you forget to write it down, you forget to buy it.

And the next night, when Jonathan goes to brush his teeth, there's no toothpaste.

Sorry!

But Jonathan, ten, is an ingenious kind of guy, as well as being responsible. So when he went to bed that night (unbrushed), he came up with a great idea—stickers that say "I Need More ________." In the blank, the manufacturer prints the name of the product.

Then, when you use up whatever you bought, you peel off the sticker and stick it on your shopping list. It sort of systematizes the whole shopping list business.

Jonathan, who lives in Willmar, Minnesota, won national honors in the 1990 Invent America contest for his pantry stickers. If "I Need More . . ." reminders make it to the marketplace, he'll also win the thanks of forgetful shoppers everywhere!

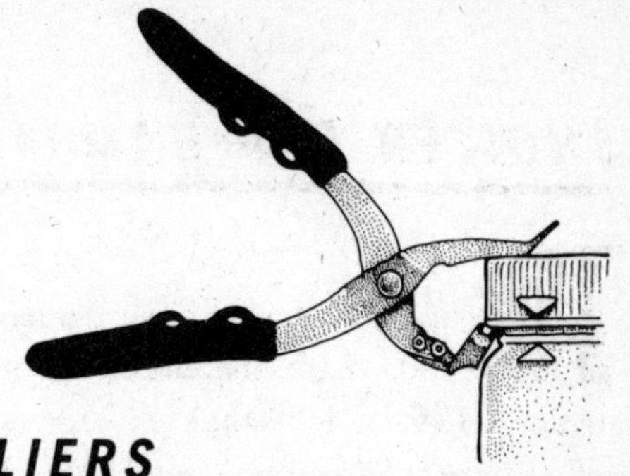

PILL-BOTTLE PLIERS

ODDS: 100%

ETA: 1992

PRICE: $15

Drug companies have made their pill bottles so safe that the people who buy their products the most can't get them open. Sounds like a joke, but it's not.

August Pomante, a sixty-five-year-old, semiretired pharmacist living in West Palm Beach, Florida, had been noticing this for years. "Old people would come in and say, 'I can't open that bottle.' And I thought, 'There better be a way to open that bottle.' " There wasn't.

So Pomante devised a way, and his newly formed company, Chem-Pharm Corporation, has begun selling the revolutionary Helping Hand Pharm-A-Tool. The device, which looks like a pair of pliers, is 7 inches by 2 inches and made of pressed steel with red plastic handles. It can cut through the outer safety cap on pill bottles, or it can snap them off like a bottle opener would.

The tool can also be used to cut tape and the seals off bottles and packages. And it has a V-shaped tip that can pick the cotton out of pill bottles. Unlike pliers, it has a little spring at the fulcrum, which, Pomante says, allows it to open and cut more easily.

The problems the elderly (and the not-so-elderly) have getting past those safety caps are widespread and well known. Complaints have led the Consumer Product Safety Commission to consider a proposal requiring manufacturers to test their packages with people aged sixty to seventy-five. But drug and packaging companies are resisting the notion. At this point, that's probably a good thing for August Pomante and his ingenious Helping Hand Pharm-A-Tool.

SHOWER-CAP BANDAGES

• • • • •

ODDS: 50%

ETA: 1995

PRICE: 30 CENTS EACH

• • • • •

Trying to take a shower when you have a wound that's bandaged is no picnic. Homemade sandwich-bag-and-rubber-band contraptions rarely do the trick. Everything you are trying to keep dry usually gets wet first.

This is what Jeffrey Estrella, a mechanical engineer from Lowell, Massachusetts, found after suffering a knee injury. Rather than just bemoan his fate, Estrella invented a shower cap for knees.

"I was on crutches," Estrella recalls, "and didn't have anything to do but sit around and watch soap operas. I had trouble taking a shower and had to do something to keep the bandage dry."

The "something" he came up with is a simple 15-inch-by-29-inch rectangle of clear plastic wrap bordered by adhesive strips that hold the plastic in place when the bandage is wrapped around the knee. Nothing could be simpler. "It's been very effective," says Estrella.

Estrella is pitching his shower cap for the knee and other injured parts to orthopedic surgeons. "After a knee operation, when a surgeon tells his patient to keep the bandage or cast clean and dry, he can just give him this wrapping and tell him to cover the dressing with it whenever he takes a shower."

ROLL-UP GRILL

"Family snowmobile cookouts have always been a big part of our lives," says LeRoy Shinler, Minnesota inventor and father of seven. "But hauling a grill was always inconvenient, and finding a place to store it after a hot dog roast was generally a problem, and messy as well."

ODDS: 75%
ETA: 1993
PRICE: $40

Made of lightweight stainless steel, the EZ Roll-Up Grill is supported by fold-up legs. There's no bottom. You simply build a fire on the ground beneath it. Afterwards, you roll up the grill and store it in its plastic carrying case. The whole thing weighs 3 pounds.

So simple, so obvious (after the fact), the invention has been patented by Shinler, who hopes to have it on the market soon.

BANK CHECKS WITH PHOTOS

This is such a logical idea for preventing bank crime that you wonder why David Rockefeller, J. P. Morgan, or J. Edgar Hoover didn't think of it first. Instead it was Niki Jo Lindstrom, a sixth-grader from Fargo, North Dakota, who came up with the notion of putting the owner's photograph on checks.

ODDS: 25%
ETA: 1994
PRICE: NA

Think about it. When you cash a check with your picture on it, you have instant ID. If your checks are lost or stolen, no one (except a twin) could use them.

"I got the idea from watching my parents write checks in stores,"

Niki Jo explains. "It takes a long time. People have to dig through their purses to find their ID."

Her idea was also partially inspired by a "true story" that went around her hometown a couple of years ago. It seems a man moved to town, opened a checking account, joined a lot of clubs, and closed the account. "Then he went through town and started writing bad checks," Niki Jo relates. He skipped town without ever being caught.

With Niki Jo's photo-checks this couldn't have happened. His photo would have been circulated by the bank. Store owners would have been able to match the picture with the photo on his checks.

Niki Jo's idea won a regional award in the Invent America contest for schoolkids. It's certainly worth serious consideration from adults.

SCENTED CLOTHES DRYER

ODDS: 85%

ETA: 2000

PRICE: $450

While Americans like to smell nice, the Japanese adamantly believe that certain aromas have a beneficial effect on the human psyche. To appeal to this desire for pleasant smells, Sanyo Electric Company introduced a new clothes dryer onto the Japanese market. The dryer imbues laundry with the user's favorite scent.

For Americans tired of "the great smell of freshly laundered clothes," Sanyo intends to market the aroma dryer in this country as well.

Called the Kaorinse, it comes with what Sanyo calls a "fragrance memory metal alloy" to attach inside the door of the dryer. You simply place a dab—about 0.1 cubic centimeters—of your favorite perfume on the metal alloy, hook it on the inside of the door and start the load. As the clothes dry, they're infused with the scent, which will last for about two days.

According to Itaru Ishizawa, a Sanyo spokesman in Tokyo, "This extra function of aromas is intended for those who want to add pleasure to the clothes they wear."

In the future, your clothes (or those of the person crammed next to you in the elevator) may smell of Tea Rose or Shalimar instead of Tide.

MOUTH FRESHENER TEETH CLEANING BISCUIT

ODDS: 75%

ETA: 1994

PRICE: $3.50 FOR BOX OF 50

"Yes, I brush after every meal" must be one of the world's ten most-popular lies. It is repeated thousands of times a day to deludable dentists, from Dubrovnik to Des Moines, by fibbers from nine to ninety.

We all know that brushing is good for us, but it's such a hassle, especially when you're dining in a good restaurant. If only we could clean our teeth the way Fido does—by eating dog biscuits—life would be so much easier.

Victor Powell, an entrepreneur from Liberty, Mississippi, had that thought. Then he did something about it. He developed the Mouth Freshener Teeth Cleaning Biscuit.

"Why should our canine companions be the only ones to have crunchy biscuits that scratch away plaque and freshen breath?" he asks.

His biscuits will come fifty to a box in appealing shapes for kids; "grown-up" biscuits will come in shapes that "interest adults," Powell promises.

For the time being, Powell is keeping the ingredients of his biscuits a secret. But he does guarantee that they will be all-natural and nutritious. They will come in chewing gum–like flavors, such as cinnamon and peppermint.

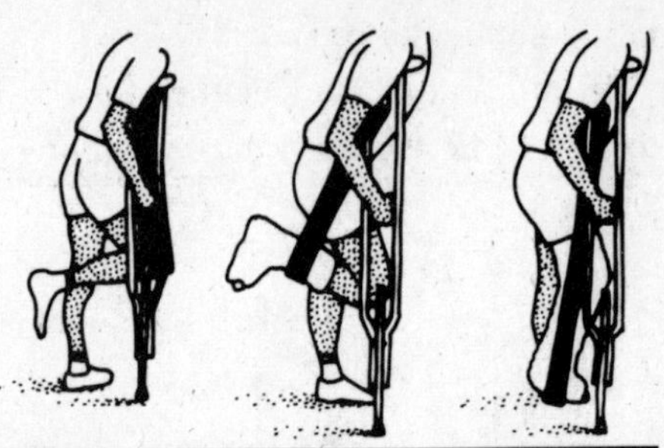

CAST SUPPORT

If they have slings for broken arms, why not for broken legs?

ODDS: 50%

ETA: 1994

PRICE: $22

This question crossed the mind of Ignasio Perez of Miami after he fell off a ladder and broke his ankle. He limped around on crutches after his misfortune, and the cast was uncomfortable.

Then Perez and his friend Steve Calderon came up with a remedy. It's an adjustable strap that hangs from under the rubber pad at the top of a normal crutch and wraps under the foot (or ankle, or knee, depending on how you want to hold your leg). The strap is wide enough and strong enough to hold a leg wrapped in a cast of any size.

According to Calderon, their invention helps to distribute the weight of the cast onto the crutch and take some of the pressure off the other side of your body. "You can dislocate a vertebra after a time with some casts," he claims.

With their patent in hand, Perez and Calderon are trying to get their sling to market. "Everything in life has to find a niche," says Calderon. "Once we find the right avenue, it will take off." It shouldn't hurt that Calderon's father is in the medical supply business.

VEGIFORMS

Are you tired of those same old vegetables looking like those same old vegetables? Well, if you are, get ready for Vegiforms, two-piece molds that can make a squash look like Richard Nixon or your Uncle Fred.

ODDS: 95%

ETA: 1992

PRICE: $11

Now just where does one get the idea to create plastic molds capable of changing the shapes of vegetables into practically anything? Richard Tweddell III of Cincinnati, Ohio, is the inventor, patenter, and seller of Vegiforms. "I had a job one summer as a fruit picker," he explained, "and I noticed that vegetables and fruits will adhere to any change in shape if you have the right mold. Later I worked for a toy company and found three or four plastics that work well as molds."

Thus was Vegiforms born. Right now Tweddell is making molds in the shapes of hearts, diamonds, elf heads, and "grumpy pickle pusses." But he can also custom make a mold of your favorite (or least favorite) friend or relative. The key is that the mold must be placed around a vegetable while it's still young and growing.

Vegiforms will work on squash, pumpkin, eggplant, cucumber—just about any vegetable you can name. Tweddell can even make one vegetable, such as squash, look like another vegetable, like corn.

"Just pick a vegetable that wants to be a star!" says Tweddell.

CHAPTER 25

end stuff

BURIAL SAFETY DEVICE

• • • • •

ODDS: 70%

ETA: 1994

PRICE: NA

• • • • •

This one's for pallbearers, a safety device to ensure they don't trip or fall as they bring the casket to its final resting place.

Roy Kappel of Landis, Saskatchewan, Canada, inventor of the G-Frame (*G* stands for grave), wanted to be a funeral director ever since he was a child. But farming got in the way for a couple of decades until health problems forced him to seek less strenuous work. Eventually he was able to pursue his childhood ambition at the Unity Funeral Home in Unity, Saskatchewan.

The big problem that Kappel saw in the job concerned the practice of setting down wooden planks around an open grave. The pallbearers (three on each side) have to walk across those loose planks to deposit the casket in the automated lowering machine.

The purpose of the planks is to support the lowering device and give the pallbearers something, besides loose earth, to walk on. But, says Kappel, pallbearers often complained that they were wobbly. "You were never sure what was beneath. And there have been accidents."

Preventing such accidents is the purpose of the G-Frame. "It frames the grave," says Kappel's wife, Margaret.

A flat, sturdy structure, the frame is made of ⅛-inch-thick aluminum sheets in a rectangular shape, connected by six hinges, three on each side (so it can be folded). On two sides, the aluminum is 12 inches wide, while on the ends it is 8 inches wide. The surface has a raised pattern so that it doesn't get slippery.

"It folds so that it's easily portable," explains Mrs. Kappel. "And it's lightweight, so it can be handled by one man." Folded, it makes a box that's 5 feet by 27 inches by 1 foot. It weighs about 70 pounds.

"The pallbearers can see it," says Kappel. "They know it's rigid. They know they can walk on it and be safe. And it's cosmetic. It has a good appearance, a professional look."

So, if you ever have occasion to be a pallbearer in the coming years, you might check with the funeral home to see if they use a G-Frame. You'll probably sleep better knowing they do.

LIFE COFFINS

ODDS: 85%

ETA: 1993

PRICE: $340–$480

They say that actress Sarah Bernhardt used to travel with her coffin, occasionally lying down in it to get the feel of the thing. Carpenter Keith Tibbetts of Cummington, Massachusetts, shares the view that coffins aren't just for the hereafter; they're also for the here and now.

Making his point in a practical way, Tibbetts created the Life Coffin, a bookcase for now, a casket for later. Philosophically speaking, the coffin-in-the-den serves another purpose—to remind us daily that life is precious and should be lived to the fullest, says Tibbetts.

At present, Tibbetts is custom making his coffins one at a time. Available in pine at $340 or oak and cherry at $480, they are made according to the owner's height and come with shelves. The box is 16 inches deep and 28 inches wide, and it weighs about 350 pounds. Shipped sanded but unfinished, the coffin can be urethaned or oiled. It looks like a bookcase with handles on the side, says its inventor.

The lining is left to the buyer to supply. When the time comes, says Tibbetts, people often use a favorite blanket or other personal item. For an additional $200, though, the future occupant can have his or her name carved on the lid.

The most unusual inquiry? It seems a Brooklyn therapist had an idea about having two of his patients lie in coffins during their sessions. Tibbetts never did get the order. Either the shrink or his patients got cold feet.

DRIVE-THROUGH "VIEWING"

ODDS: 90%
ETA: 1992
PRICE: NA

How will folks of the future pay their respects? Instead of going inside the funeral home, people will merely drive through, like at a bank or fast-food restaurant. A TV monitor will display a picture of the deceased!

This service is presently being offered with a minimum $5,000 funeral by the Gatling Funeral Home in Chicago. Lafayette and Marguerite Gatling added their high-tech service in 1988, and ever since, the bereaved have had the option of drive-through viewing. "Roughly 25 percent of the families we work with use it," reports Marguerite.

"And most who decide to view the body this way are the handicapped and the elderly."

Those who choose to pay their respects without leaving their cars simply follow a sign that reads DRIVE THRU VISITATION in front of the funeral home. They are directed to a 25-inch video screen alongside the funeral home's driveway. Visitors drive up to a speakerphone where they communicate with an attendant and identify which body they have come to view (the home has three video cameras in three parlors). They then sign the memorial register and see a close-up of the deceased transmitted for fifteen to twenty seconds. "We can re-trigger the camera as many times as necessary," adds Marguerite, for those who want to view the body longer.

How has the concept gone over in Chicago? "People are curious about it and have come to see how it works. Some think it's great, although others have a negative attitude about it," says Lafayette. "People who criticize have said things like, 'Why should it be so convenient for those who, rather than pay respect to the family, merely sign the register, get a quick glimpse from the car, and speed off?' But it's not intended for those people. It's really for the elderly and handicapped—those who aren't strong enough to park and get out of the car to walk inside."

The video viewing is also available late—from 10 P.M. until 6 A.M.—for those who can't make normal viewing hours.

Will drive-through viewing catch on nationwide? The idea is slowly gaining ground. In the first two years, about half a dozen of the 22,000 funeral homes in the U.S. added the service, says Bob Harden, director of the National Funeral Directors Association. "It's really a matter of whether the consumer feels it's an appropriate way to view the deceased. It is a plus to a service; however, it might take away from the personalization of greeting the family."

MUMMIFICATION

"It's like flying first-class instead of coach," says Corky Ra, president of Summum, the only company in the world with a patented process for mummification. "We are all going to the same place, anyway."

ODDS: 80%

ETA: 1992

PRICE: $26,000

Mummification hasn't been used much since A.D. 400. But Ra and John Chew, a professor of mortuary science at the College of Boca Raton, think it has a big future. After a slow start—it took ten years to develop the process and secure the patents—their company, Summum of Salt Lake City, Utah, has taken off. It now has registered agents in twenty-seven states, and more than 100 people have signed up.

Who wants to get mummified? "Doctors, lawyers, hardworking people who have a need for fulfillment in life as well as after life," says Chew. Many of Summum's clients are relatively young for such stuff—in their thirties. No one is older than sixty.

The actual mummification process involves soaking the body for several days in a trade-secret solution that includes nearly thirty chemicals. The body is soaked anywhere from one week to thirty days, depending on how much it has decomposed. Then the body is wrapped in a powdered thermal linen, which can be treated with herbs and spices and sealed in a polyurethane membrane. All for about $8,000.

And for $18,000 more, clients can order a customized Mummiform, an airtight casket molded in human shape that's welded shut and purged with the inert gas argon to prevent growth of bacteria.

Summum also offers a special funeral service in its own twentieth-century pyramid.

So far, Summum's actual mummifications have been confined to dogs, cats, and cadavers. Not a single client has died. "Maybe," says Ra, "if you sign up, you live forever."

ALPHABETICAL LIST OF PRODUCTS

Afterglow Light Bulb 236
Air Travel Safety Course 141
Airplane Convenience Modules 133
Airplane Crashproof Pods 6
A la Carte Hotels 136
Amplified Stethoscope 223
Anti-Aging Chair 65
Anti-Aging Substance 55
Anti-Aging Therapy 64
Aquaband Bandage 219
Artificial Pianist 104
Artificial Surfing 150
Automatic Basketball
Rebounder 191
Automatic Mood Music Finder 303
Baby-Feeding Nipple 252
Baby Safe 250
Bank Checks with Photos 321

Bathtub with a Door 80
Beach Brush 147
Bed-Wetter Clock 249
Better Baby Seat 245
Bicycle Wheel of the Future 199
Blue Roses 93
Braille Handrails 164
Built-In Child's Car Seat 310
Bulletproof Clothing 124
Burial Safety Device 327
Caffeine-Free Coffee Beans 237
Camcorder Zoom Sound 106
Car Parts Made from Recycled Soda Bottles 44
Cast Support 324
Château Bow Wow 129
Child's Handrail 248
Cholesterol Reducer 218
Cholesterol-Free Milk 264
Cholesterol-Lowering Peanut Oil 260
Cigarette Case for Quitters 221
Clean Air Machine 90
Clip-On Bicycle Motor 201
Computerized Shrink 20
Computer Job Interviewer 161
Computer Safety Glasses 295
Computer That Reads Lips 292
Computer Tracker 296
Controlled-Release Birth Control Pills 215
Convenient Home Blood Test 209
Cooling Coil 138
Crispy Canned Vegetables 256
Customized Textbooks 172
Deep-Sea Walkie-Talkie 152
Designer Sound 102
Diaphragm with Spermicide Sponge 217
Dirtboard 197
Disposable Video Cassettes 111
Diversified Furniture Unit 91
Divers' Rate of Ascent Meter 151
Dog Toilet 89
Do-It-Yourself Acupuncture Wand 66
Double-Looped Pretzel Bicycle Lock 206
Driver's TV 26
Drive-Through "Viewing" 329
Easy-Off Labels 50
Edible Pencils 29
Edible Insects 281
Electronic Bike Derailleur 204
Electronic Echo Pathfinder 228
Ergonomic Keyboard 294
Exerlopers 25
"Exercise" Wheelchair 225
Exit Traveler 241
Eyeball Sculpting 212
Eye-Operated Computers 16
Fashion Try-On Simulation 162
Fast-Food Piroshki 276
Fat Prevention Drink 220
Feeling Phone 116
Feminine Hygiene Padette 61
Finsurfer 145
Fish Dogs 258
Flarecraft 1
Flatless Bicycle Tires 203
Flavor Enhancer for Leftovers 262
Flavored Barbecue Blocks 265
Floating Furniture 76
Food Tape 9
Foolproof Car Suspension 307
Friendly Wheelchair 224
Gas-Free Beans 240
Golf Training Harness 186
Graphite Baseball Bat 188
Guardian Angel Smoke Alarm/Fire Extinguisher 231
Gutter Cleaning Machine 82
Hair-Growth Stimulator 57
Hamster Fitness Center 284
Hands-Free Phone 119
Handyman Robot 73
Hangover-Free Wine 239
Healthier Salmon 211
Heat-Storing Device 306
High-Altitude Safety Bag 193
High-Tech Matchmaking 157
Hip-Guard 210
Holographic Food 23
Holographic Windows 87
Hot Carpet 81
Hot/Cold Food Container 31
Hot/Cool Walls 74

Hot Pink Mini-Excavator 125
Human-Powered Flashlight 49
Hypercube Puzzle 177
Ice-Powered Vehicle 43
Improved Staple Remover 317
Improved Ballet Slipper 178
"I Need More" Stickers 318
Indestructible Lawn 94
Instant-Response Sunglasses 146
Interactive Books 173
Iridium Cellular Telephones 4
Jet-Lag Pill 135
Jet-Lag Watch 140
Knee Pads for Toddlers 247
Level-Enhanced Golf Putter 183
Life Coffins 328
Life Detector 232
Light Engine 302
Liquid Sunglasses 155
Literate Computers 170
Litmus Test for Hair 71
Long-Lasting Vegetable Snacks 274
Machine-Washable Wool 92
Magnetic Childproof Plug Protector 251
Magnetic Razor Blade Conditioner 70
Manual Garbage Compactor 40
Mayhaw 261
Melon-Sweetness Meter 268
Mental Fitness Gear 59
Microwave Fryer 78
Minimelons 271
Motorized Shelves 85
Mouse Repellent 283
Mouth Freshener Teeth Cleaning Biscuit 323
Mummification 331
Mush-Free Tomatoes 267
Nail-Polish-Remover Wand 32
Natural Gas–Powered Cars 37
Neon Bike Lights 202
New Contact Lens Cleaner 214
New, Improved Deodorant (Really!) 60
New Migraine Medicine 207
New Product Stores 167
New, Safer Antiwrinkle Cream 68
Noise-Dried Orange Juice 255
No More Coke-Bottle Eyeglasses 69
No-Mistake Steak Cooker 316
Nonchlorine Pool Cleaner 51
Nonsurgical Incontinence Cure 222
One-Hand Dispenser Packs 14
One-Handed Golf Putter 184
On-Time Delivery System 159
Orange Cauliflower 259
Ornithopter 179
Painless Periodontal Treatment 208
Paris in a Box 169
Parking Space Doubler 130
Peanut-Oil Breast Implant 58
Permanent Buttons 314
Personal Hovervehicle 123
Personal Submarine 131
Personalized TV 97
Photo CDs 109
Pill-Bottle Pliers 319
Popcorn Packing Pellets 41
Popped Nuñas 273
Potato Plastic 39
Razor with Counter 27
"Real 3-D" Laser Display 100
Rearview Mirror Radar 305
Recyclable Car 52
Refrigeration by Sound 46
Remote Control Call Forwarding 118
Remote-Control Vacuum Cleaner 84
Removable Steering Wheel 311
Rhubarb-Based Frozen Treats 275
Roach Repellent Insulation 286
Roadway-Powered Cars 299
Robot Bartender 12
Robot Guide Dog 229
Robotic Luggage Carrier 137
Roll-Up Grill 321
Safe Flea Trap 285
Safer Chicken 263
Salt-and-Water Air Conditioner 39
Scented Clothes Dryer 322
Scrap-Heap Homes 35
Scratch-Free Eyeglasses 213
See-Through Convertible Toaster 313
Self-Contained Portable Vacation Homes 121
Self-Heating Can 278

Self-Parking Car 7
Self-Watering Plants 182
Shark Repellent Belt and Cuffs 143
Shooter Maker 128
Shower-Cap Bandages 320
Side-Impact Car Air Bags 304
Singing Pillow 235
Six-Sided Tennis Racquet 194
Smaller Headlights 308
Smart Lighting Systems 45
Smart Telephone 114
Smoke Protection Pillow 230
Smooth Ambulance Ride 227
Softer Hardball 189
Solar Beach-Umbrella Fan 149
Solar-Powered Parking Meters 160
SongWand 175
Spaghetti Sipper 33
Star Nails 83
Stationary Infant Walker 243
Stinky Garbage Bags 287
Stolen Vehicle Location Service 165
Straight-Line Pool Cue 196
Strawberry-Flavored Bananas 269
Sun-Safety Watch 153
Super-Fast Battery Charger 48
Super Lightweight Battery 107
Supersweet Sugar Substitute 266
Superscreen Computers 289
Super "Tide" Teller 154
Swing-Strengthening Baseball Bat 187
Synthetic Vocal Tract 3
Talking Car Navigator 300
Tanning Umbrella 148
Team Chess 180
Telephone for the Deaf 117
Telesketch 113
Therapeutic Earrings 67
3-D Advertising 112
3-D Glasses That Work Anywhere 28
Three-Piece Rowing Shell 192
Time-Release Flavored Chewing Gum 279
Tiny TV 99
Tobacco Food 17
Total Infant Organizer 253
Totally Popped Popcorn 277
Trailer/Houseboat 139
Train in a Coffee Table 79
TV That Puts You in the Picture 10
Two Cars in One 18
Ubiquitous Computing 13
Ultimate Exercise Machine 126
Ultraviolet Headlights 309
VCR Lock 108
Vegetarian Village 53
Vegiforms 325
Videoharp 105
Vitamin A for Acne 62
Voice-Activated Microwave Oven 77
Voice Box 30
Voice Credit Cards 166
Voice-Fax Machine 291
Walking, Talking TV 101
Womb-Simulating Crib 246
Write-On Calculator 293